A Long Way from Tipp

Chapter 1.

A Welshman from Ireland

Leaving Ireland

William Murphy regarded himself as a Welshman; he was brought up in South Wales as a strict Catholic by his parents who were both of wholly Irish origin. William's DNA was therefore Irish and his bloodline came out centuries of repression of his forebears by the Anglo - Irish ascendancy. But at a personal level, Williams' loyalty lay with Wales. He was a fluent Welsh speaker, who fought in the First World War with a Welsh Battalion and for the whole of his life supported the Welsh Rugby team. His upbringing imbued him with a

A Long Way from Tipperary

strong sense of duty to his country and especially to his family. He was fortunate after surviving the Great War to find himself a loving and supportive wife whose premature death at the age of 49 left him devastated. This is his story and his times.

Thomas Murphy, my grandfather, was born in Tipperary in Graiguepadeen outside of a small village called Gortnahoe in 1842 as a member of a large Irish family of smallholders. His parents were Thomas and Ellen nee Connors married in 1829 in Urlingford, just across the border in Kilkenny. Thomas senior was born around 1810. They survived as subsistence farmers relying heavily on the potato and seasonal work – their property was on the edge of extensive peat lands. Thomas leased one and a half acres and a house in the Fennor town land and also used a disused school house nearby. It is probable that he was the son of William Murphy who held an acre of land in Fennor in 1827 according to the land survey. Thomas Murphy of Fennor had eleven children in total and their baptisms occur in parish records between 1830 and 1852. Margaret (Thomas's eldest sister) married in Gortnahoe in 1859 a John Murphy in the presence of John Mahoney and Johanna McNamara; this couple had a daughter, Ellen who was baptised on the 30th of April 1860.

We know from land records that my great grandfather Thomas did not depart himself from Gortnahoe as a consequence of the famine of 1845. He was there until much later. But it is certain that his extensive family had to leave to survive. Thomas is shown in the Griffiths evaluation of 1850, the revaluation of 1856 and the further land census of 1866. In 1867 however, change of ownership of his land was noted and Thomas died in

A Long Way from Tipperary

The Fields of Fennor

Kilkenny in 1867; Ellen appears to have died already as she was not on the death certificate.

The primary valuation of Ireland or Griffith's Valuation - carried out between 1848 and 1864 was to determine the liability to pay the Poor rate (for the support of the poor and destitute within each Poor Law Union) . It provides detailed information on where people lived in mid-nineteenth century Ireland and the property they possessed.

Irish genealogists tell us that there are no relevant entries for the Murphy's of Graiguepadeen in the 1901 Irish census which is the earliest complete one to have survived, so the whole family had moved on. There are still recent traces of Murphys in the area however so it is possible that some members of the family drifted back in the course of the century. Family visits to Fennor have lead to locals commenting at various times on the facial similarities between William's children and grandchildren and former Murphys who once lived in the hamlet

A Long Way from Tipperary

The Old School House in 1992

without in some instances the locals even knowing that they might be kin.

To understand the traditions which governed the lives of the Murphys during generations, it is necessary to look back over the previous centuries, Tipperary represents the eastern half of the former kingdom of Limerick. Sometime between 1206 and 1211 the great Norman honor of Limerick which had been taken from the Irish King Donagh Canbragh O'Brien, was formed into the County of Munster and subdivided again by 1254 into Tipperary and Limerick. Donagh had already left his mark on the county however by the foundation of the Abbey at Kilcooly for Cistercian monks, in about 1200. This survived as an Abbey until the Reformation when it was granted to the Earl of Ormonde, and subsequently became an outpost of the Protestant ascendancy, casting its influence over the adjoining parish of Fennor.

A Long Way from Tipperary

The Irish were lost in the Norman invasion; they had kept no records and lost their clan identities as they were absorbed into the Manorial system with its heavy dependence on tillage and sheep. On 2 November 1328, Edward II gave the title of Earl of Ormonde to James Butler and his heirs who had unparalled authority as Seneschals of the Liberty of Tipperary unfettered by parliamentary legislation until the second Duke of Ormonde made the mistake of backing the Stuarts in 1715. The Butlers ran their vast estates through close kinsmen as revealed in the hearth tax rolls, and with cadet branches of the family located in strategic locations. Viscount Ikerrin, for example had a great deal of land in Slievardagh on the eastern flank of the county, his property at Clonamicklon in Fennor faced the woods and bogs of Ely, which stretched into Cashel.

By 1640 Tipperary exhibited an extraordinary mosaic of property structures, some reflecting the feudal order and others showing strongly residual Gaelic features. Murphy and other Gaelic names, for example, appear prominently in Hearth Tax Rolls. Fennor had 12 Hearths in 1667 which indicated a significant settlement attracted no doubt by the centralising power of the landowner, his castle, townhouse and mills. A new layer of change was superimposed on Tipperary following the Cromwellian conquest. The country was settled by incomers who arrived with a retinue of retainers, family and stock. By 1667, the alliance between the new political/military order, the landed/commercial system and the Established church had stabilised its base. Towns acquired a central role, settlements fanned out along the major route ways, and there were many garrison centres. The country side was dotted with Majors, Colonels and Captains and many of the old elites were stripped

A Long Way from Tipperary

out. But Fennor was little disturbed by the new English settlements. The Butlers and their kin retained influence. The Barker family, who occupied Kilcooly until modern times, had pre-Cromwellian roots in the county. The Barkers derived their interests in the lands of the suppressed Cistercian monastery through Sir Jerome Alexander, who had purchased them from the Duke of Ormonde. Elsewhere, the Barony of Slieverdagh was allocated extensively to Cromwellian soldiers and to "the adventurers" who supported Cromwell's cause.

There were however crucial continuities beneath the elite layer; Tipperary was at best, only half conquered. The Hearth Money records point up the continuing strength of both the middle and lower levels of society. The descendants of the (old) Irish represented about 70% of the population and still retained 40 % of the more substantial two-hearth houses. The descendants of the Old English, comprising 25 % of the population, actually commanded an impressive 48% of the better houses. The New English, whilst only representing 5% of the population had come to represent 12% of the total number of houses with more than one hearth but 70% of the houses with five or more hearths. The great phase of their rule was to last only 150 years but underneath forces survived that would eventually coalesce and destroy this superstructure.

From the 1760s to the 1840s popular protest was almost a constant feature of Irish society with varying foci of grievance. Surprisingly, however, religious suppression was not a major factor. The penal laws against Catholic practice were neither consistently nor strictly enforced. When they were, this tended to coincide with fears of Jacobite invasion but after 1745 had

A Long Way from Tipperary

passed without reaction from Ireland, the Catholic clergy were generally thought to have passed a major test and were allowed thereafter to get on with their Ministry. By the mid 1750s, the archdiocese of Cashel (in which Gortnahoe /Fennor was located) had a recognisable parish system and 73 catechism teachers. The effect of the penal laws on Catholic property was more serious; the amount of land held by Catholics declined from 14% in 1703 to 5% in 1776, but there was a corresponding increase in the commercial middle class as they exploited loopholes in the law.

Economic factors were at the root of the Whiteboy disturbances. The demand for meat arising from cattle disease on the continent and from the 7 Years War (1756 -63 principally between Britain and France but also involving other continental powers) lead to pressure to convert land from tillage to pasturage; this in turn produced enclosure of common land and increased rents for arable land which put pressure on the poor. The practice of canting, by which leases were auctioned on expiry to the highest bidder exacerbated matters. And to all of these problems was added the issue of tithes. Since 1735 pasturage had been tithe-free, thereby establishing the tillage farmer and cottier (the class to which the Murphys belonged through the ages) as the tax base of the Established Church (whose religion they did not share) and liberating the better off graziers from payment. The target of the Whiteboy movement (so called because of the white shirts that they wore over their clothes, an early version of the Klu Klux Klan uniform) was the Proctor who assessed and collected the tithes and the landowners involved in enclosure and other extortionate practices. The Whiteboy operations ranged from razing

A Long Way from Tipperary

enclosures, to turning up ground, maiming horses and cattle, destroying crops, firing shots, attacking and setting fire to houses and intimidation that ran the gamut from building gallows as a warning to outright murder.

The basic injustice at the root of the tithe system can be gauged from the fact that a census of 1831 registered 4.4% Protestants in Tipperary compared with 95.6% Catholics. In Fennor, there were 2015 Catholics compared with 58 (or 2.7%) Protestants, which explains why it experienced intense Whiteboy activity. The Whiteboys in their various guises , however, were not a confessional movement inspired by Catholicism; if anything, they represented a challenge to the established Catholic leadership. Only the savagery of the system in targeting for execution a number of prominent priests suspected of sympathy with the Whiteboys gave the movement a false religious character.

The largest single social class in pre-Famine Tipperary was that of the labourers and cottiers. Those who held less than 5 acres and who had to supplement their income by off farm work are within this group. They were locked into a love/hate relationship with the farmers and middlemen who gave them access to work and land. This group was notoriously vulnerable to market changes, more especially the oscillation between arable and pastoral regimes. From this class was recruited a disproportionate percentage of 19th Century emigrants. The lowest social group was the landless labourer and his ancillaries, consisting of "spailpins", or mendicants and other displaced people. Deprived of any stake in the status quo, their natural response to dislocation was violence. But the traditional

A Long Way from Tipperary

image of Catholicism as the spokesman of a uniformly downtrodden and poverty stricken peasantry is wrong. Catholics came from a wide band of social classes, including the gentry. Catholicism provided, however, a common identity, as much ethnic as religious, to those nursing a sense of historical resentment at their perceived dispossession. The sense of unity that these feelings provided was rooted more in emotional and symbolic factors than real loss - the penal laws only hit the professional classes in reality and dispossession had only been visited on a minority. Catholicism was essentially a vast trade union which became the badge of those nursing a historical grudge and as such it represented the shared interests of this dispossessed group.

The Catholic Church that emerged from the upheavals of the 18th Century was ill equipped to support its adherents. There was a lack of churches, few priests, an absence of formal educational facilities and scarce financial resources. But by the 1790s concessions to Irish Catholics designed to attach them more securely to the Establishment, had eradicated the necessity for strategic conformity and the picture began to change. In the diocese of Cashel and Emly, the church in the mid 18th Century had about 50 simple Mass houses, each with thatched roofs and perhaps two windows. In some instances they were made of brick, and in others of mud. Later in the century they were replaced by barn chapels which were larger, had higher roofs, galleries and a cruciform plan. The pennies of the poor were conspicuous by their absence in financing these constructions which were paid for by farmers, artisans and the commercial classes. After Catholic Emancipation, the scale and pretensions of chapels became even greater; church

A Long Way from Tipperary

architects appear, the Gothic revival began and triumphalist notes sounded as the Church began to build large chapels in the towns from which it had been excluded since medieval days. In the countryside, the chapels begin to act as nuclei around which new villages developed (as occurred in Gortnahoe where the chapel was raised in 1820) during a period after the Napoleonic War when the estate system with its own church and colonial trappings was beginning to collapse. The tight link of the Established Church to the estates and the resulting dependence that this brought on sponsorship by the local landlord family brought inevitable decline in a church that was already a minority interest.

It would be wrong to give the impression that there were not also deep class based divisions even in the Catholic Church. The labourer and cottier class often remained outside the reach of formal Catholicism, locked behind the walls of an oral, intensely local world in which primitive belief, the faction fight as a ritualised method of settling disputes, keening, the pattern and the culture of drink all played a major part. The famine marked both symbolically and literally the death of the cottier and labourer class, aided by the impact of post-famine selective migration. The Catholic church moved forward into the vacuum created by the collapse of the traditional world which had been embedded most strongly in the lower social classes.

In the 1820s the politico religious struggle for Catholic emancipation was exacerbated by the acrimonious proselytising campaign of the Evangelical missionaries in Ireland, funded by mainland benefactors nourished on post-Reformation prejudice against Catholicism. The Tipperary factions saw the issue as a

A Long Way from Tipperary

heaven sent opportunity to demonstrate their power and the size of their assemblies became a major source of alarm to Westminster as well as a powerful tool in the hand of Daniel O'Connell in his campaign to win Emancipation. On the other hand, the Protestants began to fear the consequences of emancipation for their privileged position in society; their response was to form Brunswick Clubs composed of aristocrats, gentry and to a lesser extent, working class protestants.

Gortnahoe was involved in one of the early sectarian clashes between the factions; the Slievardagh Brunswickers held a meeting at Ballynonty on 1 November 1828 which included the Palatines of Kilcooly. The latter were displaced Germans who in 1772 had been induced by favourable leases to settle in Kilcooley when Sir William Barker decided to establish a Protestant colony on his estate. Such immigration had been a feature of the Protestant ascendancy as being the most convenient means of strengthening its adherents as they were not going to get any converts from Catholicism locally. The Brunswickers were met by a large and hostile crowd, only dissuaded with difficulty by the parish priest of Gortnahoe, Dr Michael Meighan, from setting upon them. More telling ways of countering the anti-emancipation effort was the use of a consumer and business boycott against those identified as hostile. This phase of the struggle ended with the reluctant assent of King George IV to the Roman Catholic Relief Bill on 13 April 1829.

Tithes now became a live issue. It had festered as a major grievance since 1690 fuelled by the rural poverty that made it

A Long Way from Tipperary

so burdensome. Emancipation now sharpened the sense of injustice at having to pay for an alien church. Most Protestant ministers in Southern Ireland occupied parishes which had small protestant congregations; many parishes were without Protestants altogether. Thus the parsons relied heavily on tithe income from Catholics for the maintenance of their families, without which they would have been destitute. The hostility was such that Protestant clergy were shouted at by men, women and children "as though they were dogs". The campaign of tithe resistance exploited ambiguities in the law; every device was employed to prevent tithes being collected. Livestock were locked into sheds to prevent distraint in lieu of tithe, early warning systems were instituted to outwit the law, and when this failed, the mobs turned on process servers and the police; violence sometimes ended in the murder of Proctors which was met in response by legalised vengeance from the authorities. Eventually, even the magistrates turned against enforcing arrangements to which such odium was attached and the clergy became powerless to enforce their rights.

The tithe war in Tipperary was only the latest manifestation of a disregard for constituted authority which was a feature of life in the county from medieval to modern times. The inevitable consequence of an impoverished agricultural economy with rapid population growth was an intense and bitter competition for land which assumed the proportion of a life and death struggle. Fierce competition for land lead to high rents and subdivision of tiny holdings. To be without land in rural Ireland was to be dependant on day labouring for survival - a notoriously seasonal occupation. Living on the margins of danger, less than perfect health , or creeping malnutrition could

A Long Way from Tipperary

mean an early death. The possession of land, either to obtain it or to keep it, coupled with the lack of mutual confidence in landlord tenant relations was the critical quintessence of agrarian turmoil in pre - famine Ireland. Most landlords travelled heavily protected by armed guards, their houses were like virtual fortresses with steel shutters affixed to their windows. They were overwhelmingly different in origins and creed from the tenant farmers cottiers and labourers who owned land in inverse proportion to their numbers. The Catholic tenantry were inclined to regard the land that they farmed as their own private property; a lively oral tradition enabled them to trace back ownership to the land settlements of the Cromwellian period and to regard any title granted at that time as based on usurpation. The notion prevailed that one day, in the not to distant future, the land which rightly belonged to the dispossessed would be returned to its owners. The high percentage of absentee landowners in Tipperary which stood at around 50% gave strength to this conviction.

The Earl of Clonmel whose heir is registered in the Griffiths evaluation as the owner of Thomas Murphy's smallholding in Fennor is a good example of the breed. John Scott was born in Tipperary in 1739 and studied at Trinity College Dublin where he graduated in law. He practiced as a barrister, rose to Attorney General and in 1783 became Chief Justice of the Court of the Kings Bench. He was given a baronetcy in 1784, in 1789 he became Viscount Clonmel and in 1793 was made an Earl. He died in Dublin in 1798. His heirs (a 7th Earl was still around in the late 1890s) owned 16,000 acres in Tipperary, as well as 2,000 in Kildare, 2,200 in Kilkenny, 3,300 in Carlow and more in Limerick, Monaghan and Dublin. His landed income

A Long Way from Tipperary

amounted to 17,140 acres and his principal residence was in Kildare. These are the facts. As for colour, the Dictionary of Irish Biography recorded in 1928 that " he amassed a great fortune by questionable means". Burkes notes that "his bronzed visage and his reputation for effrontery lead to his being called " copper faced Jack", or "Jack the Petulant"...he affected to despise the people from whose dregs he had lately sprung, and had indeed an utter contempt for everything, danger only excepted. He was flippant, pert and overbearing and a disgrace to the peerage". Clonmel was the kind of ruthless Protestant parvenu that the system needed to function well, particularly at the apex of the judicial system when the revolution in France was causing tremors throughout Europe.

It was more convenient for most large landowners however to operate through lessors or middlemen. Thomas Leahy who was the lessor of the Murphy smallholding for a number of years was of this class. This tendency lead to a web of cumbersome leasing arrangements which impoverished further the vitality of an estate system which was already weakened by absentee landlordism. As the estates declined and their surrounding villages fell into disuse, the landlord system lost its ability to cope with the consequences of the changing social, economic and political conditions that prevailed in the post-famine years. By the end of the century Tipperary was strewn with abandoned estates and secular power had transferred itself back to the towns and villages which could trace their origins back to medieval times. 61 of the 186 parish centres that the Anglican Church had taken over in the 16th Century had deserted or ruined churches. The ruined church and its abandoned graveyard came to become a poignant symbol of a

A Long Way from Tipperary

divided Ireland. As for the rehabilitated Catholic Church, it sought sites away from the historic parish centres and built its churches to become the foci of new settlements (as occurred with Gortnahoe).

Interdenominational rivalries still dominated politics at the 1841 election when two liberal candidates were challenged by conservatives, the leading candidate of the latter group being Ponsonby Barker, the son of William Barker of Kilcooly. The Catholic mobs gave Barker a hard time, urged on by the Archdeacon of Fethard, Michael Laffan who said at a dinner for O'Connell in Cashel that " the gentry are the sworn foes of St Patrick, the descendants of bloody Cromwell and his ragged regiments - the men who stained the green fields of Tipperary with the blood of our forefathers". Ponsonby's Palatine supporters were forced to retreat to the sanctuary of Kilcooly after a clash in New Birmingham and the liberals won the election handily. O'Connell feared that failure to make progress with Repeal of the Union, the next campaign following Emancipation, through Parliamentary means would lead to violence. The rising of "Young Irelanders" in 1848 proved his point. The rising failed because of the total demoralisation of a famine stricken people, who did not have enough to eat, let alone to fight, as well as the restraining influence of the clergy whose deeds showed more commitment to restraint than their words.

The great potato famine of 1845-9 opened an abyss that swallowed up many hundreds of thousands of impoverished Irish people. By the 1840s the potato was a dietary staple which enabled subsistence on a tiny holding, provided food for 9

A Long Way from Tipperary

months of the year and could at a pinch support life as a sole diet. Certainly supplementing it by milk and fish had become a rarity for the poor by the 1830s. The favourite method of conversion to other food was by raising pigs, an important part of the potato ecology. There had been fourteen partial or complete potato famines in Ireland between 1816 and 1842, but in autumn 1845, a new fungus disease struck the crop, reducing it rapidly to rottenness. The blight redoubled in 1846, preventing a new crop being sown, it declined in 1847 but returned in 1848-49. The result in areas of potato dependency, was a subsistence crisis that was beyond the powers either of the existing state apparatus or the prevalent conceptions of social responsibility.

Not all of Ireland was equally effected, but the famine hit hard in the West and South West and in the upland areas of Tipperary. The labourer class was most badly hit, followed by the smallest farmers. The impact on the population was dramatic; it has been estimated that 2,225,000 people were lost to disease, starvation or emigration over the period 1845-51. The overall population of Ireland would sink from 8.2 million in the early 1840s to 4.4 million by 1911. Statisticians argue about the death toll which varies in estimates between 1 and 1.5 million. But no amount of disagreement can conceal the devastating extent of depopulation, nor the horrific conditions in which lives were lost. The horror was compounded in many instances by evictions for failure to pay rent which added to the numbers of victims wandering the highway.

The governments efforts to deal with the famine are well documented and over the 150 years since there has been

A Long Way from Tipperary

much retrospective condemnation of its policies. In fact they were more effective that has been generally allowed in the view of more recent historians. But humanitarian impulses came up against a violent disapproval of subsidised improvement schemes; beneath the surface on the mainland there was also often an attitude that Irish fecklessness was bringing its own retribution. Public works schemes were doggedly adhered to, notwithstanding the widespread weakness of the population, and the question of payment became an obsession, expressed in the conviction that relief should be provided from the rates. Above all there was lack of an organised food distribution system. In many parts of Ireland where landlords became involved and where the level of subsistence was not perhaps as high, the local population weathered the crisis. Tipperary's death rate from 1846 to 51 however, put the county in the top 30% of those effected.

What were the longer term effects of the famine? Holdings of small farms declined drastically (from 45% to 15% over the period 1831 to 1851); larger holdings increased. Livestock farming expanded at the expense of subsistence. Catholicism increased its hold, with more priests, more chapels, and greater devotional activity at the expense of the ancient magical beliefs which had failed in the trauma of the famine. The small farmer ethos took over society, postponing fertility, avoiding subdivision and insisting on a firm material base for marriage. Sexual Puritanism was part of the package. There was more investment in Education - half a million people in 4,300 schools were funded by the National Board of education in 1849. An abiding resentment of "England" coupled with even greater hostility to landlordism generated bitterness and began to find

A Long Way from Tipperary

expression through the political system as a result of the 1850 Franchise Act which widened the electorate. The values, beliefs and influence of the farming class, which was no longer threatened by the decimated labourer and cottier class, began to enter their own ascendancy.

Finally there was emigration, which was the great fact of Irish social history from the early 19th Century, preceding even the famine. The 1840 census in Britain recorded 400,000 Irish born people on the mainland; by 1851 this had risen to 750,000. Some of the emigration was seasonal and to many Irishmen had been an inevitability even before the famine as a consequence of continuing crop failures. However, the Irish "Catholic" world view was not conducive to enterprising emigration - the philosophical acceptance of stasis, the tendency to defer to established authority and the low tolerance for individual deviation were all handicaps. Emigration also conflicted sharply with the high value that the Irish placed upon communalism, kinship and a sense of place.

North America was of course a favoured destination, especially as shipboard conditions improved following the exposure of some of the horrific conditions that prevailed on board the "coffin ships" in the 1840s. But the mainland was closer and easier to reach; the Cork - London passage dropped to a halfpenny a head in the 1840s. The Irish monopolised at first the unskilled and menial jobs but they also became involved in radical movements and maintained a strong sense of community, which provided a degree of group strength. They entered the Army and Navy in large numbers (peaking at 55,000 in 1861) and as artisans became known for masonry

A Long Way from Tipperary

and shoe making. There was also a vibrant middle class. At the heart of their culture however was an implicit reluctance to identify with Britain. Home remained Ireland, which was preserved in their imagination as it had been when they, or their parents left.

So many people died from starvation and disease that in some towns in Ireland, there were not enough people left alive to bury the dead. The best description of the horror of the famine and of the effect of starvation and of the louse-borne diseases of typhus and relapsing fever that accompanied it as a consequence of sanitary and social degeneration was contained in an open letter in the Times on December 24 1846 to the Duke of Wellington from a Cork magistrate who had visited Skibbereen in West Cork which is 160 miles due west of Fennor..

"My Lord Duke, I went to Skibbereen on 15 December and was surprised to find the wretched hamlet apparently deserted. I entered some of the hovels to ascertain the cause, and the scenes which presented themselves were such as no tongue or pen can convey the slightest idea of. In the first, six famished and ghastly skeletons, to all appearances dead, were huddled in a corner on some filthy straw, their sole covering what seem a ragged horsecloth, their wretched legs hanging out, naked above the knees. I approached with horror and found that they were alive - they were in fever, four children, a woman and what had been once a man. In a few moments I was surrounded by at least 200 such phantoms, such frightful spectres as no words can describe. Their demoniac yells are still ringing in my ears, and their horrible images are fixed in my brain....My neck cloth was seized from behind by a grip which compelled me to turn, I found myself grasped by a woman with an infant just born in her

A Long Way from Tipperary

arms and the remains of a filthy sack, her sole covering across her loins. The same morning the police opened a house on adjoining lands and two frozen corpses were found, lying upon the mud floor, half devoured by rats."

A Long Way from Tipperary

Chapter 2

Wales - The Promised Land

Between 1845 and 49 large numbers of Irish people half starved and near naked arrived on the Glamorgan coast. The Cardiff and Merthyr Guardian wrote in 1849 "upwards of 50 Irish wretches in a most deplorable plight were landed on Penarth beach ...Some check must be put to the thousands of Irish paupers who flock into the country". These people were of course absolutely desperate and the majority had suffered traumatic experiences having lost relatives and friends to starvation and disease. They were prepared to endure anything to exist. They were the poorest of the poor and ignored the fury of the farmers as they scavenged for root crops as they moved inland. They took work no matter how poorly paid and lived anywhere, however squalid as they sought out the developing towns of Glamorgan. The Welsh were also on the move looking for work and so employers found themselves with ample reserves of cheap labour which they ruthlessly exploited. Forced removals back to Ireland were futile but nonetheless attempted.

It is tempting at this distance to be critical of the Welsh for their unfeeling attitude to the impoverished immigrants pouring into their homeland but it needs to be remembered that notwithstanding official efforts in Ireland over decades to extinguish the use of Gaelic, the majority of the poor people fleeing Ireland at this time were primarily Gaelic speakers especially, according to a Government survey of 1871, Irish from the southern counties such as Southern Tipperary, Cork,

A Long Way from Tipperary

Waterford and Kerry etc. So not only were these poor people Catholics but they did not share a common language with the Welsh whose first tongue was Welsh and their second English. A moment's thought about public attitudes to the Immigration issue in Britain today, let alone hostility to economic migrants trying to enter the UK from Calais and feelings about families fleeing from famine and war in the Middle East to Italy in ill prepared boats , should inhibit high mindedness.

The cheapest way of coming over to Ireland in those days was as human ballast in the coal boats that plied their trade between Wales and Ireland. Indeed Irish landlords often paid sea captains a head fee to take the indigent and starving out of Ireland so as to reduce the pressure on the Irish Poor Law and therefore their local taxes. When regulations were introduced to control this trade and fine skippers transporting people in inhuman circumstances, they avoided embarrassment from landing their human cargos in ports and harbours, by shoving them off in creeks and onto beaches. Only one skipper was fined for this illegal trade and he had the effrontery to unload a cargo just short of Newport. Church archives record that many parentless children turned up on the beaches with instructions that they should make their way to Bridgend and sit on the town hall steps until someone from the Irish community took them in.

It may well be that the Murphys had coped better than most with the heart rending consequences of the Great Famine - their lease of a small parcel of land raised them a fraction above the level of desperation of most peasants. They certainly seem to have hung on in Ireland after 1845. But it is certain in view of the impact of the famine that William was not the first

A Long Way from Tipperary

of his family to set foot in Wales. He must have followed older brothers. There are indications in the Church records in Maesteg that at least two of his nephews migrated to the Llynfi valley both called John who were cousins of my father William. They form a link to their respective fathers, Dennis (born 1834) and Michael (born 1833) who could have settled elsewhere earlier in South Wales.

Thomas is probably in the 1861 census for South Wales. But the first indisputable entry is in the 1871 census, 4 years after his father's death. We find him at Number 11 Commercial Street Maesteg, 28 years old and working as a labourer in the Iron works. He married Margaret nee Hayes the previous year who was 6 years younger than himself. Richard and Margaret Hayes, Thomas's in laws live just up the road at Number 57 having moved from nearby Post Office Court where they were located in 1861. The Hayes were both Irish born and Richard had also worked at the Iron works since at least 1861. The Parish records show intimate connections between the Hayes and the Murphys right throughout the rest of the century as witnesses to each other's baptisms and marriages; it is clear that they were both very active in the Church.

Thomas and Margaret move to 45 Rock Street by the time of the 1881 census. By this time they have four children Catherine, aged 8, Margaret aged 5, twins aged 1, Richard and Thomas. Both Rock and Commercial Street are close to the Catholic Church. One of the first enterprises that the immigrant Catholics had achieved in the Bridgend valley as their community grew and prospered was the construction of a Church, at first in Bridgend and later in Maesteg. The Earl of

A Long Way from Tipperary

Dunraven who had estates in Ireland put up an endowment to build a church, house and school at Maesteg. This was constructed in 1872 and dedicated to Our Lady and St Patrick. It became the Church Hall when the present Church was built in 1907 in Pugin style. This was built right in the heart of the congregation and must have played a major part in forming the solidarity that characterised the Irish as they dealt with the many tragedies that afflicted miners in the 19th century as a result of the dangers of their occupation. The Church was also a shield against the hostility of the Welsh who felt inevitably threatened by the incursion of thousands of poor, uneducated Irishmen. The local press in the 19th Century has many examples of the patronising attitudes of the Welsh towards the incomers, which was an improvement on earlier feelings of downright hostility after the famine when the Welsh knew that the Irish gentry were simply dumping the poor and indigent on them. I can understand their anger. The Irish brought with them their own traditions amongst which were a strong sense of solidarity, unreasoning faith, fecundity and a propensity towards violence, largely attributable to a weakness for strong drink.

The Catholics banded together in overcrowded houses made worst by lots of single lodgers. The priest became a pivotal element in the community; Father Glassbrook, who married Thomas and Margaret, took charge at Aberavon, Maesteg and Neath in 1858 and remained until 1870. He was large and jovial and travelled about his parish on a pony, often followed by a gaggle of children. The Benedictine Order to which Glassbrook belonged was in the vanguard of the Church in Wales at this time. The priest as the Catholic spokesman had a lot to deal with; Catholicism was regarded by the Welsh as alien to their

A Long Way from Tipperary

Rev. Edward Anselm Glassbrook, O.S.B.

tradition of nonconformity and both communities were rock like in their attitudes. The Bible versus Doctrinal beliefs imposed by Rome was the chasm separating them. The immigrant was blamed for many of the problems of the new towns, real or imaginary. The Priest had to control the warring factions from different counties in Ireland who when not fighting each other, would fight the Welsh. Both sides needed little encouragement to have a go, often sparked by disputes sparked in the workplace. The Irish however were always in the minority and had to fight hard for their position as the Welsh did their best to prevent them from getting the better paid positions underground.

William described his origins as deriving from "Tipperary Stone Throwers" without knowing the origin of the term. The men of

A Long Way from Tipperary

Tipperary had taken some unusual steps at the beginning of the 19th Century to institutionalize their regard for violence which earned them the nick name "Tipperary Stone Throwers". In the first decades of the Century they invented a cult of stick fighting in which tenant farmers and their sons dressed up to confront other farmers in open spaces towards the end of public gatherings such as fairs, markets and wakes. Two lines met in face to face fighting for no reason other than a love of violence; rules were agreed by the team captains, the most basic one was that no one should back off if a fight was offered. They fought with large sticks, some hardened and tipped with lead, the shaft usually made from the blackthorn. A contemporary commentator noted "To be sure, skulls and bones are broken, and lives lost; but they are lost in pleasant fighting – they are the consequences of the sport, the beauty of which consists of breaking as many heads as you can".

The "Rawlins" and "Cusheens" featured in south Tipperary and in 1836 alone 100 faction fights were reported, the groups numbering sometimes between 200 and a 1000, turning their ire on the police if they tried to interfere or even on the Army. Most factions were distinctly tribal, joining together family clans with a history of cooperation The biggest faction fight took place on June 24 1834, the Feast day of St John the Baptist at Balleyveigh in Country Kerry; when the bleeding stopped, 20 men were dead.

It was Thurles, not far from Gortnahoe however, that has the dubious honour of giving Tipperary its "Stone Thrower" title. In 1826 in the course of a faction fight in the main square, some of the supporting wives had brought baskets secretly loaded with

A Long Way from Tipperary

rocks which they started to throw at the opposing faction. In the general melee, targets were missed but windows broken, the police attacked and then fled (but not before shooting three miscreants dead) ; the day was only saved by the 15th Royal Foot who were stationed in Thurles. By the end of the Century, the influence of the Church, the growth of Fenianism, offering a political outlet for violence and the foundation of Hurling as a national sport with rules in Thurles in 1884, put an end to this activity. But the title stuck and William, my father remembered it somewhat ruefully. He had no taste for violence other than participating in the organised mayhem of the rugby field.

The eventual power of the Irish in the valleys was as much attributable to their willingness to join with others in asserting their rights as it was to violence. In the 1820s Iron making had transformed the Llynfi valley which was an agricultural valley

Maesteg Deep Pit 1916 (Drift Mine)

with a scattered population before the development of coal and iron. The early development of industry was through open cast

A Long Way from Tipperary

mining of coal on farmland via simple excavations. Coal and later smelted iron was drawn to markets through horse drawn wagons which took them to the coast. The valley was fortunately located as the coal and ironstone measures surfaced in the Llynfi and were therefore initially accessible through shallow pits and later drifts, punched into the sides of the valley in order to follow the coal seams as they tracked downwards. A railway and port at Porthcawl followed and the population boomed. There were simply not enough Welsh people in the valley to exploit these riches at the beginning and so labour was drawn in from Bristol and the West Country and then the Irish arrived. Initially the mine owners had things very much their way but even before unionised labour became a potent factor, the miners learned to stand up for themselves. This was not only reflected in pay and safety but also by breaking the pernicious practice of "Truck", a system of paying miners at long intervals in an invented currency that was only useable at the company store where prices were of course controlled by the owners who therefore had a double financial hold on their employees.

The "Truck" system ran from 1828 until it was abandoned in 1869 after legal challenge. In an area without shops, and with the propensity of wages to be "blown" on booze, the scheme was not without merit. But it was clearly exploitative - it was a great vehicle for profit and overcharging. In the 1830s it made up to 20% of the Ironworks profits! It also meant that the miners never accumulated the wherewithal to withhold their labour. By 1851 the population of Maesteg was almost 5,000 and it doubled within 5 years. In 1856 there was no lighting and no sewage disposal, work on which only started in 1858, but

A Long Way from Tipperary

there were 47 pubs which had grown to 64 by 1880. The main employers were the two large iron works, the Llynfi (1828-1870) and the Cambrian (1939-1970). Some 1500 men were employed at the Cambrian alone. But iron was reaching the end of the road when Thomas first appears irrefutably in the census in 1871, through a combination of falling demand and uneconomic conditions. Fortunately the coal mining industry then began to form the backbone of the prosperity of the town.

With the collapse of Iron in the early 1870s following a decade of uncertainty, the steam power revolution dawned just in time to generate a demand for steam coal which existed in abundance in the valley. A major driver of this development was the entrepreneurial genius of John North who made a fortune in the Chilean Nitrates industry but realising that the bubble was about to burst, moved into coal by acquiring collieries in the Llynfi valley in the mid 1880s. Having acquired a mining capability, North then muscled his way into the lucrative London coal market as well as getting himself on the coveted Admiralty List of the best steam coals for the Navy. Notwithstanding various mining accidents and indeed a two year strike in 1894, he gave a major boost to Maesteg. North, who lived in a mansion in Avery Hill Eltham, London, now occupied by the University of Greenwich died in 1897 but by 1899, 2,286 men were employed as miners, twice the figure for 1891 and there was a housing boom especially in Caerau. A new mine was opened at Cwmdu and by 1913, the company employed 5500 workers and was amongst the ten biggest miners in Glamorgan.

The valley avoided the major disasters that struck other communities, although a naked light explosion at Gun Pit in

A Long Way from Tipperary

Miners - South Wales 1876

1863 killed 14 miners, and a further 11 men died at the Oakwood mine in an explosion of methane at midnight on 10 January 1872; fortunately most of the workforce were absent as the force of the blast mangled the headings and the thunder could be heard for miles. There were a string of smaller accidents punctuated by an unusual accident at the Garth Colliery in 1897 when the winding engineman responsible for hauling the men up the shaft allowed the cage to over run at the pithead – the haulage rope became detached and the cage plunged, killing all nine men inside. Public attention was inevitably focussed on explosions but the far more insidious killer was the high incidence of prolonged and debilitating illness associated with dust related disease. It was not until 1942 that pneumoconiosis was acknowledged as a hazardous disease – in the meantime, thousands of miners had their lives cut short by a condition that turned their lungs into concrete and made it impossible to breathe.

A Long Way from Tipperary

Dead Miners – Aftermath of an Explosion 1880

In the earliest phase of mining, the miners were employed by the iron companies and they had no collective strength. Strike leaders were arrested for "deserting their work". Although there is some evidence of trade union activity in the valley by the 1860s it is not until 1872 that we find a substantial number of around 900 miners in the union. There was a strike in 1872 for better pay which was settled in 1873. Various local formulas for relating pay to the price of coal failed to produce stability. It is clear that Thomas was trying to establish himself in Maesteg during a period of industrial unrest – every improvement in conditions had to be extracted under pressure. Miners were working a six day week but through strikes squeezed a concession from the owners of a day off a month in 1888. The 1890s saw lengthy stoppages over coal cutting rates – the problem was that conditions were so varied in the mines that no single negotiation could meet could meet all contingencies. The Caerau miners went out in June 1884 and forced the recalcitrant to join them by dragging strike breakers from their homes in Maesteg, dressing them in sheets and parading them

A Long Way from Tipperary

Miners - Oldster, Youngster and Mule

around the town (this seems like a throw back to the "Whiteboy" days of Tipperary). Striking miners at this time were able to hold out through support payments made to families from subscriptions contributed by miners in non striking mines But after 12 months the owners outmanoeuvred the miners by closing all the mines, thereby creating equality of misery and distress. The result was that the men were starved back to work in February 1896. The industry was expanding rapidly and pressure for change was growing; the Coal Owner Associations answer to pay demands was a lockout in 1898 which had a disastrous effect on the community; soup kitchens were opened and families scavenged on the coal tips for fuel. After 22 weeks the miners reluctantly returned – the owner's response was far from magnanimous. They abolished the concession of one day off a month conceded ten years earlier. This was however a Pyrrhic victory as the South Wales Miners

A Long Way from Tipperary

Federation was formed a month later – there was a new determination to form a united front against the owners and they would live to regret their triumph. Militancy had been born in South Wales that would endure until the end of the coal era.

It is quite likely that my grandfather played a leading role in the union as he was clearly well respected and something of a natural leader. The evidence for this is that when he died he was one of the rare Irishmen who were buried at the Parish Church in Llangenydd which does not have a Catholic plot but where respectable people aspired to be interred. The Murphys lived close to the foot of the stone stairs that led up to the Church from Commercial Street. It was the custom in those days to expose the deceased in his coffin to his family and neighbours in the parlour and there to hold the wake, a celebration to wish the dead well on their way to the next life. This could get quite boisterous in the Irish tradition but the men were expected to be sufficiently recovered on the following day to carry the coffin to the graveyard. In the case of Thomas Murphy, this was a formidable haul up the hill for several miles to the churchyard and my father was proud to say that none of his father's friends and admirers had to carry twice - this was an important statement. Thomas was in his mid sixties when he died in 1906. His wife Margaret followed him shortly thereafter. The family gravestones look unexpectedly affluent in the social context of the time.

Margaret came from wholly Irish stock, her maiden name was Hayes and her parents had immigrated also to Wales from Ireland via London in search of work. Her parents were amongst the first to be buried in the new cemetery in Maesteg

A Long Way from Tipperary

in the 1880s; her father Richard had worked as a labourer manufacturing nails in one of the iron foundries in Maesteg. She had 11 children of which Catherine (1873-97) died in childbirth; her baby James (born 6/3/97), died after a further 3 months; Margaret (born 1875) married Michael Keefe in May 1898; they had four children James, John (born 1913); Patrick (born 1915 and Margaret (born 1916) ; Mary (born. 1878) died as a baby; Richard (1879 - 1949) never married; Thomas, his twin, married Kate McGuire and had several children; Joanna (1883) died as a baby; James (1881 - 1893) died in the pits; Helen (1885 -1960) had a single illegitimate son Thomas (raised by Margaret); John (1890-1955) never married; William (1891 - 1965)) married Alice Maud Turner; Edward married but had no children.

What is unusual about this Irish family is that only 5 of the children of Thomas and Margaret produced children who survived and of these Nell had only one child. Two of their children died as babies, one died in childbirth, one died in an accident aged 12 and two never married. The death of James during his first week at work must have been particularly difficult for Margaret to bear. He was suffocated to death on 4 October 1893 in North Navigation Colliery No 9 as a result of a roof face fall in the Victoria seam after a prop collapsed. According to the Mining Accident report, he was filling coal at the face in a narrow gallery with another boy whilst the collier responsible for him was in the main gallery, too far away to save him. He was 12 years old. The death of Thomas, Margaret's husband was also connected to the pits as he had thrombosis in his legs attributed to injuries in the mine which undermined his health, migrated to his heart and eventually killed him in 1906. By this

A Long Way from Tipperary

Underground Gallery

time he had climbed up the mining hierarchy to become a colliery platelayer – which meant that he took care of the tracks underground on which the coal wagons ran.

The lot of a child in the Irish community was not a happy one. The first Catholic school in Maesteg was opened in January 1875. There were 67 children being taught in one room, the youngest 4 and the oldest 14. By 1876 the roll had increased to 80 but the following year it was observed that " many children are absent owing to sickness and poverty amongst their parents. The parents are receiving scarcely any wages and the little ones are being kept at home because they have not sufficient clothing to save them from the inclemency of the weather. There are many children absent through lack of sufficient food" To add to these problems, children were dying as a result of the many epidemics of the period, smallpox, diphtheria, measles, scarlet fever and whooping cough. In

A Long Way from Tipperary

1887, the parish priest recorded that "there are 40 children in desperate circumstances, Six or eight are actually so naked that for decency's sake, I could not allow them to attend school." . At this time, the death rate throughout the country amongst children of generally sober and employed working classes family was one in four, or double the death rate of males in the Armed Forces between 1914-18.

William had a difficult relationship with his mother who was said to be a tough and uncompromising woman – her life gave her no quarter. It might be too much to attribute to her influence the fact that none of her children produced families on the Irish

The Bath After Work

scale but it is the case that only William had a family big enough to gladden the heart of Mother Church - 7 children in all if we include the two who died shortly after birth. It appears that William left home as soon as he was able, probably to lodge

A Long Way from Tipperary

with another family. He is described in his Army attestation document in 1908 as a miner and also appears in the 1910 census in this role. We know that he followed the mining apprentice route that was common in those days in the pits of serving initially as a small boy; he was probably 13 when he started around 1905. Not that many years before, little lads as young as 7 or 8 controlled the wooden ventilation doors below ground which shut off sections of workings in order to prevent fire damp explosions from flashing through the galleries and killing everyone. The children opened and closed the doors as the horse or man drawn wagons went along the tracks to the pit bottom. As the children grew up , they were used to excavate coal from small seams and also to pull wagons (known as drams) along by straps attached to their waists. They were probably doing man's work by the time that they reached 15.

William was a small man ; his attestation into the Air Force in 1918 shows that he was 5ft 6 inches in height, had dark hair, a fair complexion and blue/grey eyes. His chest measured 32 inches - he was quite wiry. He did not enjoy the pits and once described with little pleasure his job of working narrow seams little more than shoulder width which he could only tackle by laying on his side on the ground. As he hacked his way along the seam with a pick, the coal was pulled back by his partner using a shovel to a third miner who would load the coal into a truck, He had to stop periodically to drive in wooden props to support the roof a s he penetrated further into the seam. He would find himself eventually working deep inside a propped gallery, not a place for anyone suffering from claustrophobia.. He and his mates would swop roles throughout the shift. They took meals, which my father called "scran"- a military term,

A Long Way from Tipperary

Working a Narrow Seam

underground and drank copious quantities of water to replace the sweat and wash the coal dust from their mouth and throats.

Food was taken underground in tins called "Tommy Boxes". The miners ate by the light of carbide safety lamps attached to their hats which burned a chemical with a bright flame. These had been invented decades earlier by Humphrey Davey and were designed to avoid coal damp explosions which were usually fatal. It was a penal offence for a miner to take matches or a lighter underground for obvious reasons In the case of one notorious explosion at the Sengennydd colliery in 1913, 440 men were killed, almost 10% of the population of the village. William was lucky in Maesteg - he only suffered minor accidents but these left coal scars on his forehead and his forearm where open wounds had absorbed coal dust which remained visible under the skin. There were no pithead baths in those days so the tub had to be drawn up for each miner in the family when they got home.

A Long Way from Tipperary

William on the Eve of War.

The coming war probably held few fears for William when he joined his regiment in 1908 but by the end of 1914 the Old Testament words in Revelation 6:8 would have come to mind;

"I looked, and there before me was a pale horse! Its rider was named Death, and Hades was following close behind him. They were given power over a fourth of the earth to kill by sword, famine and plague, and by the wild beasts of the earth."

Notwithstanding his terrible experiences with the Welch in 1914/15, William said that he was glad to have joined the Army early on when he had the chance of being an infantryman. Later, he would have had less choice as the Army was keen to

A Long Way from Tipperary

recruit experienced miners for mining and counter mining operations which became such a major feature of warfare on the western front and which is well illustrated in the novel "Birdsong". William said that he preferred to take his chances in the trenches rather than face death fighting the Germans underground where no quarter was given and there was the constant fear of being blown up and suffocated by the enemy's counter mining operations.

A Long Way from Tipperary

Chapter 3.

Going to War

William Murphy (164900 formerly 260) Second Battalion Welch Regiment 11 September 9 August 1908 to 10 September 1915 (France). Enlisted Private 2nd Class in the Royal Air Force 8 May 1918, Discharged 30 April 1920 Awarded 1914 Star, British War Medal and Victory Medal. Born 1891 – Died 1965.

William Murphy was only 17 when he joined the 3rd (Special Reserve) Battalion of the Welch Regiment on 11 September

A Long Way from Tipperary

1908. This Battalion was the direct successor of the 3rd (Militia) Battalion, formerly the Militia of the County of Glamorgan which was transmuted into its new incarnation at midnight on March 31st 1908. This transformation was the product of the Haldane Reforms which were initiated when Haldane took over responsibility for the War Office following the Liberal Victory at the polls in November 1905. Haldane's plans were based on the idea of using the Militia to become a real reserve of officers and men for the Regular Army with the general role of providing complete units on mobilisation if required, but more importantly, of maintaining a regular flow of reinforcements to replace casualties and other wastage when the Regular Army was committed to war. The Special Reserve Battalions were to be administered in all respects through Regular Army channels. Training was to be based on the appropriate Regimental Depots which in the case of 3rd Welch was Maindy Barracks, Cardiff. The need for the Haldane Reforms was amply demonstrated in 1907 when the Regular Army found itself unable to meet its establishment of 6,494 officers and 160,200 Men. The Militia and Volunteers, in spite of their enthusiasm were not considered to be sufficiently well trained to meet the demands of warfare of the day.

William's commitment to the Third Battalion involved him in completing 6 months initial training and thereafter a further 27 days annually. It is likely that he continued working in the pits in the prelude to war. The family had no record of military service and probably had little regard for an institution that was synonymous with repression in Ireland. Later of course, William's brother Edward joined him in the

A Long Way from Tipperary

Army after the outbreak of war by enlisting in the Royal Horse Artillery.

At the declaration of war all members of the Third Battalion were sent telegrams to muster at Maindy Barracks. They were now effectively on the fighting strength of the Regiment and any failure to appear would have attracted a charge of desertion. According to Captain HC Rees, the Battalion was greatly below strength and a large percentage of those serving were too young to take to the field. The result of the shortage was to fill the ranks with reservists like William who had not had time to get marching fit before being called up to endure the terrific strain of what was to become the Retreat from Mons. The practice was to send men up to the Battalion as soon as they were fully kitted out. This could not have been an easy time to join "the old sweats" who tended to have a superior attitude to reservists but such feelings were not fated to endure as only a handful of those who fought with the Second Battalion as either professional or reservist survived until Christmas 1914. Thereafter, any survivor had the right to consider himself a veteran.

It is unlikely that William Murphy appreciated in the summer of 1914 that the assassination of Archduke Franz Ferdinand the heir to the monarchy of the Habsburgs in Sarajevo on 28 June was going to have any effect on his life. The 2nd Welch were at Aldershot carrying out Brigade training with the Third Brigade. On I August they were ordered back to their peace station, Borden in Hampshire and on 4 August mobilisation was ordered. The Battalion was despatched post-haste to Le Havre where it arrived on 12 August.

A Long Way from Tipperary

Franz Ferdinand was a brutal and obstinate man, impatient with opposition and unsuited to the democratic age. Bosnia and its sister province Herzegovina were recent Habsburg acquisitions. Formerly Turkish and the scene of many rebellions, they had been administered by Austria - Hungary since 1878. The people were southern Slavs, Serbs or Croats, many of them resentful at having been brought under the Habsburgs instead of being allowed to join Serbia, their national State. Gavrilo Princip, a schoolboy conspirator took his chance and killed both the Archduke and his wife during a visit to inspect the Army in Bosnia. Austria had had trouble with Serbia before and as a declining power was anxious to assert its authority. It turned to its German ally who promised backing if Russia threatened to support Serbia. Although the Austrians had no proof that Serbia was involved in the assassination, an ultimatum was despatched with Serbian humiliation in mind. The Serbs were slow to respond and the Austrians declared war. This was fatal. The Austrians were not looking for a real conflict and were not in fact ready to fight, but the reaction was catastrophic.

Now it was Russia's turn - she claimed to be the patron of Serbia and could not allow Austro-Hungarian domination of the Balkans because of the need to control the Straits of Constantinople, her major outlet to the sea. The Russians only wanted to answer the violent diplomacy of the Austrians with a demonstration of their own-to mobilize. But their problem was that the mobilisation of their great conscript army rested on railways and once started it could not be stopped. Moreover the Russians realised that if they only mobilised against Austria, they would be defenceless against

A Long Way from Tipperary

her ally Germany unless they undertook a general (as opposed to a partial mobilisation). Their intention was again not to fight but to engage in a diplomatic demonstration. Their bluff was called.

The second factor of high strategy intervened at this point. All the military in Europe had failed to learn the lessons of recent wars, including the American Civil war, that defence was getting stronger and attack more difficult. The Germans did not believe that they could conquer decisively if they had to fight on two fronts against both France and Russia. They assumed that once they were embroiled with Russia, France would attack. Whilst all chiefs of staffs had offensive plans, the Germans had planned ever since 1892 to attack heavily in the West before the Russians could become a factor. All powers except Germany could mobilize yet get on with diplomacy. The Germans had run mobilisation and war into one. They gave Russia 12 hours to demobilize - the Russians refused and on August 1 Germany declared War on Russia and; two days later with hardly an attempt at an excuse, on France.

The German War Plan was the concept of von Schlieffen, Chief of the German General Staff from 1892 to 1906 and already dead by 1914. The short frontier between France and Germany was heavily fortified on both sides, so there was no chance of a quick victory there. To the north of it lay Belgium, making a sort of funnel through which the German armies could pass, then flood out onto the plain to encircle the French. On 2 August they demanded free passage through Belgium. The Belgians refused and this

A Long Way from Tipperary

brought Britain into the War. Austria declared war on Russia on 6 August. France and Britain declared war on Austria on 10 August. On 3 August the Turks allied themselves with the Germans.

All over Europe conscripts joined their units - the war was met with great enthusiasm. There had been no major war since 1871....no man in the prime of his life knew what war was about. But there was confidence that it would be over quickly. Men did not debate why they were fighting. They knew.... It was to defend the Motherland. The British were a different case. They were in no danger of invasion. They had gone to war for the neutrality and independence of Belgium. They talked from the beginning in idealistic terms. This was "the war to end wars". ...to make the world safe for democracy. They would not be content with victory.....the disillusionment afterwards was correspondingly greater.

The British Generals had seen real fighting over vast spaces against an unseen enemy in the Boer War...a Cavalry war. In France, horses were everywhere, but the infantry depended on railways to get close to the theatre of battle, where this worked. Otherwise, they slogged everywhere on foot. Both sides could reach the battlefield with speed but once they arrived, their speed across the ground slowed to walking pace. The practical effect of this was that reinforcements could always arrive fast enough to a threatened position to prevent the attacking side breaking through on foot in a sustained manner. This is the strategic reason why defence was stronger than attack throughout the war. Defence was mechanised, attack was not. Supplies

A Long Way from Tipperary

were pulled along by horses, in every Army forage took up more space than ammunition or food. Armies had to be fed not from the land but from the homeland. The very size of the Armies made it difficult for them to move and thence to win.

There was a real war of movement, however, for the first month or so, then followed four years of deadlock. The French were aware of the Germans plan but thought they had an answer. As the Germans struggled through Belgium the French planned to strike them in the flank in the Ardennes and also attack in Lorraine. The offensive was launched on 14 August..... it was a disaster. The French shattered themselves on the German defences, losing the flower of their armies. The Germans had an easier time in their advance through Belgium, the French were bogged down in Lorraine and the small Belgian Army drew back into the fortress of Antwerp. Liege fell and the Germans ploughed on into France on foot at a terrific rate, Kluck's First Army often covered 30 miles in a day. The Belgians pulled off the important stroke of wrecking the railways but only fatigue seemed likely to delay the Germans from reaching their target of Paris. As the Germans crossed the River Meuse a feeble attempt was made by the French to attack them in their flank from Verdun, but it failed. In the meantime discussions took place in London about the best place for the B.E.F. In fact, there was no choice as the imetable had been prepared since 1911 for drawing up the British on the left of the French. The British therefore lost their freedom of action from the very start.

A Long Way from Tipperary

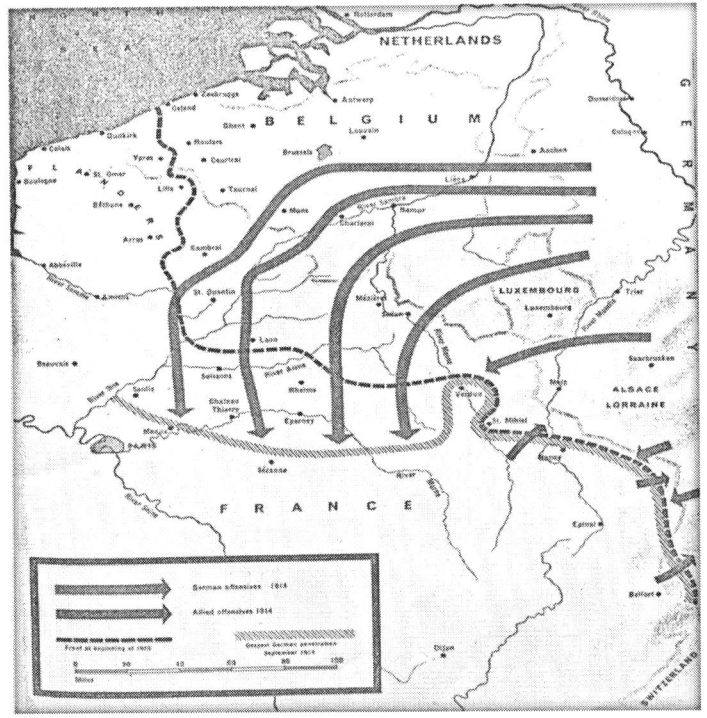

The German Plan

The B.E.F. was in position by 20 August and advancing, reached Mons on 22 August where it collided with the Germans. Two British Divisions were attacked by two German Army Corps and held them off on 23 August. General French intended to stay and fight but discovered during the night that he had nothing on his left and the French on his right were falling back fast. He retreated but on 26 August had to fight again at Le Cateau. No further fighting took place for ten days. The BEF. hung on tight to

A Long Way from Tipperary

the French on the right. The French were falling back due south, drawing the British with them, away from their lines of supplies and communications which ran to the west. The Germans on the other hand were marching first due west and then inclining south west.... the opposing forces were thus moving away from each other. General French was so worried that he had to be stopped from clearing off to St Nazaire altogether by Kitchener. The French Government fled from Paris to Bordeaux.

As the Germans swung round into France, there appeared the great flaw in Schlieffen's plan.....Paris. If Kluck's Army on the German extreme right went west of Paris there would be a great gap between it and Bulow's Army which came next in line. If Kluck went east of Paris, he would be attacked in the flank. The Germans were unable to contain Paris because their lines of communication were already stretched and they had insufficient forces. Kluck's advance waved about then he decided to go east of Paris in order to encircle the French Armies before the Paris garrison broke out. General Gallieni, the Military Governor of Paris saw the Germans exposed flank and wanted to let it go beyond Paris in order to catch the Germans in the rear. But Joffre resisted the German advance. When Kluck realised what was happening, he turned West again towards Paris. Further East Bulow held firm against Joffre, but an enormous gap opened up between the two German Armies into which the British advanced....they went forward into emptiness whilst the French fought fiercely on either flank. The BEF advanced with light casualties in crossing the Marne. General Moltke was worried about the extension of his forces and after an

A Long Way from Tipperary

inconclusive engagement against the French, authorised a general retreat. The Allied advance in pursuit lasted five days.

The Germans reached the Aisne and were so exhausted that they could march no more. They dug in and set up machine guns. Trench warfare had begun.....the machine gun completed the contrast between speed of arrival on the battlefield and slowness of advance on it when the dominance of the machine gun could only be overcome (until the arrival of the tank) by massive bombardment and the accumulation of Reserves, warnings which always gave the other side the chance to bring up reinforcements.

There was a last splutter of movement because both lines still hung in the air. Both tried to turn the flank, to get ahead of the other. This was called the 'race to the sea' although it was an open flank not the sea that both sides were aiming for. The Germans were distracted however by the Belgian defence of Antwerp, which fell on 10 October. But the Belgians, by holding the Germans on the coast, principally by flooding the country, pushed the German advance inland and the latter moved in mid October towards Ypres, meaning to outflank their enemy. There they met the BEF which in turn was moving up from the Aisne in its own outflanking manoeuvre. The Germans were stronger and at one point punched a hole in the British defences, but the position held as reinforcements were brought up by rail. The mutual battering however produced great slaughter in this the First Battle of Ypres as men were fed in day after day on a narrow front. The British regular Army was shattered

A Long Way from Tipperary

leaving only a framework for the mass armies to come. The Western Front was now drawn from the Channel to Switzerland.

At the outbreak of the war the Welch Regiment consisted of the 1st Battalion in India, the 2nd Battalion in the Aldershot Command, the Depot at Cardiff, the 3rd Battalion at Cardiff which provided reserves for the two regular Battalions, and the 4th, 5th, 6th and 7th (Cyclist) Territorial Battalions in South Wales. By the end of the war, there were 34 Battalions of the Regiment which took part in all the principal battles and campaigns and lost 355 officers, 1,244 warrant officers and NCOs and 6,180 other ranks, killed or died of wounds, a total of 7,779.

The 2nd Battalion, commanded by Lt Col C.B. Morland, went to France in August with the 3rd Brigade of the 1st Division and served throughout the war in France and Belgium. It formed part of the BEF that consisted of a Cavalry Division and six Infantry divisions-all of which included Artillery, Engineers and RASC, together with a small Flying Corps, numbering about 160,000 all ranks. The Welch were hardly engaged at Mons, the opening battle of the war on 23rd August, as the German attack fell almost entirely on the 2nd Corps on their left, but they took part in the ever memorable "Retreat from Mons" - a march of over 200 miles in 13 days, after which they turned around on 6 September and advancing alongside the French attacked strongly across the Aisne. They crossed the Aisne under considerable fire and assaulted entrenched German positions along a long ridge known as the "Chemin de Dames" (Ladies Road). They

A Long Way from Tipperary

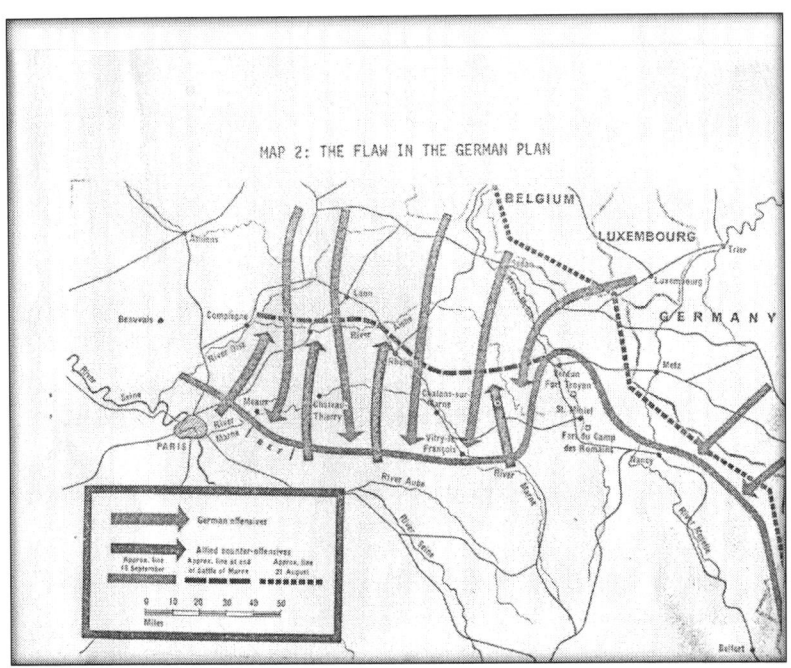

The Flaw in the German Plan

lost 11 officers and 210 other ranks. They later moved north as the front extended to participate in the First Battle of Ypres which lasted from 19 October to 10 November. The memorable actions of this period took place at Langemarck, near Ypres on 23 October when they mowed down a massed enemy attack (by the so-called German "Student" battalions); on 29 October when they made a long advance and recaptured the village of Givenchy, from which the BEF had been driven by a heavy German assault and finally, on 31 October in the critical defence of Gheluvelt on the most crucial day of the war.

A Long Way from Tipperary

A detailed explanation of Gheluvelt comes later but essentially the Germans were seeking a breakthrough and concentrated their fire on the village that was held by the Welch with the Queens on their right and the South Wales Borderers on their left. The Germans were held for three hours, but the line was broken and only a handful of the Welch escaped, the survivors reforming at Veldhoek, half a mile back. Gheluvelt was retaken by the 2nd Worcesters who rejoined half of the SWB who had held on in the grounds of Gheluvelt Chateau. They were too few to hold the position however, so during the night the line was redrawn further back. At nightfall on 31 October, the Welch mustered only 3 officers and 50 men of who William Murphy was certainly numbered. In the fierce fighting of First Ypres, which went on until 15 November, the 2nd Battalion had lost 6 officers and 197 other ranks killed with many others wounded.

The 2nd Battalion was so badly mauled that it had to be withdrawn from the line and organised on a two company basis until it was replenished in December, reaching again around 1000 men. The dying down of the fighting at Ypres was largely due to the transfer by the Germans of forces to the Russian Front. This prompted a half hearted allied offensive in December and a retaliatory attack by the Germans which saw the Battalion again in action in appalling mud and water at Givenchy and Festubert. By the end of January, the weather had become too bad for attacks by either Army. The German advance in 1914 had made a large salient between Rheims and Amiens, which threatened the communications of the French with their Northern front. If

A Long Way from Tipperary

this salient could be successfully pierced, the Germans would in turn be threatened. Joffre decided to attack from both sides with the French and the British cooperating in their own area. The French Tenth was to capture the Vimy Heights and the British First Army, the Aubers Ridge, the attack was to start in March. As a preliminary, the BEF took the village of Neuve Chapelle, to which the 2nd Battalion moved up after its capture. The attack at Aubers was another disaster in which the Battalion attempted to advance over waterlogged ground against protected machine gun emplacements. Within 24 hours of the opening attack on 9 May, the Battalion lost 11 officers and 245 other ranks out of a total of 24 officers and 838 other ranks. The Battalion was again reinforced and Lieutenant Colonel Prothero appointed to command.

In spite of the failure of Joffre's futile offensives in May, he was eager for fresh onslaughts. The British Government were against further operations until Kitcheners New Armies were ready on a large scale in 1916. The British had landed in the Dardanelles in April and in spite of the obvious difficulties there, the British preferred to push the attack to a conclusion before embarking on more adventures in France. Kitchener promised Joffre however at the Chantilly conference in July that he would support a new offensive on the Western Front in September, after Gallipoli. By August, it was clear that the attack at Gallipoli had failed and Joffre now presented his post-dated cheque. When British Ministers resisted, Kitchener replied "We have to make war as we must and not as we should like to". He believed that unless the British gave support to Joffre, he would be

A Long Way from Tipperary

overthrown and the French politicians would make peace. British soldiers died so that France could be kept in the war.

Joffre's plan was to launch a combined offensive- attacking in Champagne on the right and Arras on the left. Although initially the French tasted success by overrunning the German front line, they found a fully prepared second line behind it...defence in depth turned offensives into pointless slaughter. Joffre had laid down however that the British should attack at Loos in spite of the objections of General French for whom it meant advancing across coalfields and a wilderness of miners' cottages. Kitchener ordered French to fall into line and at first the British did very well, breaking though the German line on the right, and almost penetrating the second line. Haig called for reserves, but French who was jealous of him, had kept reserves at his own hand and too far to the rear. As they moved up they tangled with troops coming out of line. The result was chaos. During the confusion the Germans counter- attacked and threatened a breakthrough in turn. The British renewed their efforts, whilst the French looked on. The fighting petered out early in November with no strategic gain. The British lost 50,000 men as against 20,000 Germans; the French 190,000 as against 120,000.

Loos cost the Welch dear...the 2nd Battalion alone lost 12 officers and 224 other ranks out of a regimental loss of 41 officers and 872 ranks. It is not clear at what stage William Murphy left the battalion but it appears from the record that he was saved from the carnage by the enteric fever that sent him to hospital on 10 September. It is nonetheless quite

A Long Way from Tipperary

extraordinary that he managed to survive thus far in view of the losses that his battalion suffered in the first year of the war. He was an extraordinarily lucky man, as an account of the battles in which he was engaged shows, based on the regimental diary and other material. Before we move on that however, it might be interesting to look at the history of the 2nd Battalion as well as the kind of soldier that it produced.

A Long Way from Tipperary

Chapter 4

Origins of the Modern Army

The origins of the modern army date back to the Civil War when Cromwell trained and equipped his troops so well that they became known as "Ironsides". After Cromwell's death Charles II thought it safer to create new regiments which existed only to form bodyguards for the King but by degrees they increased to become the permanent Army. In 1681 Charles built Chelsea hospital which was used by military pensioners who had become infirm in his service. Many were fit enough for garrison duties and it was from these that the 41st Foot, so called the Regiment of Invalids was formed in 1719. In 1787 it was turned into a Marching Regiment and its invalid status abandoned. In the meantime the 69th Foot was raised in 1756 and was used as a Marine Force. The two regiments had separate careers until 1881 when they were amalgamated into the Welch Regiment as the 1st and 2nd Battalions (the 41st having been granted the title in 1831).

The 69th Foot as the precursor of the 2nd Battalion is of particular interest to this story. It had a distinguished fighting history and saw a great deal of action during the 7 Years war. It took Martinique from the French in 1762 and was active in skirmishing off the west coast of France. 20 years later during the American War of Independence it participated in one of the few bright incidents from the British standpoint when it served under Rodney at the Battle of the

A Long Way from Tipperary

Saints off of Dominica which defeated the French in the West Indies. During the Napoleonic Wars it served on the Agamemnon under Nelson at Toulon in 1793 and later again in the West Indies. Two detachments served again under Nelson in the Captain at the battle of Cape St Vincent on St Valentines Day 1797 when the Spanish Navy was destroyed and prevented from joining with the French to control the Channel. The 69th were in India from 1805 to 1825 at various periods seeing action at the Capture of Mauritius and also the seizure of Java from the Dutch (in 1811). A detachment of the 69th was present at the Battle of Quatre Bras on 16 June 1815, a costly victory and curtain raiser for Waterloo at which the 69th was also involved.

The period from around 1825 until 1881 seems rather quiet for the 69th. On the other hand the 41st was involved in the acquisition of Burma in 1826, battles in Afghanistan, including the relief of Kandahar in 1841 and the ferocious battles of Alma, Inkerman and Sevastopol during the Crimean War from 1854 to 1856. After its formation into the Welch Regiment, it served as the 1st Battalion in the Boer War and took part in the relief of Kimberley and the fighting at Paardeberg that lead to the capture of Bloemfontein and later Pretoria.

From the soldiers standpoint, in 1914 the Battalion of around 1000 men at full strength (they seldom were) was the unit that provided his prestige as a fighting man, sometimes lead by a Major but more frequently by Colonel (who sometimes commanded a regiment of 2000 men). The company imposed itself powerfully on the men, it consisted

A Long Way from Tipperary

of 250 soldiers, and was commanded by a Captain who signed a man's pay book each week. Company NCOs detailed parades, ration parties and fatigues. Group loyalty depended heavily however on the section (15 men under a Lance Corporal) and the platoon (about 60 men under a Subaltern). Armies and Corps meant very little, the biggest unit with real meaning was the Division consisting of 12,000 men under a Major General which moved as a single whole, occupying about twenty miles of road and needing 188 lorry and wagon loads of equipment a day to keep it functioning.

It is reasonable to assume that as William Murphy was a committed soldier having been in the Militia since the age of 17, his uniform was slightly better fitting than that of the thousands who came after him. It was nonetheless a most uncomfortable outfit for war, consisting of heavy serge trousers, a rough woollen shirt, blouse and puttees which dated back to the Indian Mutiny. His boots would have been the bane of his life. Unlike the German boot, the British boot did not extend up the leg but was still of an enormous size and far less suitable than the enemy's boot for marching. It was made of Indian roan leather and ideally should be a tight fit forward but loose at the rear with a low heel suitable for downhill marching. In spite of such tricks as putting wet soap on the feet, wearing two pairs of socks and never removing the boots until feet were cooled, blisters, calluses and nodules under the pressure of the laces were common to all.

The discomfort of the march was compounded by the weight of the pack that each man had to carry which weighed in at

A Long Way from Tipperary

around 55 lbs before any extras were shared around. This was broken down into about 12 lbs of clothing, an 11lb rifle, 100 rounds of ammunition, trench tools, webbing, the pack itself and rations/water. The extras, apart from personal items, were such things as Verey pistols (for firing signal rockets) periscopes and wire cutters. No wonder strong men staggered. During the period of mobile war, the Second Battalion did an awful lot of marching. The routine never changed during the whole war. Men marched for 50 minutes in the hour, covering in that time around 3 miles and 12 to 15 miles in a day. Each Regiment of 4 in the Brigade took it in turns to head the march so as to set its own pace and avoid the choking dust that the column threw up. Officers on horseback lead the men whilst NCOs took the rear to ensure a proper gap of 7 paces between platoons. A whistle blew every 50 minutes and men collapsed, slackening their belts and using their packs as a pillow. A battalion lavatory would have been dug in advance of the line of march. The straight roads of France made each kilometre seem like four. Roads were often unsurfaced and in dry weather produced choking dust whilst when wet became rivers of mud. The steep camber tipped the weary off to the side. Water could only be taken with permission.

The infantry weapon carried by Private Murphy was the Lee Enfield which was conceived initially during the Boer War as a Cavalry carbine. It was fitted with a magazine of 10 bullets and consisted of 131 separate parts - no wonder it was inspected so frequently. Used by an expert it was a precision tool. Amateurs were thought capable of hitting a 5 centime

A Long Way from Tipperary

piece at thirty yards with 6 out of 10 in rapid fire. The weapon was considered effective up to 1400 yards but Colonial

Edward Murphy- Royal Horse Artillery

experience had placed a premium on rapid collective fire rather than accuracy in order to produce a beaten zone, which was effective against both natives and the Germans

A Long Way from Tipperary

when they attacked obligingly in close formation as the battalion experienced at Langemarck. But in trench conditions and with only average ability, the results were very variable. Oil in the barrel would throw the first shot wide. Light breeze would add 6ft at 1000 yards while rain made bullets fly high. One participant reckoned that other than during the opening campaigns, a German was fairly safe from single shots at around 200 yards (a lower level of accuracy than the archers at Crecy in the 14th century).

The other basic front line infantry weapon was the grenade which was distributed to all ranks but was the principal domain of specialists. It could be thrown 40 yards and could kill in the open at a range of 100 yards. Each company also had Lewis guns (four by 1917) which could fire 550 rounds per minute but jammed in mud and required large ammunition stocks. The dominating force on the battlefield however was the machine gun. It need 16 men to sustain it and was a temperamental weapon but its accuracy on its tripod (fields and angles of fire were predetermined) made it a nerveless weapon that even the most terrified soldier could fire on target, even at night. It could either rake the opposing parapet or pile lead into a predetermined gap. Six machine guns could hold up a brigade, one could stop 2 battalions before they advanced 200 yards from their own line. The Germans unfortunately had more of them and used them to greater effect as they were never fully integrated into British military thinking.

I remember talking to Uncle Harry Cainey in the 1960's (who with his wife Auntie Minnie were my parents best

A Long Way from Tipperary

friends) about his experience with the Machine Gun Corps; he wept even then at the slaughter that he had visited on the Germans in the trenches and their courage in advancing into the storm. He was a countryman with a deep Somerset accent which made his account seemingly even more poignant. He was still traumatised by his memories of war.

The final front line weapon was the mortar - 545 were fired by the BEF in 1914, a mere 6 million by 1916.The main British weapon was the Stokes mortar which could fire 22 rounds in a minute. The crews were normally in the support line until called forward to take out a target. The Germans version was more potent. The charge weighed 200lbs, carried for 1000 yards and was often laid to a pattern of one missile per ten yards at three minute intervals. The charge was so big that it could be seen arriving, and left a house sized hole.

Artillery fire was by far and away the principal cause of both wounds and death in the war - estimates range from 60% to 80% of all casualties. The artillery used in the Great War could be broadly classified as guns, howitzers and mortars (plus rather specialised rockets). The howitzer has a fatter barrel and a higher trajectory than a gun - it is classically employed in indirect fire, dropping on its target rather than hitting it directly. . At the beginning the artillery of the Regular British Army was organised into batteries (a battery had strength of about 5 officers and 200 gunners) of the Royal Horse Artillery (RHA) and the Royal Field Artillery (RFA). In principle, the Regular RHA battery deployed the lighter calibre field guns (six 13-pounders) that were normally

A Long Way from Tipperary

attached to the cavalry. But, due to the limited possibilities of the operational deployment of the cavalry generally as the war progressed, elements of the RHA were also widely used to support the RFA. The Regular RFA had batteries with the heavier field guns or howitzers (six 18-pounders, or 4.5-inch howitzers). William's brother Edward in the RHA would have initially galloped into battle riding a lead horse pulling his gun limber, deployed to fire and then moved on. But once trench war began, his role would become static.

In the early years of the war the Territorial and New Army batteries only had four 15-pounder guns or four 5-inch howitzers. In 1916 there was a general re-equipment and all field batteries were given six up-to-date 18-pounders. These two corps of artillery were made mobile by the use of teams of horses and, increasingly by motorised transport. Additionally, some of the heavier calibre guns, howitzers and mountain guns of the Royal Garrison Artillery (RGA) were deployed in a strongly supportive role from two miles, or more, behind the Front Line.

Effectively, in 1914, neither the British nor the French had any of the specialised weapons which became known as trench mortars, whilst the Germans had developed a whole range of 'mine launchers' (Minenwerfer) as close quarter support for the infantry. These projectiles ranged from the huge 42cm Morser to the highly portable 7.58cm model. Bitter battlefield experience quickly taught the British Expeditionary Force that it urgently required versions of these weapons for trench warfare. But it wasn't until mid-1915 that a tried and tested weapon emerged. It was

A Long Way from Tipperary

designated as the 2-inch Bomb H E Trench Mortar - or 'Toffee Apple'-

When the BEF first went to France in 1914, the shrapnel shell was by far the most frequently projectile that was deployed; both the 18 and 13-pounder field guns fired shrapnel shells exclusively. The shrapnel shell was an empty metal casing filled with spherical lead/antimony balls and an explosive burster charge. At the designated distance and height above the target, this charge exploded expelling the shrapnel balls forwards and downwards in a 100-yard cone, rather like that of a shot-gun blast. The shrapnel shell was patently an anti-personnel weapon, and the British steel helmet, introduced on the Western Front in 1916, was expressly designed to protect the head, face and neck from the equivalent projectiles of the enemy. Until then William and his comrades wore clothe caps which offered no protection at all. The efficacy of the shrapnel was dependent on the proximity of the ground- or aerial-burst to the intended target. Ground bursts were particularly effective when the shrapnel caught its victims at close range in open country. However, the shrapnel shell was also extensively used against specific other targets - particularly barbed-wire concentrations - with highly variable and unpredictable results that caused frequent operational set-backs to the advancing infantry when they failed . E.g. the Somme

High explosive shells with impact fuses had several operational purposes on the Western Front. For example, they could: seriously damage, or even obliterate trench works and dugouts, often killing or burying alive their occupants; destroy civilian residential and commercial

A Long Way from Tipperary

buildings preventing their use as strong-points, areas of troop concentration and defence nuclei; break-up concentrations of barbed wire or fortified purpose-made strong-points (particularly the 18-pounder); eliminate huge numbers of the draft animals involved in all kinds of military activity including transportation of weapons, munitions and the essential commodities required for the prosecution of the war-effort.

But perhaps most importantly, the HE shells were highly effective against the troops themselves on the battle-field. Apart from the highly destructive effect of the blast of the HE itself, which could itself maim or completely disintegrate the human body, the sturdy metal casing of the HE shell would be reduced to fragments. These ragged metal splinters were hurled by the gas produced by the explosion of the HE at tremendous velocities - typically several thousand miles an hour - to a considerable distance from the point of the explosion. They caused all manner of frightful injuries, even total dismemberment of humans and military animals alike which, along with the trauma of the explosion itself, were the cause of much of the psychological distress suffered by so many soldiers on active service on the Western Front. Indeed, 'shell shock' was initially described as 'shell concussion' since the condition was thought to be brought on by close proximity to a shell explosion – i.e. a 'near miss'. Add to this the trauma of being buried alive, or plastered from head-to-toe by the pulverised remains of one's former comrades, and the shock reaction is not difficult to understand.

A Long Way from Tipperary

Chapter 5.

The Welch go to War

The Battalion landed at Le Havre on the 13th August and entrained on the following day for Etreux from whence it marched on through the fortress of Maubeuge to Grand Reng. Half the battalion established themselves at Fauroeulx and the rest at Peissant. The Allies failed to foresee that the violation of Belgian neutrality provided the Germans with a wider arc on which to pivot their envelopment operation than Metz, and Liege therefore fell quickly to the German Army. The Allies realised too late that their northern flank was very vulnerable. The Germans advanced on Namur, the Belgians fell back north towards Antwerp and the enemy began to appear on the banks of the River Meuse near Dinant. Joffre sent the Fifth French Army northwards toward Namur and the BEF was asked to prolong the left of the French. The Germans in fact allowed the French First and Second Armies to penetrate into difficult terrain in the south, before counter-attacking and forcing them back into France. The Germans moved over 750,000 men into Belgium and instead of outflanking the Germans the allies found themselves dangerously exposed. The French Third and Fourth Armies moved into the Ardennes to engage the enemy's right wing and all might still have gone well if General Lanrezac, the Commander of the French Fifth had left his position overlooking the River Sambre and occupied Charleroi. The Germans beat him to it, crossed the Sambre between Charleroi and Namur, and then attacked the heights south of

A Long Way from Tipperary

the river. The Third and Fourth Armies failed to break the German Centre and the Fifth was thrown on the defensive.

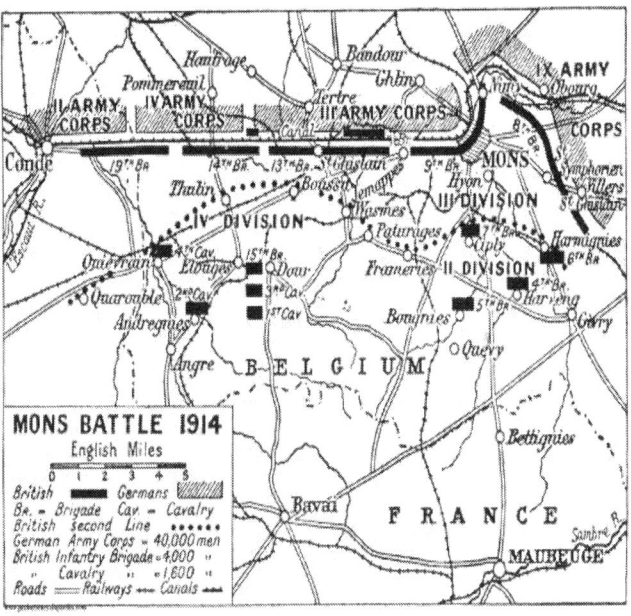

Mons - Welch Positions to the South East

The left Corps of the Fifth on the BEF's right flank retired to a new position some 12 miles south of the river, but Lanrezac failed to inform General French of his intention. On 22 August therefore a nine mile gap opened between the British and the French with the British on the wrong side of the river. Cavalry fighting took place on 22 August and French made the decision to stand his ground and protect the disappearing French flank. There was nothing on the left flank of the BEF between it and the sea, and it was about to

A Long Way from Tipperary

receive the full weight of the 250,000 men of Von Kluck's First Army. French took up the best defensive position available and stationed II Corps on the southern bank of the Conde Canal between that village and Mons. From Mons, the line ran forward in a salient and was then withdrawn south-east towards the Sambre. II Corps took the thrust of Von Kluck attack. First Corps, including the Welch were scarcely engaged. During the whole of 23 August the battle raged, the canal bank was held easily with heavy German losses but the 3rd Division in the salient were overpowered by German Artillery. At nightfall the BEF fell back to prepared positions some three miles south of the canal. The onward drive of the Germans was arrested and there was nothing for it but to retreat. On 23 August the Welch who were holding a front of about 3 miles, a manifestly impossible situation, were in action against German Cavalry at Fauroeulx. They had no orders but could hear intensive firing from Mons and also from the direction of Charleroi.

On 24 August the Battalion held an entrenched front of 3 miles through the villages of Fauroeulx and Peissant (see Mons map). Machine guns covered a railway line in front and the village of Merbes St Marie. As the Germans were principally engaged with II Corps along the Conde Canal and the area immediately north- east of Mons, the threat to the battalion came from the east of this village which constituted the beginnings of the gap between the British and French Forces, and through which in due course the French retreated and the Germans advanced. The Welch cut down a German Cavalry patrol on 24 August unaware of the fact that, as the Queens observed who were on higher ground,

A Long Way from Tipperary

around 10,000 German Cavalry were on the other side of this engagement hidden by a wood. By now the Germans had abandoned their mass attack formations as they were mowed down by rapid rifle fire, giving rise to the belief that the BEF was well endowed with machine guns and the Welch were therefore able to escape, joining the Queens.

The battalion was eventually ordered to retreat through Croix and Rouveroy, and arriving just north of Grand Reng on high ground was heartened to be encouraged on by a voluble peasant on a bicycle, who emerged breathless from Rouveroy to tell it the location of the Germans. When heavy artillery fire subsequently fell on their positions, they realised that they had been "had" by a German spy! Detouring Maubeuge, the battalion reached Neuf Mesnil that night, having marched 45 miles in two days and after three hours rest, continued on to Le Grand Fayt. There they were asked to support the 3rd Coldstream Guards under attack at Landrecies, but the Germans withdrew. They went on to Favril and then Petit Cambresis near Fesmy, arriving at dark on 26 August. The heavy firing at Le Cateau could be heard where on the morning of 26 August, British forces commanded by General Sir Horace Smith-Dorrien engaged the Germans in a rearguard action to facilitate the retreat. Le Cateau was an artilleryman's battle, demonstrating the devastating results which modern quick-firing artillery using air bursting shrapnel shells could have on infantry advancing in the open. Smith Dorrien bought 5 days by his action in which 40,000 British troops were involved losing almost 8,000 as casualties or prisoners of war.

A Long Way from Tipperary

On 27 August the Welch were told to "prepare to be sacrificed", according to Rees, as the flank guard designated to cover the First Corps. They had one battery of Artillery and were ordered to cover the retreat down the line of Boue, Iron and Guise. Locals advised them of a rapid German advance, so they picked up speed and as they turned the corner on the road from Fesmy le Star to Boue, the German advance guard approached from the north from the direction of Le Sart, arriving just too late to catch them as they turned The Welch in combination with the Munsters, also designated rearguard held them off, but they were involved in continuous if light contact with German Cavalry. They had to turn down a request from the Munsters to give them more support as if they had done so, the flank of the Division would have been exposed – the Munsters were nearly destroyed subsequently as they failed to receive the order to retreat and after 12 hours fighting, with only 250 men left, and after running out of ammunition, were overwhelmed.

German pursuit of the Welch culminated in charge by a small detachment of Lancers in the streets of the village of La Neuville. The officer in charge got within pistol range and was killed with his men, his horse becoming a battalion trophy which survived the war and was dubbed "The Ooolan". German shelling accompanied the battalion through Iron to Guise, where they crossed the Sambre, blowing the bridge en route, and reached Bernot. On 28 August, the retreat was resumed and in a terrible day of heat and dust, the Welch marched through La Fere to

A Long Way from Tipperary

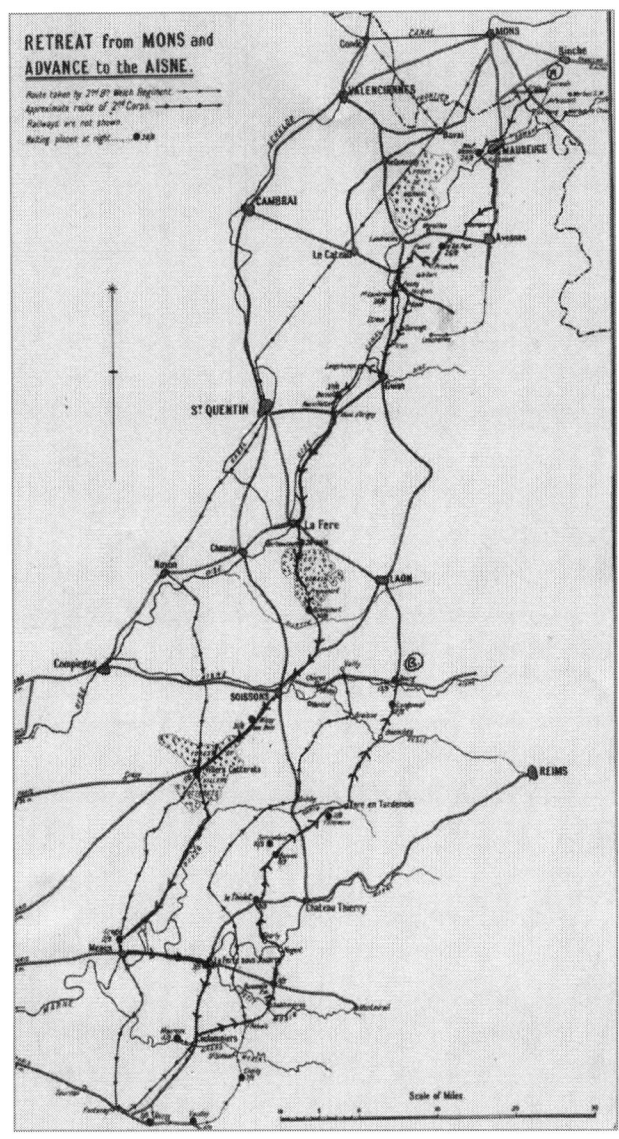

Retreat from Mons, advance to the Marne

A Long Way from Tipperary

Berteaucourt. The worst of the retreat was now over as the B.E.F. had outpaced the Germans who were already opening the gap between their First and Second Armies which was to prove fatal to their ambitions. Their advance was in any event slowed by fresh French forces constituting the Fifth Army, who moved up through the exhausted BEF to stem the Germans at Guise. 29 August was a real day of rest.

Whilst the Welch had been retreating with the I Corps, II Corps had fallen back in parallel through Le Cateau, St Quentin and Noyon. General Joffre decided at this point (or, so he would have history believe), that it would be tactically sound to drop back a further 40 miles to put the Marne between the Allies and the Germans, whilst drawing them in to the point where they would be exposing a vulnerable flank. The French, it must be said, had ambitions to clear off even further.

On 30 August the retreat continued through the Forest of Gobain. At A large convent called Premontre, relief came in the shape of nuns bringing soup and coffee. I visited the Convent in the 1990s and left an account of this story with them. The night was spent at Bretancourt and on 31 August (again in awful heat), the battalion passed through Missy au Bois and crossed the River Aisne at Soissons. On 1 September I and II Corps were united for the first time since Mons at Villers Cotterets. The March continued through Cregy, near Meaux, to La Ferte sous Jouarre, crossing the River Marne at Germigny and the Petit Morin. The

A Long Way from Tipperary

Grand Morin was crossed at Moroux and on 5 September the retreat came to and end at Rozoy.

The Battalion diary claims that between 22 August (when the Welch were still advancing) and 5 September, it marched

A Long Way from Tipperary

about 240 miles. Rees wrote that during the retreat " *The determination of the men passed all belief. The reservists were not in anyway fit for such a terrific test of endurance. Between the 22nd of August and the 5th of September we marched about 240 miles and only on one day did we have a semblance of rest. The men were absolutely tired out before the actual retreat began on the 24th. At the end of some marches, it was impossible to maintain our formation and the column became merely a crowd flowing slowly along the road, the men looking as if they neither saw, nor felt anything. Almost without exception, heir feet were raw and bleeding and many marched with puttees wrapped around their feet. Their one desire was to halt and fight the enemy and not being allowed to do so was the cause of bitter complaint.*

Casualties in battle were negligible and on 5 September, the 73 men missing from the establishment from sickness, wounds or death were made good. It was the battalion's good fortune to be not only in I Corps, but to be on the inside or eastern flank of the retreat and therefore protected from the flank attacks of Von Kluck's First Army, which had been hotly pursuing II Corps from the West and North. The issue now however was, could the Battalion now go forward, as it was their turn to launch their own offensive?

On 4 September Joffre ordered the B.E.F. to advance to the North East in order to attack the right flank of the German First Army. The attack commenced at Rozoy on 6 September and the Germans began to fall back. On 7 September it reached Choisy and on 8 September crossed

A Long Way from Tipperary

the Petit Morin, "a stream running through a narrow valley with steep wooded sides, approachable only through close intricate country, studded with innumerable copses, villages and hamlets and with only six bridges in that part of the front

available to cross. The diary records that part of the 1st Division saw some sharp fighting with the German rearguard but the Battalion was not engaged.

By one of those extraordinary quirks of fate, it is evident that William marched through the village of Sablonnieres on the way to the bivouac at Bassevelle Farm on the Montmirail Road only a few hours after the action in which Captain John Norwood V.C. lost his life on 8 September. Rees recorded that *"There was some sharp fighting at Sablonnieres at the passage of the Morin. We pushed forward to the line of the*

A Long Way from Tipperary

Montmirail road, with heavy rifle fire going on over on our left just over the brow of the hill. "

This must have been the fatal action in which John was killed as the only Commonwealth graves in the village belong to John and his companions John had won his Victoria Cross at Ladysmith in the Anglo-South African War and having left the Army in 1908, rejoined again in 1914 to support his Regiment, the Fifth Dragoon Guards who were essentially Mounted Infantry. The significance of this strange proximity at Sablonnieres is that William's son married Gay Norwood, the granddaughter of John, some 55 years later. John's medals are owned by the family and are on loan to the Imperial War Museum's VC and GC Collection..

The account of Captain Norwood's death from the history of the 5th Dragoon Guards reads as follows ;

"On September 8 the regiment marched at 2.30 a.m. as the leading Regiment of the Brigade whose duty it was to cover the advance of the 1st Army Corps. The order was B Squadron on the right, C in the centre and A on the left. On approaching Sablonnieres, on the River Morin, Captain Norwood reported the village to be lightly held, but Lt. Williams with his troop was unable to advance along the road in front of the village owing to rifle fire. Captain Norwood with three Troops of B, and Captain Partridge with 2 Troops of C were sent to Bellot, which was held by the French, with orders to cross the river there and attack Sablonnnieres from he east. Both Captains were killed in the subsequent action. It would be interesting to know what

A Long Way from Tipperary

Approaching Sablonnieres from the south, September 1914 Overlooking the site of John Norwood's Death

information Captain Partridge, who was the senior officer present and in command of the force, received from the French at Bellot to cause him to modify his plan of attack. To the east of Sablonnieres, on the north side of the river, the ground is very steep and covered with thick woods. There seems reason to believe that he learned that the Germans had strongly entrenched positions there, covering their left flank, and that the best way of carrying out the spirit of his instructions was to attack along the railway on the south side of the river so as to enfilade these positions. Sadly in doing so he came under severe fire from the village and wood immediately north of the river, with the result that he was killed, as were Captain Norwood and Privates Wisdom and Fishlock, while Lieutenants Martin and Nettlefold and 12 men were wounded."

A Long Way from Tipperary

It is clear from other documentation that I have seen that John Norwood had dismounted to go the aid of a wounded NCO when he was killed; this was exactly the same action that had earned him the VC in South Africa. When we visited Sablonnieres in 1978, we gained access to the parish records at the Mayor's office where the burial arrangements are recorded. All those concerned are buried in the village churchyard. A monument to them all stands in the village. A poignant note in the records that 20 horses had to be disposed of, suggesting that the troop was hit by heavy machine gun fire.

At daybreak on 9 September the advance continued to the Marne where to everyone's great surprise the bridges were captured intact because the 11th Hussars had prevented their destruction by getting early into position overnight. The third Brigade had experienced some heavy fighting as did 3 Corps but by evening the BEF was dug in along the Chateau Thierry-Paris road and the Royal Flying Corps reported that the German First and Second Armies were in full retreat.

The explanation for these unusual developments lies in a failure of intelligence. The Germans had concluded from the French retreat that the 5th French Army was a beaten force

A Long Way from Tipperary

and that the BEF had been practically annihilated. This lead the German High Command to come up with a strategy that required the German First and Second Armies to wheel to the South West and drive the "remnants" (as they conceived it) of the French and British forces into Paris. Meanwhile the remaining German Armies would push the other French armies south towards the Swiss frontier. Unfortunately for the Germans, the Fifth and Ninth Armies pinned the Second German Army to its ground and prevented it wheeling south west, whilst the German First moved away and opened a gap which allowed the BEF to force its way forward, roll up the German's left flank and threaten an attack in the rear. Von Kluck could not believe his force's failure to hold the Marne and Petit Morin crossings, which precipitated the imperative to fall back and regroup. Paris was saved.

The battle of the Aisne was preceded by small scale actions involved in the crossing of the River Vesle. The Welch furnished the advanced guard of the First Division on the right. On turning the corner on the road leading down to Bazoches from Fere en Tardenoise, excited French troops who had been mauled by the Germans reported enemy forces on top of the round hill over which the road ran. They retreated under artillery fire. That night the Welch were at Longueval, two miles short of the Aisne.

The engagement to capture the high ground beyond the Aisne is often described as the battle of the " Chemin de Dames" from the name of the road that runs along the edge of the plateau and which was a fashionable carriage way in earlier times. In fact this battle was just the first of a long

A Long Way from Tipperary

series of engagements between the Allies (subsequently only the French) and the Germans for this strategic position. The battle plan was for the right of the Force, the 1st Division, consisting of 2 and 3 Brigades to break through the German positions on the crest in the area of Cerny and with a French Division on their right flank, to insert themselves between the German First and Second Armies, thereby rolling them up the left flank of the German First. After the British First Division in the opening moves had achieved its goals, the strategy was for the British Second Division lead by the 1st Guards Brigade to take the vanguard role and plunge through the gap.

The Aisne favoured the defence as it was a sluggish river, some 200 ft wide and unfordable. It had steep sided wooded valleys cut by tributary streams into the plateau. There was little cover on the low ground for infantry and no place for artillery until the plateau was gained. The Germans had destroyed all 7 road bridges in the sector allotted to the BEF but left an aqueduct at Bourg carrying a canal over which the Battalion crossed with little opposition before digging in that evening on the high ground south west of Moulins. General French's instructions were to push forward about five miles to the high ground north of the Aisne on a frontage of 10 miles with the right thrown forward so as to envelop the left of the First German Army. The Welch were part of this right.

At the outset of the action on 13 September, the First Division was charged with following the road that lead up spurs to the crest and the Second to take a deep valley to the left (leading to Braye) which also opened to the crest.

A Long Way from Tipperary

During the night it was discovered that the Germans held a sugar beet factory just below the crest of the hill half a mile to the northwest of Troyon (a stone pile marked the spot in 1979). The Germans had also entrenched themselves at crossroads just beyond, thereby blocking the road. The 2nd Brigade was ordered to clear the road and started at 0300 am in mist and rain to do so. The 1st Sussex took Troyon and hundreds of prisoners and cut down a counter attack by German field guns, leaving the guns derelict on the plateau. The attack continued against the sugar factory by First Coldstream but by 0700 am little progress was being made so the First Guards Brigade from the Second Division was asked to move to the left of Second Brigade to outflank the Germans. As their leading battalions emerged, they received a mauling from German guns on the crest. The Cavalry however secured the right flank at Paissy. The Queens came up on the right of the Coldstream Guards, and they managed in the mist to occupy Cerny, cross the Chemin and take a farm about half a mile to the north east of it. They were isolated all day however and finally extricated themselves at dusk.

The Third Brigade was designated as the Reserve with the Welch on the left, the South Wales Borderers on the right and the Gloucesters in reserve. On the morning of the 14th they were ordered to advance from near Moulins, cross the valley to the Beaulne spur and prolong the line of the First Guards Brigade. Advancing to the North West, they left the village of Beaulne on their left and were covered by the steep slope of the Vendresse ridge on their right.

A Long Way from Tipperary

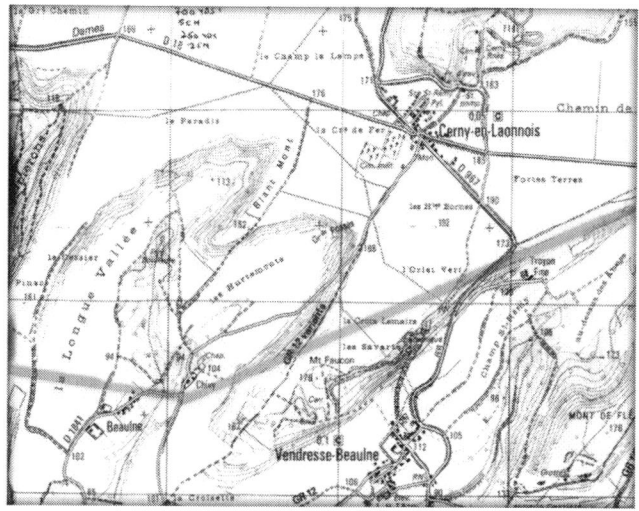

The Troyon Sugar Beet Factory

Major Kerrich, commanding the leading platoons, saw a strong German attack by three German battalions developing on the opposite ridge and moving east with the aim of taking 1st Guards in the flank. The direction of the advance was north west at this point but Kerrich changed direction to the west, apparently to gain height quickly, so as to take the Germans in the flank by firing across the valley. A gap speedily opened up between the Welch and the SWB who were bogged down also in deep woods. Rees recorded that the Welch crossed the Chivy valley at right angles, exposed to long range rifle and machine gun fire. But they then firmly established themselves on the south east slopes of the Beaulne spur and from holding a steep bank near the crest, charged Germans among corn stooks some 150 yards away who fled, leaving their dead. They continued their

A Long Way from Tipperary

advance until reaching a line of apple trees on the further side of the Beaulne spur (probably along the track that ran on top of the spur) when a storm of shells burst around them, causing casualties. As Rees noted, they were moving at right angles to their intended course at this point – he having established contact with the Highland Light Infantry who were proceeding up the west side of the Beaulne spur.

D company had reached the crest of the ridge and were firing furiously but were taking casualties and running low on ammunition. Major Moore the Company Commander ordered all to withdrawal 250 yards to the bank from which the charge had been made, and this was done in small groups. From there they saw that desperate fighting was going on around the Troyon factory where the ground was covered in bodies; British artillery was playing havoc with German troops on the forward slope of the Chemin de Dames just above the wood at the head of the Chivy valley and Melville's machine guns had done great execution on the right of the Battalion C. But the price paid was high – Kerrich had been killed, Haggard mortally wounded and C Company had 50 casualties from shell and rifle fire.

The Battalion won its first V.C. in the actions on this day. This was one of the few episodes that I can recall being mentioned by my father concerning his experiences in the war. He had the greatest regard for Captain Mark Haggard who had been detailed to take his company with the other companies attacking up the Beaulne spur. The Germans were well entrenched on the ridge and beyond it. Ordering his company to lie down, he advanced to reconnoitre then,

A Long Way from Tipperary

observing a German Maxim gun, gave the order to "fix bayonets" and charge. He was 30 yards ahead of his men and engaging the gun when it cut him and others down.

Fuller Supporting the Dying Haggard

Between consciousness and spasms of pain, he is said to have urged "Stick it the Welch". His men were unable to move and in spite of being ordered to withdraw, Lance Corporal William Fuller of Laugharne, went back for him. He picked up Haggard, carried him 100 yards to shelter where he dressed his wounds and, at Haggard's request even returned again to the killing field in order to retrieve

A Long Way from Tipperary

Haggard's rifle. Subsequently, Haggard was carried to a barn where he died, being buried nearby (he is now in Vendresse cemetery).

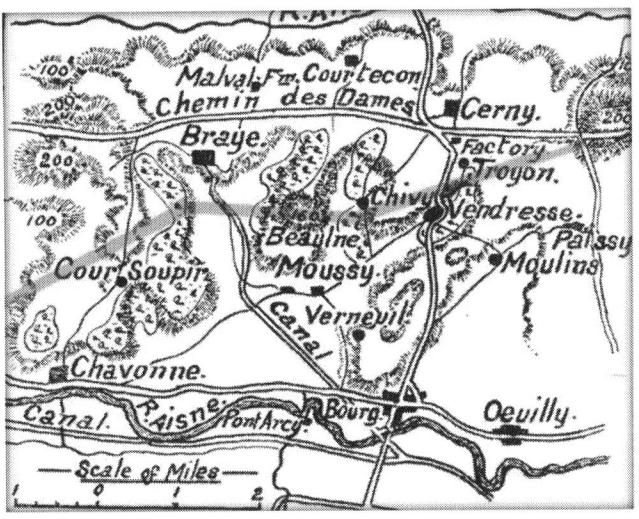

Chemin des Dames.

Haggard was the nephew of the novelist (author of "King Solomon's Mines" etc) and was immensely popular in the Regiment into which he had been Commissioned during the Boer war. He had only married the year before. His rallying cry was later inscribed in gold under the barrack clock at the Cardiff depot. Fuller was wounded gravely in the neck at Gheluvelt 6 weeks later and sent back to Wales where he was found unfit for service and moved to recruiting duties. He attended the famous Garden Party at Buckingham Palace in 1920 for surviving VCs and their families. He died in 1974 and his grave at Mumbles was unmarked until 2005.

A Long Way from Tipperary

Haggard's behaviour seems today to be somewhat quixotic, as does his exhortation to the Welch (although you only have to look at the example of Colonel H Jones of the Parachute Regiment at Goose Green in the Falklands War to find modern parallels). The attitude to the war at this stage however was still a mixture of boyish enthusiasm and sporting metaphors among the officers, as the following extract from the diary of Lieutenant Melville, who was commanding the machine gun section on the right of C Company on the Beaulne spur shows concerning his actions that day. ;

Lieutenant Melville's Account *"I made my way to the front line but quickly realised that machine guns were of no use there as we could not put our heads up. I observed a German officer leading a platoon towards our right flank, obviously with a view to attacking us. So I crawled down the ridge a bit and moved to the extreme right to engage him. I got my guns into action and told my men to open fire as soon as I gave the word, watching the German carefully through my binoculars. As he jumped up, my guns opened fire and the poor fellow pitched forward dead, the spike of his helmet burying itself in the ground...one of my men later handed me his sword and belt as a trophy. Having wiped out this little counter attack, I saw to my intense excitement, the German trenches on my right filled with troops prepared to repulse the attack of the South Wales Borderers. Ranging very carefully with my Barr and Stroud, I started vertical searching from both guns. As the range was about 700 yards, the execution was terrible. Eventually the Germans could stand it no longer, and breaking from their trenches, ran back over*

A Long Way from Tipperary

the crest of the hill like a football mob, both my guns pumping into them .I then saw the most beautiful exhibition of shooting by the 113th Field Battery, which was supporting us in the valley below, As soon as they broke from the trenches, the guns opened up with shrapnel. The slaughter was terrific. Later the drama was repeated, the Boches being force back into their trenches only to break once again and retire over the hill.....the hillside was thick with their dead and wounded." (NB – Ordnance, including examples of live 303 rounds and shells could be found on the ground close to the track up the Beaulne spur even in the 1990's).

The machine guns had now expended their ammunition but more was brought up and moving the guns to a new position, the SWB were brought up and both Battalions had a combined shoot in enfilade against heavy attacks against the 1st and 2nd Brigades in the failing light. This German counter attack had driven the 2nd Brigade from the sugar factory but their casualties were so large that there was a lull. The light was fading fast when, the 3rd Infantry Brigade pushed forward between the 2nd and the 5th and carried the line forward to within 300 yards of the Chemin de Dames. The Welch with A and C companies of the SWB pushed up along the Beaulne Ridge capturing 100 prisoners and a machine gun, and reaching the top of the Chivy valley. There was practically no opposition.

On the left of the 1st Division, the 6th Brigade had advanced as far as Braye by noon but was driven back to the spur above Moussy where it established itself; heavy fighting occurred around El Soupir ending with the 4th Guards

A Long Way from Tipperary

Brigade holding the farm called La Cour Soupir, one and a quarter miles to the north east of the village and on the west of the Beaulne spur. So ended the 14th September with the Germans firmly established on the Chemin des Dames and First Corps holding a line from 1000 yards north east of Troyon to the ridge and then down across the Beaulne spur to La Court, Soupir and Chavonne.

German determination to hold the allies on the Chemins des Dames was fuelled by the recognition that its possession by either side ensured command of the southern part of the Craonne Plateau from Soissons to Berry au Bac. The fall of the French fortress at Maubeuge had enabled them to rush up troops to defend the position and they arrived in the nick of time. On 14 September their determination to break through might have prevailed had it not been for the actions of the 1st Division and Melville's machine guns. The 1st Division had been opposed by no fewer 18 German battalions and suffered more than the 2nd Division. Combined casualties in the two Divisions amounted to 3000 men and the Welch had not seen such intensity of action since their forerunners experiences at Waterloo and Inkerman or suffered such grievous casualties.

The Battalion spent the night of 14 -15 September on the Beaulne ridge - the actual ground was wooded to a certain extent which provided some cover - and they were about 100 metres from the crest line. It was impossible to sleep because of the moans and cries of the German wounded and dying out on the ridge on their front. At dawn, a decision was made to advance the Battalion by 150 yards where they

A Long Way from Tipperary

laid down in the wet grass but this movement attracted machine gun fire and as they had both flanks in the air, an immediate retreat was ordered to the sunken road in front of Beaulne. But before they left, as Melville says the Welch machine gunners had a wonderful target "On top of the ridge about 1000 yards away were two large haystacks beyond which were a large number of Germans, probably staff officers with range finders and binoculars, recce'ing our position. Ranging on them carefully I opened up with our machine guns with combined sights and caused great execution." The Welch then beat a retreat to the road under sniper fire.

At nightfall, A and C companies were pushed up with the SWB to the northern edges of the wood that covered the Chivy spur. Here they were completely cut off from Beaulne, one and a half miles away, and at some distance from the left of the SWB. It rained continuously and some British shells fell short on them. They remained there for 8 days, finding it a great nuisance to be with 300 yards of a German field battery whose observer operated from the top of a hay stack and who refused to be moved by either rifle or shell fire. There was a daily duel with some other Germans at a haystack 700 yards distant which was eventually resolved when one night, a Sergeant crawled out, bayoneted a guard and set fire to the haystack.

It became plain that there was no point in holding the Welch and the SWB in their precarious positions unless they were going to attack the Chemin de Dames. On the night of 20-21, they were withdrawn to Beaulne with the SWB holding

A Long Way from Tipperary

the southern end of the Vendresse spur and the 1st and 2nd Brigades holding the ridge to the north east. On 25 September, the Welch were brought into reserve at Vendresse just in time to join the SWB in fighting off an attack from the Germans who had massed in the woods of the Chivy valley during the night and rushed their forward posts. A and C companies moved round the southern edge of the Vendresse spur and attacked the Germans in the flank. They retreated into dead ground leaving the eastern slope of the Chivy littered with bodies. When the fog lifted, the Cameronians on the right of the SWB could see into dead ground where strong reserves were present. Under machine gun and rifle fire, the opposition retreated having suffered more destruction. The SWB had lost 7 officers and 200 men in the action.

There was a final flurry of machine gun activity on the Vendresse ridge on 15 October before the Welch moved out; their machine guns held off heavy attacks. By this time, the British front line reached the Chemin des Dames about a mile east of Cerny, passed through Troyon going west, shaded the southern edge of Chivy and crossed the valley bottom before climbing the Beaulne spur which ran on a south west – north east line, south of Braye and north of Court Soupir.

The Southern flanks of both Armies now rested on the Swiss frontier - their Northern flanks were in the air. The Germans were dependant on the railway from San Quentin to Belgium for supplies, whilst the BEF ports of Calais and Boulogne were undefended. Identical interests therefore drove both

A Long Way from Tipperary

sides north. British desire to sustain the Belgians in their defence of Antwerp was frustrated when it fell. It was decided to withdraw the British gradually from the Aisne. By now there were sufficient men engaged on either side to place 30,000 soldiers per mile on the entire Franco German border and even 15,000 per mile on the Franco Belgian border. The fighting on the Chemin Des Dames bought to an end a period of mobile warfare. It is generally considered that 15 September marks the beginning of trench warfare, for which the BEF with inferior numbers, lacking heavy artillery and trench equipment was sorely ill equipped. As the battalion headed back towards the flatlands of Flanders, it left casualties behind that would later be considered light: 55 dead, 28 missing and 132 wounded.

The terrain on which these battles were fought is virtually unchanged, so it is possible to walk up the narrow ravine along the farm track that the Welch followed to reach the plateau and to see across the Chivy valley to what would have been the German lines observed by Melville. This chalky upland is a far cry from the glutinous trenches that would eventually become the home of the battalion for four long years. The debris of war, including intact 303 rifle rounds that evidently spilled from the belts and pockets of nervous young infantrymen can still be picked up in summer under balmy skies and to the sounds of songbirds. Ploughing reveals shell cases and unexploded war heads that are placed at the sides of the fields for collection and there is now a war memorial and French War Graveyard at the Troyon cross roads.

A Long Way from Tipperary

Chapter 6

The First Battle of Ypres

The battles for Ypres were confusing for the Generals of the day and remain so even now for contemporary historians - there is a considerable overlap between events and the first part of the battle was not so much a series of discrete engagements as a tide of rolling encounters forming part of a general struggle. The importance of Ypres to the Armies of 1914 arose from a number of factors; it was a road, rail and canal centre and the nearest town to the channel coast; the port of Dunkirk was just 30 miles away. Surrounded by an encircling ridge to the north, east and south, the Ypres salient was a bastion for any force that held the city. But the true importance of Ypres lay in political and emotional factors. It was the last major town in Belgian hands, the only bit that remained of "poor little Belgium". The battles around Ypres were in the main "soldiers battles", attempts to take ground and hang on to it – the weight of responsibility for doing so resting on the battalion commanders and company officers.

Ypres is best envisaged as lying in the centre of a saucer; the eastern ridge of this runs from Messines to Paschendaele. The most significant physical factor is the high water table. When it rains any undrained land floods quickly and with most of the ditches destroyed by shelling, the countryside becomes a quagmire. Soldiers digging

A Long Way from Tipperary

struck water after a couple of feet – at the beginning there were no sandbags or trench equipment. Once trenches and dugouts were excavated they rapidly filled up until men were standing for hours or days knee or waist deep in chilly muddy water. Apart from a lack of basics such as buckets, barbed wire and shovels, there was a grave shortage of artillery ammunition – Britain had not geared up for a prolonged war. To compound the artilleryman's problem, the terrain was flat and as the Great War was essentially an Artillery war, the ridges of Ypres involving small elevations became very important. Whoever dominated the Ypres ridges dominated the salient, so the battles became attritional battles for position on the ridge.

By mid October the Germans could count on 16 Infantry and five cavalry divisions with another five on the way. The BEF now mustered four Corps, amounting to 7 Infantry, 3 Cavalry and one Indian Division - all these were severely under strength and they had no reserves. On 14 October the High Command, the German 6th and 4th Armies were told to position themselves to the north and east of Ypres and from this start point attack the BEF like a battering ram so as to crush the allied flank and then wheel south and west to pin the British against the Channel coast, taking Calais and Dunkirk and then pressing south to roll up the Allied line. The French Cavalry under General Mitry were the first to discover the German intentions when they ran into elements of the German Army outside of Roulers on 19 October. On that same day, the British sent forces down the Menin road as

A Long Way from Tipperary

far as Gheluvelt where they came under fire from heavy artillery.

Location of Actions around Ypres

General French now realised that he was facing not one Army but two. The weather was misty and cloudy, the Germans had moved at night to avoid Royal Flying Corps reconnaissance. It is easy to see how French misread the battle, encouraged no doubt by General Henry Wilson

A Long Way from Tipperary

who was no more than a mouthpiece for General Foch who was constantly urging the British to press on to the east. Even so French stuck to his conviction that the enemy force in front of him was negligible and on 19 October, ordered 1 Corps under Haig to march out of Ypres and take the approach to Roulers, taking stock of the situation on reaching the salient ridge but moving on to capture Bruges if the route was cleared. The rest of the BEF was to lean on the enemy line to the East to prevent them moving to 1 Corps front. Another Commander might have considered the mounting evidence of German strength but French pressed on blindly until disaster confronted him in the face.

The first bad sign occurred when the British advance by 3 Corps at Armentieres, about 15 miles south of Ypres was checked on 20 October and then pushed back in continuous fighting in which the troops fought for every metre of ground notwithstanding the fact that over - sized cartridges had been issued which stuck in the breech when the rifle was hot. At La Vallee, the 2 Battalion of the Sherwood Foresters were reduced to two officers and sixty men before they surrendered. Allenby's Cavalry Corps of 9.000 was attacked by 24,000 men and fell back to Messines and Ploegstreet. Rawlinson's Fourth Corps was acting as the right flank of Haig's First Corps and on 19 October Major General Capper's 7th Division pushed patrols up beyond Gheluvelt along the Menin road but then had to draw back.

At the north end of the line, the 2nd Division of Hague's for

A Long Way from Tipperary

force, obeying instructions to head for Roulers crossed the Zonnebeke-Langemarck road 4 miles east of Ypres encountering strong German forces which they routed through Field Artillery and rapid rifle fire which carpeted the ground with German dead - the British then entrenched around Zonnebeke. German pressure on Three Corps and the Cavalry Corps continued at Messines, La Gheer and Armentieres. By the end of the day although the Germans had suffered heavy losses, the British had suffered too and were in a precarious position. They were much reduced in numbers and 7 Infantry Divisions plus 5 French and British Cavalry divisions were holding a front of some 35 miles against 19 German Divisions backed by heavy artillery and machine guns. The British advance had stalled and they only had 93 heavy guns in France of which 54 were deployed along the Ypres front; ammunition was so short that they could only fire 8 shells per gun per day. Everything now depended on the Infantry.

British defences around Ypres at this time must be imagined as at best short disconnected stretches of trench, three feet deep, no wire, no dugouts, no communication trenches and no defence line; the troops were using bayonets, sharpened stakes, looted spades and their bare hands to dig holes. Shells took a heavy toll of the shallow trenches which could not be dug deeper because of the water table; the troops fought in small scattered groups, their trenches not continuous but sometimes separated by as much as several hundred yards.

A Long Way from Tipperary

First Corps, which included the 1st Division and the 2nd Welch had had detrained at Hazebrouck on 18 October and had marched up to Ypres in time to participate in the action with Haig's 1 Corps. After resting in Poperinghe, the Welch advanced on the left of the attack and on 21 October were in reserve with 3 Brigade which captured Langemarck village. In the meantime, the French cavalry had been driven out of Houthulst Forest leaving the road clear for the German advance. Pressing beyond the village, the lead Battalions found the enemy in strength and the Welch were called up to support the Queen's who were hard pressed. A German sniper was shot out of the church tower in Langemarck which itself was destroyed by German Artillery on the following day. At dusk on 21 October the line was withdrawn about 300 yards northeast of the village with the Welch in the centre. The Division as a whole was strung out over 4 miles, holding shallow trenches.

On 22 October, the Germans reduced the village to ashes in 4 hours of shelling. But the day for the Welch was otherwise a quiet one. Not so for the Green Howards, the Royal Scots Fusiliers and the 2nd Wiltshires. This was the day that German historians have come to call the "Kindermorde", the "Slaughter of the Innocents" of Langemarck. On that misty morning the German Infantry advanced in small clumps. Silhouetted against the eastern sky they made perfect targets and some infantrymen fired as many as 500 rounds that day, their rifles became too hot to handle. The German regiments consisted of volunteers, many of them students and they

A Long Way from Tipperary

marched forward singing, with arms linked. The British Official History records; " Struck by gun and machine gun fire as soon as they came into sight, the German masses staggered...their dead and wounded were piled into heaps...some struggled on and a few got to within 200 yards of the Wiltshires and even penetrated a gap but...they were driven back by shrapnel and rifle fire." These attacks continued all day. There has been some scepticism amongst historians as to whether the student battalions were as naïve as portrayed but on 27 October 1914 a German Cavalry Officer, Captain Rudolf Binding wrote " These young fellows that we have just trained are too helpless, especially when their officers are killed. Our light infantry Battalion, almost all Marburg students have suffered terribly. In the next division, just such young souls, the intellectual flower of Germany, went singing into attack at Langemarck, just as vain and just as costly"

On 23 October the Germans again attacked, this time in force against the angle held by the 1st Coldstream, the 1st Gloucester and 2nd Welch from the village of Koekuit at 2000 yards distance. Their losses to heavy rifle fire were catastrophic as Captain Rees recorded in his diary;

" At the corner of my hedge we had a machine gun. I stood by this gun for about an hour. We saw the Germans forming up for attack and we opened fire at 1,250 yards. We had every form of target from a company in mass, to a battalion in fours near the edge of Houthulst Forest. Sergeant Longden reckoned by that evening that we had killed 1,000 Germans. I put it at 4 to 500 casualties. The

A Long Way from Tipperary

enemy who had not properly located us before the action began, started shelling but fortunately caused only one casualty.....I never saw the Germans make a worse attack or suffer heavier losses." As one German General recorded" *Boundless enthusiasm could not compensate for insufficient training."*

All of William's sons found Langemarck a sombre place, for all of the subsequent reconstruction of the village including the church. It left all of us moved when we visited the cemetery in the early 1990s. It is the only German cemetery in the salient proper and contains 44,292 burials as well as long lists of the missing. The headstones do not mark but symbolise the dead as the Belgians were less generous about giving land to their former enemy. During the Second World War it was visited by Hitler who fought in the salient. The so called "Student Battalions" were in fact quite close in character to the later "Kitchener Battalions" of the British Army; about 30% of the rank and file were old trained soldiers and all the platoon leaders were trained NCOs. The COs and Adjutants were regulars but the balance consisted of volunteers who were young men of good education. A German historian observed recently that all nations need potent unassailable myths and Langemarck has the same force for Germany as the Menin Gate has for Britain.

The last word, albeit a jingoistic one goes to the Brigadier who commanded 3 Brigade and who wrote in his diary;" *We had a great fight yesterday and were attacked all day. The Brigade did splendidly and inflicted great loss on the*

A Long Way from Tipperary

enemy. The Queen's made a gallant charge, the Gloucesters fired over 500 rounds per man, lost all their officers and many NCOs, had the Germans within 50yards and not a man retired. Some of their bayonets were shot off their rifles and they had over 60 casualties – a grand performance. The Welch also sat out an attack by mobs of Germans and downed them gallantly"

The German attack had been thrown back so decisively that French judged it safe to withdraw 1 Corps and hand over it's trenches to a French Territorial Division. I Corps were therefore withdrawn on 23/ 24 October and moved to Ypres-Hooge-Zillebeke to be ready for the next offensive. The French Territorials did not endear themselves to the Welch however by blazing away at the handover, resulting in C Company losing 39 men to artillery fire provoked by their zeal. Thus ended the first phase of the battles of Ypres with the French holding the northern portion of the semicircle around Ypres and the British, the south where there had been desperate fighting at Polygon Wood and where a German break through was narrowly averted at the point of a bayonet with huge losses for the Wiltshires, and the Warwicks. The critical point of the battle was now coming. Some relief or reinforcement was required - but where was it to come from? A large number of rifle battalions had been gravely reduced, some had lost more than 50% of their strength. As the fighting men were killed off, the BEF line began to weaken. Territorial Battalions were only just arriving in the field, artillery ammunition was low. On the other hand, the

A Long Way from Tipperary

Germans had suffered losses too and the British had a tactical advantage in that they were now on the defensive.

At this moment, General French came to the extraordinary conclusion that *"it was only necessary to press the enemy hard to achieve a complete success and victory"* The idea was that the British along the line of Broodseinde to Neuve Chapelle should advance East, keeping step on their left flank with the French. This tactic meant that by keeping pace with the French and refusing the opportunity to exploit breakthroughs, the action was doomed from the start. And why French imagined that a smaller force with minimal artillery could achieve what the Germans with more of both could not, remains a mystery. At Paschendaele, movement was brought (not for the last time there) to a shuddering halt; large German formations were found to be massing along the Menin Road in the centre, and at La Basse and Armentieres, there was bloodletting on both sides but little movement.

On 27 October, French sent a cable to Kitchener saying that the enemy had sustained such losses in recent weeks that they were now *"quite incapable of making any strong or sustained attack".* Three days later, the Germans bludgeoned their way into Gheluvelt in an attack that endangered the whole British line.

Von Falkenhayn was handling his forces with great skill transferring his efforts up and down the line. He could not attack across all fronts because even the Germans did not have unlimited artillery ammunition. He wanted to

A Long Way from Tipperary

keep pressure across the entire front in order to prevent the transfer of allied forces to his chosen point of attack, but unfortunately for him, this exhausted his own men and required more guns and units than he had. He therefore formed a Third Army under General von Fabeck consisting of 6 Divisions which would work between the flanks of the other two but provide critical force in the attack. All three Armies were to be instructed to push their way through to the vital Messines - Wytschaete Ridge and so on to the Gheluvelt plateau. To keep the British off balance, a fresh attack was decided on Gheluvelt on 29 October.

As for French, he had no more Divisions available, indeed some had to be disbanded. However, he placed Haig's 7th Division across the Menin Road and it was en route to this position when GHQ intercepted a German radio message ordering the Fourth Army to attack down the Menin Road towards Gheluvelt. This was to be the decisive engagement of the First Battle of Ypres.

On 28 October the Belgians opened the sea defences near Nieuport and flooded the country in front of the Yser Canal for 10 miles, thus securing their front. On 29 October, after testing attacks earlier on other parts of the front the Germans attacked in great force in the area of Gheluvelt. Thus began the bloodiest engagement in which the original members of 2nd Battalion were involved. By the end of it the battalion was virtually destroyed, losing most of its officers and reducing its ranks to battered fragments. The village has been reconstructed, but the

A Long Way from Tipperary

major features of the original site are easily discernable including the spectral shell of the windmill.

The battle began when Germans took parts of Gheluvelt in a dawn attack up the Menin road on the 29th under cover of fog enabling them to get between the outposts of the Ist Guards Brigade on the eastern end of the village and even establish machine gun posts in Gheluvelt itself. A counter-attack by three Battalions of the 3rd Brigade and two of the 2nd including the Welch developed by 2 pm in which the Welch advanced in artillery formation between the Queens on the right and the SWB on the left, on either side of the Menin road from the direction of Ypres. For Rees, the 29th "was a day of great fighting and the last great open warfare battle that I have seen in this war. The enemy attacked all along the line and most of the First Division were thrown in to counter attack" Stragglers reported that the Germans were entering he village in force and they soon appeared advancing in a dense line at the further, east, end of the village. On seeing the British infantry, some stopped, others opened fire and a few continued to advance. The Welch had difficulty in getting into position as anyone showing themselves to use their rifles clear of the houses was met by a hail of bullets. However a thin line was established, with C company on the right, B on the left and Lieutenant Melville establishing two machine guns on the left of the advance where he was able to enfilade the Germans advancing north of the village. He brought about such execution that the Germans fell back taking with them those in front of the village.

A Long Way from Tipperary

Lieutenant Marshall leading B Company pushed forward a long way beyond the village to an orchard where he was isolated so he withdrew to a wood where he dug his rifle pits. Two platoons of A company on the right of the advance lost direction and ended up 800 yards south of the Menin road where they fought for the next few days alongside the 7th Division. At nightfall, B company were redeployed to dig a new trench with its right on the Menin Road and a barricade was placed in the road in line with it. Above them, battalion machine guns were placed to sweep the position. The counter attack had been a significant achievement as it was under heavy shrapnel fire and through a mass of stragglers. Melville's use of his machine guns had turned the outcome.

The principal adversary of the Welch in this crucial battle was the 54 Reserve Division containing the List Regiment in which Adolf Hitler was serving as a volunteer. This was one of 400 Infantry Regiments in the German Army although it belonged to the Bavarian Army which had been semi autonomous since 1871. It consisted of three Regiments of 1000 men forming three Battalions subdivided into 4 companies. Notwithstanding later efforts to propagate the notion that this was a "volunteer" regiment, intending to suggest that it was full of students, artists and graduates, more than 85% were conscripts – Hitler was a rare volunteer, accepted because he did not disclose his Austrian citizenship. They were drawn from the supplementary reserve, generally deemed to be men who were insufficiently fit to serve in peacetime but able enough to be called up for war. They

A Long Way from Tipperary

were not cheery volunteers but a medley of half fit men cobbled together to assemble a big enough force to knock out France before turning to Russia. They were unprepared and untrained for the realities of warfare. Their median age was around 25 and they were farmers, agricultural workers, and craftsmen largely drawn from rural areas, overwhelmingly Catholic and owing their loyalty to their villages and only in a wider sense to Bavaria, not to Germany nor to the Emperor. Their general attitude was one of pessimism and fear. Those deriving from Munich came from a liberal and social democratic background – no admirers of Kaiser Wilhelm, Ironically, in view of later history, Hitler served alongside a fair number of Jewish volunteers and the Bavarian Army had many Jews amongst its officers.

As the Regiment was at the lower end of the German Army food chain, it came up short when it came to equipment. They trained with outmoded rifles, were given rucksacks instead of knapsacks and instead of helmets, were issued with oil clothe hats with a grey cotton cover that fatally looked like British Army head gear. The crash training exercise on which they embarked in early October in Lechfield was a bit of a shambles – although not particularly strenuous, they suffered from the forced marches involved, the weather and fatigue – discipline was poor. They arrived en route to the front at Lille which had been badly attacked on 23 October. Here they were joined with the 54th (Wurttemberg) Reserve Division tasked to attack Ypres. Because of the German obsession with " franc tireurs", or partisans from which the

A Long Way from Tipperary

Germans had suffered heavily in the course of their invasion of France in 1870, a readily knotted noose was handed out to every three soldiers for hanging suspects. By this time however, the German Army was beginning to realise that its recent history of war crimes against civilians was doing it no favours, and so an order to the Regiment to hang the entire male population of a village en route to Gheluvelt almost certainly wrongly accused of being the origin of the wounding of a German soldier was rescinded. They enjoyed themselves at Le Halois however by killing chickens with their bayonets, as the records recalls, doing so with such enthusiasm as to risk injury to themselves and others

In the early hours of 29 October 349 men of the List Regiment woke up for the last time. Awakening in the dark, they marched silently for 4 hours towards the flickering light of burning villages. As dawn approached, they still could not see as visibility was down to 40 metres because of heavy fog. They went into battle still wearing their cotton hats - the standard battle rifle had arrived just before they left from Bavaria, but many did not know how to use it. Around 6 am Hitler and his mates arrived at the crest of a small knoll, surrounded by fresh German graves. The entire weight of the German Army was now going to be thrown at the British position in Gheluvelt. Not only was the vision of the List hampered by fog but also the landscape was dotted with hedges, fields, farm buildings and little forests. The ground was littered with dead bodies from those who had gone before and the torn cadavers of horses and cattle. Once the attack had

A Long Way from Tipperary

begun, shells rained down from the British position but the counter barrage from the German guns was awesome and allowed the Regiment to attack. They recklessly charged forward but as they overran the British trenches, by failing to check that they were cleared, soon found themselves being fired upon from front and back. Some later commented that they could not bear to look back because they did not want to see the faces of their fallen comrades. There is no evidence whatsoever to support Hitler's later extraordinary claim that the men sang " Deutschland uber Alles" or indeed any patriotic song.

As the regiment ran across the fields outside Gheluvelt, the casualties mounted. The British machine gun squads at the centre of the village had a field day, as did the British soldiers manning trenches on both side of the Menin road who under cover of the tobacco fields in front of them, shot the advancing Bavarians one by one. Due to the acute shortage of machine guns in the BEF at this moment, most of the execution was by rifle fire. Although the British eventually fell back, there was a counter attack and throughout the day, the Bavarians would be involved in hand to hand combat, but the truth was less heroic than Hitler portrayed it in Mein Kampf. The fact was that the British troops before them eventually ran low on ammunition and energy after weeks of combat but were still more than a match for the List Regiment. Casualties were light however in Hitler's own company, giving the lie to his heroic account.

A Long Way from Tipperary

Evidence from this first day of battle in the List archives suggests that after many hours of fighting and after suffering heavy casualties, the men of the List found that their nerves did not allow them to fight the war that they expected. When towards the evening Hitler's company was ordered to move, the instruction had to be repeated three times before there was a response. On the 29th of October the British received unsolicited support from the Wurttembergers and Saxons who mistook the men of the List as British because of their hats and opened fire, causing many deaths from friendly fire. The overall death toll could have been higher but the British trenches around Gheluvelt were unconnected so communication was poor, the machine guns jammed again and a large number of cartridges issued to the BEF were too big for their rifles. Their artillery ammunition was also restricted.

At dawn on the 30th October D Company had two platoons in trenches echeloned back behind a hedge to the left rear of B company in their front line trenches to guard against an advance from a nearby farm. There was 50 metres of open ground between them and Battalion HQ which with further D platoon was in a sunken lane about 40 yards long leading down to the farm. The remaining platoon was at a barricade placed in Gheluvelt at the crossroads. C Company held a little wood between D Company and the SWB with two platoons. The remaining two were in reserve at the windmill with Melville's machine guns. Digging in took place under heavy shelling including field guns firing from 1000 yards. Rees who was in the sunken lane at this point says " It

A Long Way from Tipperary

became evident that a big attack was impending. We were steadily shelled all day with guns and howitzers of all calibres.. The enemy were massing on our front"

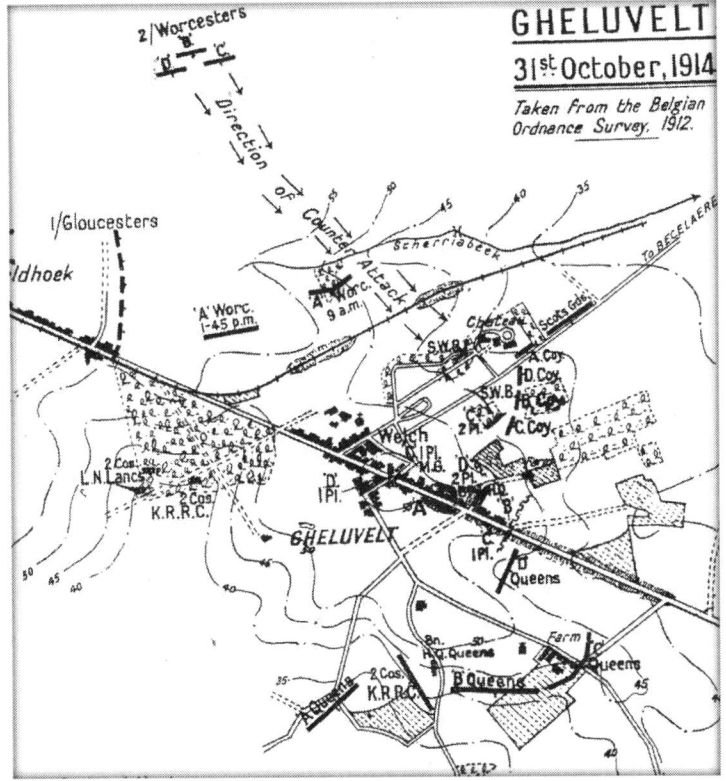

Gheluvelt 1914

(See map - Black marks Welch positions). Because the road is elevated above the plain, B company could not see the

A Long Way from Tipperary

Queen's on their right across the road is easy to understand in retrospect how the Welch and the Queens ended up in an exposed position resulting from their counter attacking efforts. But one look at the terrain suggests that they must have experienced profound foreboding from the fact that all companies, but especially B and D were dug shallowly into a reverse slope (the ground sloping up behind them) offering no possibility of tactical retreat if the enemy fire became overwhelming. Whilst the 30th of October was spent digging in and making defences, the German field guns managed not only to take out a machine gun but also disable Melville, the resourceful officer in charge. Whilst an attack on Zonnebeeke was easily repulsed on that day, the Germans attacked at a relative strength of 6 to 1 the section of front at Hollebeeke and Zandvoorde pushing it back a mile and a half.

On 31 October the Germans made their supreme effort to break through to Ypres. The whole 12 miles of front from Messines to Polygon Wood was attacked, the principal effort being directed against Gheluvelt. As one diary records "The Second Battalion Welch Regiment was annihilated. No other term can describe their casualties".

Why was Gheluvelt important? The answer lies in the topography. The Ypres Menin road reaches the top of the high ground overlooking Ypres at Kilometre 6. Thence it runs straight to Veldhoek, one mile distant and thereafter through Gheluvelt at a further mile, before dropping down. Both the latter villages were straggles of brick houses. Gheluvelt was built on a small promontory which dominated

A Long Way from Tipperary

the flat land to the East through which the Menin road ran on a causeway about 12 feet above ground level at its lowest point. Troops advancing from Ypres had the protection of the rising ground until they reached the village. Conversely, the village jutted out like a peninsula into the sea, dominating the German lines and yet it was complimentary to the three points of high ground at Zandvoorde, Kruiseecke and Becelaere which they already had in their possession. In a few hundred yards at the eastern end of the village, the ground drops 50 feet and it was here that the Welch waited. It was a most difficult position for the British to defend without Artillery, as its shape and size made large scale defensive deployment impossible. It must also be noted that no deliberate defensive action was contemplated – the orders for the 31st were for a possible advance.

It is chilling from looking at the battlefield today as local traffic lumbers up the Menin road to Ypres whilst a busy motorway skirts the village to the north to imagine the concentration of fire that waits to fall on the Welch. The 31st October was termed the most critical day of the war. The whole front of 12 miles from Messines to Polygon Wood was attacked throughout the day and the greater part of the next night. The principal effort made on each side of the Menin Road falling on the Welch and their fellow Regiments in the I and VII Divisions. During the night, the two platoons of A company which had fought with the 7th Division on the 29th rejoined the Battalion but they were severely depleted – they had been isolated and had to make a rush for it individually – and then after getting back to the British line suffered a shell

A Long Way from Tipperary

burst. Only a handful remained to dig into the sides of the hollow part of the road in Gheluvelt.

The Germans advanced under cover of night and dug in about 150 yards in front of company B. The British artillery

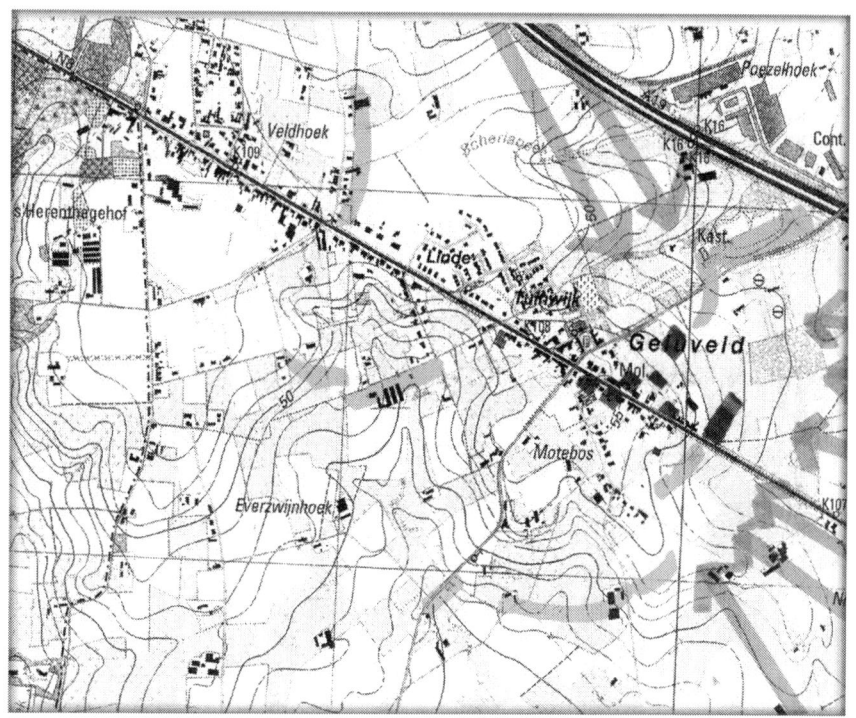

Modern Map –Welch Positions Marked

were so short of ammunition by now that they were only able to lay down 6 shells. Dawn broke and the Germans attacked all along the line, managing to establish themselves in

A Long Way from Tipperary

an orchard 800 yards south of the Menin road where they could enfilade the trenches of the Queens. At 0800 on 31 October a bombardment began which deluged the trench of B Company which was absolutely exposed, only survived by dashing between trenches and the support line as the barrage changed its target, using the traverses. At 0900 the barrage lifted to the top of the hill and German troops began to move into the wood to the left of B. A German Company advanced to within 120 yards but could not be stopped as it was armed with machine guns with heavy shields – their fire was so accurate and heavy that the company lost a lot of men and could no longer put their heads over the parapet. Mud clogged the Company's rifles and together with shell damage left only 12 weapons serviceable: enfilade fire commenced from the left flank from Germans who had penetrated the woods.

There was little cover in the sunken road, so Battalion HQ under the command of Colonel Morland moved back to the centre of the village with about 60 men. The two platoons of D company to the rear of B were enfiladed by fire, brought down by spotter plane from their left flank centred on Zandvoorde and many were killed or wounded. Those attempting to reach the sunken road by dashing across open ground were killed. Rees notes that there was a partially dug trench between D platoon and the sunken lane but instead of using it, about 25 men attempted to run and were all killed. He could not make his voice urging them to crawl heard in the noise as he shouted orders from the sunken lane. In the centre of the village around the barricade the fire was intensive, shells bringing down the houses. Rees

A Long Way from Tipperary

recorded later " The shellfire around the barricade was very violent. Two shells burst in the house where we were sheltering. Eventually I got away with about a dozen men but the machine gun tripod had been blown to pieces and we had no ammunition for the gun". By the time that a runner sent by Colonel Morland to inform the Queens that the Welch were drawing back reached their trenches, they were already being taken by the Germans.

The Battalion was now thoroughly disorganised and split up. B Company and the two platoons of C Company in the wood were pinned to their trenches. Major Pritchard with a small number of men from the reserve platoons of C was still dug in at the windmill, Battalion HQ had continued north towards the Chateau and some stragglers had joined the Gloucesters astride the road at Veldhoek. More under Captain Rees joined the 54 Battery RA a mile west of the village under Major Peel. He reported that he did not think that there were 100 men left of the Welch and had the distinct feeling that he was in danger of being arrested for spreading alarmist reports. There was a lull before 1000 hours when the final drama was played out. According to the official history, the Germans sprang up to the charge "with the greatest enthusiasm, cheering and singing, for they had been warned that the Kaiser himself was present." The Germans sent in 13 Battalions, six fresh, North and South of the Menin Road against barely 1000 men of the Queens , Welch, South Wales Borderers and Scots Guards. Rapid fire held them up for over an hour but they overwhelmed the defenders. Having finished all their ammunition, B Company fixed bayonets and waited for the German attack. At 11.45

A Long Way from Tipperary

a.m. two German machine guns opened up from <u>behind the trench</u>, and after several traverses, a German officer called out in English inviting the company to surrender or face annihilation. As the village was taken, they had no choice but their stubborn defence had bought time. 37 survivors, many wounded were taken prisoner leaving over 80 dead.

By this time, the Germans had succeeded in entering Gheluvelt from both the north and the south; they had broken the left angle of the salient held by the Queens and KRRC and got in behind them. They had infiltrated the wood to the left of B and infiltrated between B and C having wiped out the two D platoons. The Welch supports in the village delivered disconnected counter attacks and fighting continued for an hour but the Germans eventually seized the centre of the village.

A Gloucester Officer at Gheluvelt noted in his diary *"Church, houses and the windmill of Gheluvelt were reduced to ruins and the Welch were practically wiped out where they stood, and soon after dazed and broken men of this Regiment commenced to struggle back through Gheluvelt and Veldhoek. Whole companies were annihilated and the marvel is that anyone remained to help break th*e infantry attacks *that were delivered again and again."*

A Counter-attack was ordered by the GOC Third Brigade using his Brigade Reserve, the 1st Gloucesters to prevent the enemy advance. The Welch with Rees were ordered to join in. Rees felt very badly shaken, his rifle had been shot through in two places and the strap cut of his water bottle but

A Long Way from Tipperary

he got together about 40 stragglers and started to advance with the Gloucesters. His force got to the outskirts of the village before grinding to a halt, their number reduced to 13 men. Rees, pushing on alone, found Colonel Morland, the Battalion Commander who was still in the village and with others had witnessed savage fighting including an ill fated bayonet charge around the barricade in which Captain Ferrar was killed. Morland said to Rees as he approached that "these ten men attacks are no good!" It was clear to Rees, who said so, that Morland failed to comprehend that the remainder of the Battalion had been wiped out or scattered in the fighting in the village. Morland joined Rees as the Welch and the Gloucesters were forced back to the line of 54 Battery where a new line was taken up. As Morland, Rees and Captain Moore plus a few others discussed the situation in a trench, a shell burst near by and killed Moore and mortally wounded Morland. This left Rees and Corder as the only officers to survive the battle with their 25 men. Although this number rose later as a result of stragglers rejoining the Battalion the Welch had started with 600 men and ended in platoon strength.

Rees wrote that

" Colonel Morland was a terrible loss. I never saw him in the slightest degree upset by anything that happened. He remained wary and as cool and collected as if he were on parade at home. Moore was also a great loss and the Regiment lost one of its bravest officers when he was killed"

A Long Way from Tipperary

Morland's body was carried away on a door and Rees was given temporary Command of the Battalions. An eye witness to the condition of the Welch was Lt Ralph Blewett of the Royal Field Artillery whose gun with 25 men and another officer were the only survivors thus far of 54 Battery left at Gheluvelt – his guns were off the road about a mile from the village. He wrote

"I don't know what time of day it was, but I saw the first group of men properly under control come back and I saw it was Rees of the Welch Regiment. He had I suppose about 15 or 20 men with him. The Major asked me who he was, and whether he was the sort of man who would come back. As he had got a DSO only a few days before, I was able to convince him that he was one of the best and that there was no question of him coming back unnecessarily...Rees then came over to the battery – I have rarely seen a man in a more pitiable state, muddy and unshaven of course but barely able to walk for sheer weariness, his equipment had been for the most part shot off of him, and he was absolutely stunned and almost speechless. By good luck we had some hot tea going in the battery and a cup and a slice of bread and jam and a cigarette worked wonders. His regiment had apparently been in a sunken road through the other side of Gheluvelt. They had been shelled continuously from dawn and he and the men with him were the remains. After profuse thanks for the first meal he had had that day, he took his command forward to a half dug trench on a crest about 200 yards in front of the battery and manned it much to the satisfaction of the battery."

A Long Way from Tipperary

Rees survived the war to become a Brigadier General and wrote afterwards about his experiences. He said that *"at this time, myself and Corder were the only two officers who had survived the fighting at Gheluvelt and we had about 25 men. These men I spread out as a firing line across a turnip field a little in front of the guns and I went to interview Robinson, the Commander of the Battery. I suggested that he should open fire on some houses full of snipers about 500 yards away on the south side of the Menin Road. He said that he had got a few rounds of high explosive up for trial and I remarked that it seemed a priceless opportunity. He blew the houses up pretty badly and continued with shrapnel on the slope beyond them which effectively stopped the rifle shooting that was getting rather trying. At that moment Blewett appeared and asked permission to take an 18 pounder onto the road and have a duel with it. Having got permission, he manhandled the gun on to the road. The German fired first and missed and Blewitt did not give him a second chance. He put a stop to any trouble from that quarter for the rest of the afternoon. If the Germans had pushed home their attack, there was nothing to stop them"*.

In fact, Blewitt put 15 rounds in rapid succession down the road, knocking out the German gun, blowing apart the barricade and helping the Worcester's counter – attack; he was later awarded the DSO.

The first counter attack had failed but the British position was now stabilised by a counter attack by the SWB from a light railway to the north west of the village, which regained the line from the village to the Chateau. Where the remainder of

A Long Way from Tipperary

the battalion still held the Chateau grounds. The course of the battle was now about to change in a rather startling way. Every reserve of the 1st Corps had been used up except the 2nd Worcesters.....the situation seemed hopeless. The Worcesters who had been dug in at Polderhoek Wood were formed into two lines at 50 yards distance (see arrows from the North West on Modern Gheluvelt map) and in spite of tremendous artillery fire that felled 100 men, swept across 1000 yards of open ground from the north west without cover and surprised the Germans who thought the battle was over. The bare slope across which they charged was littered with dead and wounded and along its crest, German shells were bursting. The ground underfoot was rank grass and rough stubble and although men fell at every pace, they dashed on with fixed bayonets. They seized at first a sunken lane leading to the Chateau and moved on to capture the north end of the village up to the main road, joining the SWB who had held the grounds of Gheluvelt Chateau all day. The enemy fell back but hung on to the southern portion, their attempt to advance along this side being smothered by fire from the remnants of the Queens, Welch, Gloucesters, KRRC and Loyals who were now dug in just to the north of the Menin Road on the Veldhoek side of the village.

The Worcester's achievement was magnificent and exemplified the fact that proved increasingly true during the war that the moment of victory was the moment of greatest danger. The Germans made no further effort to advance that day (although an attempt to advance south along the Menin road was smothered by fire from the Welch, the Gloucesters, and remnants of the Queens and KRRC)

A Long Way from Tipperary

because they were in ignorance of the weakness of the British position. But the position was so insecure south of the Menin Road that after dark the Worcesters were withdrawn to a new position in prolongation of the line held by the remnants of the Welch and others i.e. just outside the village to the west. Further south the British held on to the Wytschaete-Messines ridge, reinforced by the French. To the north, the British were forced back to the Polygon Wood - Klein Zillebeke line.

A Long Way from Tipperary

Chapter 7 .

The Battles Around Ypres

Action was not over for the Welch survivors – during the night of 1-2 November they were withdrawn to Sanctuary Wood from trenches rapidly dug south of the Menin road which they handed over to the Berkshires. There they were reinforced by 30 men from the Third Battalion and by gathering stragglers and transport men, were able to raise their numbers to 4 officers and 140 men. They were then sent back to recover the trenches that they had just handed over to the Berkshires. The counterattack succeeded in regaining trenches near Harenthage Woods. The attack succeeded as a whole but only regained a portion of the trench.

Rees described what happened as follows; "We passed by Stirling Castle and Harenthage Chateau under a great deal of shrapnel fire. Hewitt was hit in the leg, Corder took a bullet through the arm and I was badly lamed by a hit on the foot. At the edge of the wood on the west side of Tower Hamlets, we found ourselves charging into darkness led by General Fitzclarence, with the Gloucesters on our right. We came under a storm of rifle and machine gun fire and were driven back to rifle pits at the edge of the wood. There was hopeless confusion – each pit contained representative of 6 different regiments with French Zouaves thrown in. We got straightened up and held about 100 yards of trench on either side of Zouaves , with the Loyals on our right and the 60th on

A Long Way from Tipperary

our left. The trenches were scarcely finished before dawn when shelling commenced and continued all day."

After dark the Welch were moved into support but continued to take casualties from shelling and were recalled during the night to help the Queens and SWB. On the 4th November the Battalion was sent to Bellewarde Farm to rest....this was the official end of the battle of Gheluvelt. But between then and 11 November, there was little respite. Action on the 7 and 8 November saw more casualties and on 11 November the Germans launched their final effort to break through across the whole front.

Gheluvelt saw the end of the old battalion and its epitaph is best described in a letter that I found in the Public Records Office from Colonel Marden, who wrote the official history. Writing from 7 Metropole Court Folkestone on 14 November 1932 to a fellow soldier he says;

" *Your experienced eye has hit on a weak spot in my narrative of 31 October 1914 i.e. the action of "C" Company.*

I think that you will find that the only account of 31 Oct in the war diaries which records the actions of the Welch was written by Captain Rees, who took command of the battalion at the end of the day and who afterwards attained the rank of Brigadier. After the war Rees wrote a Diary of the first Seven months of the war and amplified a little what he had already written in the official War Diary of the Battalion. Morland, the CO, Ferrar, the Adjutant and Moore. Commander of "C" company were all killed. Pritchard, Second in Command was

A Long Way from Tipperary

dangerously wounded and died in 1917 from the effect of his wounds. Marshal. Commander of "B" company was taken prisoner and can only speak of the action of his own company. Young, "D" company, was wounded early in the action and can say nothing about "C" company. Oppenheim (wounded) has disappeared. So also has Cocks, wounded) who was probably commanding the two platoons of "C" company in the little wood. Corder, who alone with Rees was left unwounded at the close of 31 October was killed at Aubers Ridge on 9 May 1915. I have said that there were about 12 officers and 600 other ranks (page 323 of the History) but I had included Gilbey who went sick the day before and counted in Hewett who was fighting with the 7th Division. There were really only 10 officers with the Welch on 31 October; 5 officers having become casualties on 26 and 29 October.

Of the NCOs mentioned in the history, none can say what happened to C company. I got in touch with CSM Saunders of "C" but he was with Moore at company on the mound near the windmill. He confirms that C company had two platoons in the little wood. Rees says that these were wiped out by shellfire. They were to the right rear of "C" company South Wales Borderers. They were probably not seriously dug in, as it was a defensive action to commence with and they would be wanted for counter attack. I imagine that Cocks was with them, but he was wounded sometime during the battle. Rees says that Moore sent a platoon from his reserve on the mount before action commenced on the 31st to keep in touch with the Queens. They must have been in a very

A Long Way from Tipperary

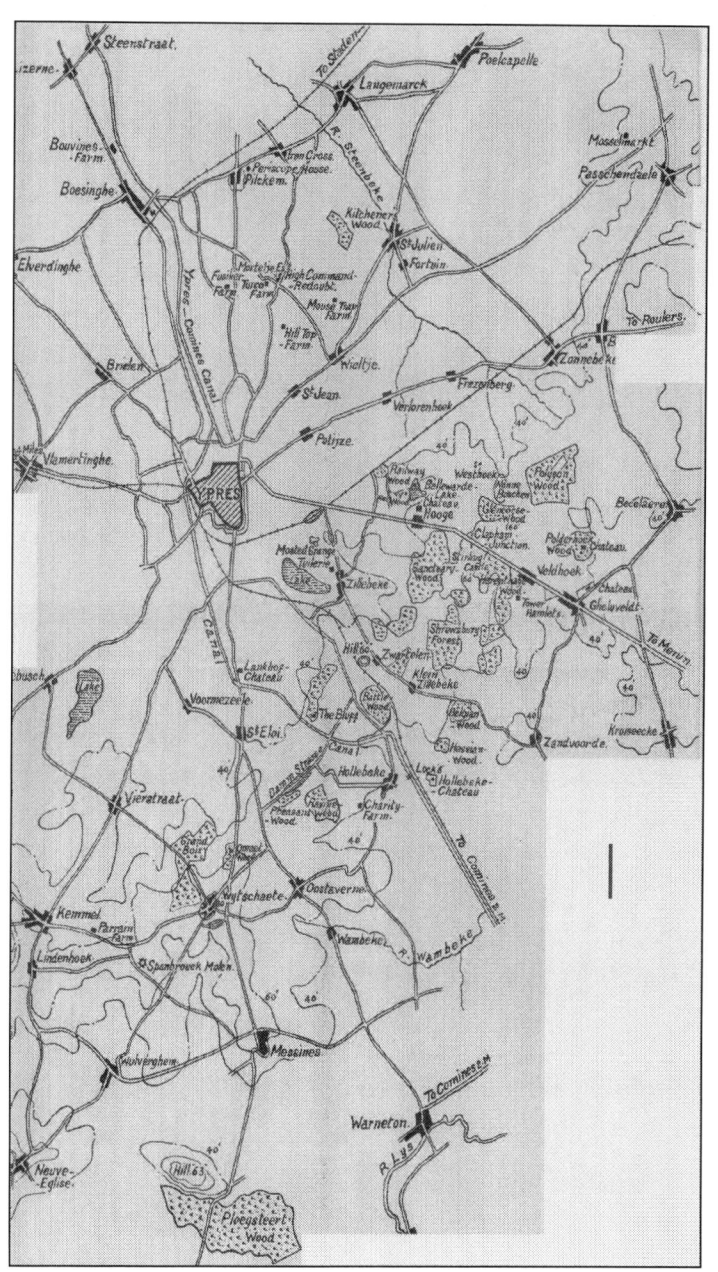

A Long Way from Tipperary

exposed position and would have had no time to dig in before the bombardment began. There is no record of what became of them. "B" Company (Marshal) was hidden from the Queens by the causeway. Morland certainly withdrew his HQ and his supports in the vicinity of his HQ to the village, as it appeared to be useless to keep them where they were and to this extent, the Queens may claim that the Welch left them in the lurch.

The note that I made when reading the Official History was that Morland was accused of withdrawing his "firing line and supports". This is incorrect. He couldn't move "B" company which was pinned to the ground or the two platoons of "D" company (badly shown by crenulations in the map but really behind a hedge on the edge of the farm) which constituted his firing line and his supports were not dug in, merely sheltering in a sunken lane in shelters in the main road.

I do not think that the SWB accuse the Welch of leaving them in the lurch. The Boche certainly did get in between the their right company and "B " company through the farm because "D" company platoons were wiped out. I have had some correspondence with Burleigh Leach who commanded and with S Atkinson, who as you now wrote the SWB history and they accept the fact that the Welch were wiped out not that they retired from their front trenches. I think that the account in the SWB history is a fair one.

It is generally agreed that the Boche got into Gheluvelt about 12.00 to 12.30pm. I imagine that if "C" company platoons were still in the wood, they would have been rounded up

A Long Way from Tipperary

from the flank, but I think that had lost heavily from shellfire being in the direct line of guns firing from Kruiseecke and that the survivors had been withdrawn to the village to join the rest of "C" company and that they had taken part in the fighting there.

The SWB state that they had only 14 officers. They were half in a position sheltered from observation and were lucky compared with the Welch and the Queens.

The impression I wish to give of the fighting on 31 October 1914 is, as far as the Welch are concerned, that they were in a frightfully exposed position, very weak in officers, and not dug in, except as regards "B" company and two platoons of D company, and not expecting a mass attack preceded by a tremendous bombardment. They did their best and the firing line certainly did not retire - they could not do so. Morland thought that it was best tactically to withdraw his supports and hold them for counterattack and it is difficult to say that he was wrong."

The Battle of Gheluvelt was the baptism of fire of Adolf Hitler. As observed earlier, the Regiment was full of raw recruits, few sharing the deep elation of Hitler at the thought of battle, At the outbreak of war, Hitler had written "*I fell down on my knees and thanked heaven from an overflowing heart for granting me the good fortune of being permitted to live at this time*" The famous photograph of Hitler in the crowd taken at Munich's Odeonplatz on 2 August on the declaration of war with Russia, testifies to his rapture, although it was doctored afterwards to suggest greater

A Long Way from Tipperary

numbers of enthusiasts for the war in the square. Hitler's feeling did not last long as in letters from the front, Hitler wrote that after four days of fighting, the List regiment had been reduced from 3,600 to 611 men, and List himself killed, partly as a result of friendly fire but also from the rapid execution of British rifle fire.

The description given by Hitler in Mein Kampf will not stand close examination of the details, which are largely propagandistic, but it shows how much Gheluvelt meant to him.

"And then came a damp, cold night in Flanders, through which we marched in silence, and when the day began to emerge from the mist, suddenly an iron greeting came whizzing at us over our heads, and with a sharp report sent the little pellets flying between our ranks, ripping up the wet ground; but even before the little cloud had passed, from two hundred throats the first hurrah rose to meet the first messenger of death. Then a crackling and a roaring, a singing and a howling began and with feverish eyes each one of us was drawn forward, faster and faster, until suddenly, past turnip fields and hedges the fight began, the fight of man against man. And from a distance, the strains of a song reached our ears, coming closer and closer, leaping from company to company, and just as death plunged a busy hand into our ranks, the song reached us too and we passed it along; "Deutschland, Deutschland uber alles, alles in der Welt!" Hitler's initial idealism however gave way on seeing thousands killed and injured to the realization that "life was a constant horrible struggle"

A Long Way from Tipperary

According to German sources, the regiment had fought in the Gheluvelt sector for three days. At the end of the second day of combat, which was rainy and cold, the List had fought their way about halfway up the hill towards the centre of Gheluvelt. By this time, the Regiment was barely the size of a company, having lost two thirds of its members. Its new Commander. Captain Franz Rubenbauer argued in vain on the evening of 30 October that his men were exhausted and should be withdrawn. To accept this proposition across the board would have meant that Germany had lost the race for the sea,(or more accurately, the Channel) so on 31 October, the remains of the List with Wurttemberg and Saxon troops, were ordered to force their way into the grounds of Gheluvelt Chateau. Their success was temporary because, as we have seen, the Chateau was recaptured by the Worcesters and German casualties included List himself. Hitler escaped the hand to hand fighting in the village, as he was nicely ensconced in a former British trench. The British had held the German attack and after they regrouped, the outcome was that the front had advanced no more than 3 kilometres towards Ypres from the opening day of battle which was where it was to stay until 1917 – static warfare had begun.

German participants in the battle, including the List chaplain, recognised that the British were both brave and skilled soldiers. The outcome had been a stalemate but Hitler and the Regiment always tried to sell it as a German triumph to justify the staggering casualties. As Hitler recorded, the regiment as a whole had been reduced to 611 effectives, and the casualty rate was 83% including both dead and

A Long Way from Tipperary

wounded. 724 – one in 4 of the Regiment – were killed. It was now less than battalion size. Nearly a quarter of all German losses in 1914 occurred at 1st Ypres.

Hitler spent most of the war as a dispatch runner, which was a highly dangerous role. He was a committed and conscientious soldier who did not lack physical courage but his tendency to brooding and introspection made him a solitary figure; about the war itself, he was utterly fanatical. No humanitarian feelings could be allowed to interfere with the ruthless prosecution of German interests. For example, he disapproved of the Christmas truce of 1914 " there should be no question of something like that during war". Hitler spent much of the war engaged with the British rather than the French. He survived Gheluvelt unscathed but was hit by French shell splinters in November 1914 near Fromelles where he spent half of his wartime service. Between March 1915 and September 1916 his regiment defended two kilometres of stalemated front near Fromelles where heavy battles were fought with the British; in September 1916 they were moved to the Somme where he was wounded again and sent home for treatment. He was back at the front at Vimy in 1917, then on to a hammering near Ypres in August. October 1917 to April 1918 brought huge German losses especially in July on the Marne, which was the last major German offensive. In August the List were moved to Cambrai to combat the British offensive at Bapaume and in September his unit was gassed on the heights south of Wervick, back to where the war started for him in Ypres. Hitler's war was now over and it was whilst he was recovering in Germany that he heard the news of the

A Long Way from Tipperary

shattering defeat of Germany, accompanied by Revolution at home - what he called the greatest villainy of the century.

Interestingly, there is some evidence that the mustard gas that incapacitated Hitler was manufactured in Bristol, William's future home. Dichloroethyl sulphide killed comparatively few people but the injuries that it could inflict were terrible. Anyone coming into direct contact with it would suffer pain in the eyes and throat, immense blisters and even blindness. The wounds it caused were comparable to second or even third degree burns. Victims were incapacitated for months and many never fully recovered often dying later of cancer. A gas mask offered no protection and it easily penetrated clothing. In late 1917 the British decided after experiencing German gas attacks (in one of which, William's brother Edward was a victim) that they needed their own which was a challenge as the British Chemical industry was nowhere near as advanced as the German. This decision took on a somewhat desperate character in 1918 as Russia had already been knocked out of the war, the British had suffered huge losses in recent German offensives and new capacity was required. By August 1918 the chemical factory at Avonmouth, the port of Bristol, was up and running producing 700 tons of gas a week loaded into shells at Chittening nearby which also took gas from Manchester and Runcorn. There is little doubt that the use of gas against the Hindenburg line which enveloped Hitler during the 100 days British and Commonwealth offensive contributed immensely to its success. Bristol also paid a price as the gas was dangerous to manage and leaked a lot – 50 to 60 employees were treated each day

A Long Way from Tipperary

and there were over 1,200 employees effected at the factories during the last 6 months of 1918.

It is fascinating to speculate how the 20th Century might have been changed if Hitler had fallen victim, like so many of his comrades to a British bullet at Gheluvelt; but even if we postulate the historical fantasy that a well aimed round from William Murphy might have saved the world, we cannot possibly know what other demonic figure would have arisen from the chaos of Germany's defeat.

It is worth noting that Hitler was considered by his superiors to be lacking in leadership qualities and that none of those who served with him thought otherwise; he received a promotion in 1914 to Corporal but this was his last, which is surprising in view of the fact that the very act of survival over four years opened up promotion opportunities. Certainly, his conviction that the German Army had been defeated by a stab in the back, which was a pure invention of the German Right but one which the Nazis would use as a central element in their propaganda armoury, was believed by many gullible soldiers. In fact, unrest at home was a consequence not a cause of military failure. Germany had been militarily defeated and was close to the end of its tether. Whilst the High Command still pumped out triumphalist propaganda, the Army was exhausted and in the last months took heavier losses than at any other time. In addition illness took its toll. Around 1.75 million soldiers had fallen victim to an influenza epidemic between March and July 1918 and around 750,000 were wounded during the

A Long Way from Tipperary

same period. It was no wonder that the Army was in a state of collapse.

Whilst Gheluvelt raged, another nasty fight was going on further south – the battle for the Messines Ridge. Defending the ridge were detachments of British cavalry and the London Scottish Regiment, a Territorial formation. They were heavily outnumbered and badly cut up but managed to escape under cover of smoke. The ridge was exchanged three times, finally being taken by the Germans. The situation was desperate for the British, they had been fighting for two weeks and many commanders thought that they could not stand another onslaught. The Official History records that "Infantry Brigades were reduced below the level of Battalions, Cavalry Regiments to below squadrons with only some thirty heavy guns available, largely low on ammunition. Haig desperately needed to relieve the 1st and 7th Divisions. But when a Division from 2 Corps was finally put in to replace the 7th, it arrived from La Bassee in the same condition.

Falkenhayn saw this attack as his last opportunity to drive the British out of the salient and take the channel ports. It was going to be a close run thing because there were no British reserves between the salient and the sea. If he was able to break through the British lines, there was little hope of an allied recovery because he would then be able to roll up the French from their flank and control of the channel would prevent further British engagement. He therefore assembled 6 fresh divisions – the strategy of attacking somewhere in the salient every day had extended the

A Long Way from Tipperary

<u>Hitler at the left</u>

British and he thought that one big push would do it. First he would keep up the pressure down the whole line from Nieuport to La Bassee 60 miles south - half a million men attacking at once - and then on 11th November the Germans attacked along the whole 9 miles from Messines to Polygon Wood, the attack being known as the Battle of Nonne Boschen. Fog and rain continued in the salient and at 9 am the soldiers of the 4th Bavarian Division marched northwest, parallel to the Menin road where the newly arrived men of II Corps waited for them. The British had been fortifying their

A Long Way from Tipperary

lines and they cut the Germans down with rifle fire - they broke and ran.

Soon the Prussian Guard had its turn – they penetrated the line between Polygon Wood and Nonne Boschen at the junction of the British and French forces but the British counterattacked and drove them back. Further north 6 battalions of the German Guards broke through near Polygon Woods, on a line manned by remnants of the Black watch and Scots Guards but they were cut up hideously by shrapnel fired at point blank range. In Polygon Wood itself as the mist rose, the grey German figures that appeared were seen to be masses of dead. A Prussian Guard Battalion that had lost many of its officers plunged into Polygon Wood and were killed, fled or captured. Then as dusk fell it began to rain heavily.

The Welch were fortunate during Nonne Boschen in that they were deployed south of the Menin Road at Shrewsbury Forest as part of Lord Craven's force consisting of the Royals, the 10th Hussars, 2nd KRRC 1st SWB 2nd Munsters and London Scottish. They were on the east edge of the woods with the London Scottish on their left and Munsters on the right. The battalion consisted of only two companies of 6 officers and 200 men. The attacks of the Germans were easily contained although sniping went on incessantly as the enemy was on the other side of the wood. On 12 November they moved to a new position in Forest which turned out to be a sniper's paradise, according to Captain Rees.

A Long Way from Tipperary

On the 13th at dawn the Germans attacked without warning, accompanied by smoke bombs; they had temporary successin taking a trench as both sides blazed away through the smoke, but it was retaken. At last the Welch were relieved and billeted in Ypres en route to Locre. As Rees recorded " *I have never seen troops in such a state of filth or exhaustion.*" Falkenhayn had had enough. His men were fought out. Some men did not get out of their trenches, others made half-hearted assaults. The youthful reserve units had seen enough death and destruction and their hearts were not in it. They had been through hell and their nerves were shot.

The BEF was withdrawn from the Ypres salient on 15 September and succeeding days. The French took over the 21 miles between Givenchy and Wytshaete. It is worth remembering that the French defended 430 miles of front at this point with the British holding only 21 miles.

The First Battle of Ypres was the death knell of the old British professional Army. The butcher's bill came to more than 60,000 men. At best, those battalions which arrived at full strength of 1,100 men (most had not because they had been fighting since August) were now reduced to a few officers and two or three hundred men. The casualties of the Welch were 8 officers and 197 men killed, 16 0fficers and 400 men wounded and 45 POWs. Only Rees of the original officers who came out from Britain remained on active duty. It was far worse for the Germans; they had lost more than 165,000 men, a great many of whom were the student battalions who were ruthlessly sacrificed. The combined

A Long Way from Tipperary

casualty rate was about 8.000 per day for the month of the battles. The salient stank with the rotting bodies of men and animals.

The Official History written in 1925 said " The British Army has fought many a defensive battle with success - Crecy, Agincourt, Albuera, Waterloo, Inkerman; and Ypres proved that the men of 1914 were fully the equals of their forefathers in valour and determination...But the cost was overwhelming. In the British battalions which fought at the Marne and Ypres, there scarcely remained with the colours an average of one officer and thirty men of those who had landed in August 1914. The old British Army was gone past recall, leaving but a remnant to carry on the training of the new Armies; but the framework that remained had gained an experience and confidence which was to make those armies invincible...If they had done nothing else, the men of the BEF would have done far more than could be expected of their numbers."

The Imperial War Museum history of 1914 records that by December 1914 those concerned with the medical and mental condition of those who became casualties of the first campaigns began to confront a new phenomenon. Large numbers of soldiers started to be evacuated back to the UK with " nervous and mental shock" amounting to 7 to 10% of all officers and 3-4% of all ranks. An experienced neurologist sent to investigate found that during Ypres there were rashes of men who became paralyzed under shell fire or were reduced to a state of collapse by exhaustion and strain. The phrase " shell shock" enter the national vocabulary.

A Long Way from Tipperary

Gheluvelt After the Battles

It may well be that after the war when William briefly worked in a psychiatric hospital, that many of the patients would have been suffering from "shell shock" as a result of sharing his experiences in battle.

It is certain that William was either among the handful of men who accompanied Rees from Gheluvelt back down the road to Veldhoek or that he was amongst the stragglers who rejoined over the next 12 hours. It is impossible for us to imagine what he experienced. The heavy artillery fire, the sweep of German machine guns, the air full of the hiss of bullets and the frightening noise of shells falling, exploding and tearing his comrades apart, officers and NCOs to whom the men looked for leadership tumbling, dead and wounded all around - an Army in the process of disintegration. His experience on the Chemin de Dames would have been much closer to the kind of open-ground peacetime exercises

A Long Way from Tipperary

in which he would have participated whilst training with the 3rd Battalion. Nothing could have prepared him for the onslaught at Gheluvelt. And yet in the midst of fear, he had to continue to play the role expected of him - the price that the List Regiment paid for their part on the attack is testimony to the fact that even in the course of their decimation, the Welch refused to capitulate. But even more was to be expected of William and his comrades.

The 2nd Battalion which owing to its weakness, had been organised on a two company basis, now received reinforcement and by 20 December numbered over 1000 men, but only four officers belonged to the Regiment. It was inspected and commended by King George at Merris on 3 December and Rees awarded his DSO. The Ypres offensive had petered out because the Germans had to transfer men to the Eastern Front. To take advantage of this supposed temporary weakness, the French decided to attack and to ask the British (who were too battered to do so) to "demonstrate" in support. The French made little headway and the Germans in retaliation attacked Givenchy, a small village rising out of waterlogged country in the north and low lying ground in the south. It was tactically important as it offered an observation point and as such was a bone of contention right through the war, being finally eliminated from the map. At day break on the 20th, the enemy exploded ten small mines under the trenches and rushed the village; they also captured the front and support trenches on both sides and drove in a pocket 300 yards deep into Indian lines to the north of Givenchy and towards Festubert.

A Long Way from Tipperary

By the time the Welch arrived on 21 December, the Manchesters had recaptured the village of Givenchy but had gradually been driven back and now held a portion of the village. To the north of the village, various portions of Indian troops with a sprinkling of British troops belonging to the Lahore Division were in the reserve trenches facing the Germans in occupation of our original front and support trenches. The 1st Guards Brigade was ordered to retake Givenchy from the Northwest whilst a French Territorial Division attacked from the south. The 3rd Brigade was ordered to operate on the left of the 1st Guards and to recapture the trenches between Givenchy and the hamlet of Rue de Cailloux by frontal assault (see map). The Artillery of the Division had not accompanied it and the Indians had no howitzers or heavy guns. There were few officers in the 3rd Brigade that had ever seen action and the prospect of attacking with only their own fire was not inviting. The head of the brigade arrived at Festubert about 1.45 p.m. The SWB were positioned on the left of the formation, the Gloucesters on the right, having received instructions to keep in touch with the 1st Guards. The Welch were at the Tuning Forks, half a mile west of Festubert, in support with the Munsters and 4th RWF in reserve. At 3pm the Brigade debouched from Festubert and Le Plantin respectively and at once a gap occurred as the front to be covered was about a mile and the Gloucesters veered away to the right to get in touch with the 1st Guards Brigade. Rees wrote;

" The advance was signalled by a hail of bullets that swept across the dead flat marshy ground and came whistling down our road. I established my HQ behind a house not far

A Long Way from Tipperary

from where the road runs into Festubert. I sent Ridewood with a platoon to establish touch with the 1st Brigade. He disappeared and I learnt later that they came under fire from La Plantain and that most were wounded"

At 3.15 Rees sent two companies to support the SWB and the Gloucesters and to fill the gap. Pushing forward in the failing light and zig zagging to avoid deep ditches, these companies lost touch. B Company came up on the right of the SWB who had reached the old support trenches after losing many men and A company, inclining to the right to tag the Gloucesters, pushed the enemy out of the old support trenches at considerable cost. C Company was thrown into the space between B and A but became came under heavy fire, lost men and became disorganised. D Company was detached to support A Company and the Gloucesters but came up between them and contacted neither in the dark. Rees, after stumbling about himself in the dark, discovered A company in the old support trenches, with the Germans a short distance ahead,. The Gloucesters were about 200 yards from A company with the Germans in front of them and B company was in close touch with the SWB who in turn had the Germans about 120 yards away. Unfortunately, this left gap of 600 yards in the centre of the Welch.

The 1st Guards had met with fierce resistance in Givenchy and had used up its reserves in taking the village. A considerable gap existed as a consequence between the left of the 1st and the right of the Gloucesters which the Munsters failed to bridge, ending up dug in 250 yards east of the road o Givenchy. At 7 am next morning, orders were given to

A Long Way from Tipperary

Plan of Festubert

renew the attack but the rifles clogged with mud and the ground was so deep that the attack became bogged. C Company was reorganised and thrown into the gap but its officers were killed and it was virtually annihilated. The survivors took up a position on the Plantin road. D company got up in line with A and closed the gap with the Gloucesters. On the left, the SWB extended their ground to the north and the B company of the Welch to the south, narrowing the gap to 500 yards. The Munsters pushed forward further than any others in support of the Gloucesters but lost 11 officers and 200 men and had to be retired. The battle came to an end . As Rees records

A Long Way from Tipperary

"no advance across the Festubert marches was possible unless supported by masses of artillery" (of which there was none).

The 3rd Brigade had recaptured the old support trenches but the original front trenches remained in German hands. Moreover there was a large gap between B Company and the rest of the Welch in the exact centre of which the Germans established a strong machine gun post in an old communications trench. The casualties of the Welch at this point amounted to 3 officers and 120 men. On Christmas day and the days that followed, attempts were made to drive deep saps towards the enemy but these were defeated by heavy fire at short range. It was evident that the ground was too deep for either side to attack successfully. Needless to day, whatever festive spirit caused troops to fraternise elsewhere on the Western Front that Christmas, did not reach Givenchy. On 26 December, B Company returned to Reserve and the Welch held their position with two companies in the front line and two in reserve. Rees commented

"The weather was atrocious and the conditions worse than I have ever seen. On one occasion it took me two hours to go along 150 yards of trench and return. In many cases the mud and water were waist deep and the men were perched on mud islands."

German trench mortars exacted a heavy toll whilst British artillery was restricted to four rounds per gun, per day. The Welch added a further 65 casualties to their toll before finally

A Long Way from Tipperary

receiving four days rest at Bethune on 8 January. It had been a grim Christmas for William.

On 12 January the 3rd Brigade was sent back again to the Givenchy sub-sector which ran from the canal on the right, round the front of the village to a point about 150 yards to the north of it where it bent back sharply for 500 yards towards Festubert (see map). All four battalions were in the line, each with two companies in front, one in support and one in reserve. On the right were the Munsters, then came the Gloucesters, while the Welch, to who were attached two platoons of the 4th RWF held the village front which included on its left French Farm, a slightly advanced post. The SWB on the left had one company forward, and one back. Battalion HQ was located in a farm house in the centre of Givenchy – it had all around defence and was converted into a keep containing about 70 men. Snipers occupied houses on the edge of the village. On 24 January there were indications of a storm brewing and Rees brought up a company of Black Watch who stationed themselves in cellars in the village.

After a bombardment at 07 30 am on 25 January, the fire lifted and 120 – 150 Germans broke through the lines of the RWF and reached HQ before faltering (some were shot by orderlies through loop holes.) French Farm took heavy casualties and the Welch right fighting alongside the Gloucesters were firing from both sides of their trenches. The Germans appeared in the village round the church and were counter attacked by the Black Watch Platoons and the Welch, house to house fighting took place around the church

A Long Way from Tipperary

before the original line was recaptured. The enemy had attacked with 1800 men in six lines and apart from their one successful point of entry where a trench had been battered by artillery, they had been simply been mown down by rifle fire. 70 Germans were captured and a number of medals won, one by Private Rogers, a man who had enlisted in 1882 and who was already a grey haired old soldier.. He led the charge to recapture an artillery observation post that had been seized by the Germans. A period of calm now ensued.

When General Sir Charles Munro inspected the Battalion on 23 February, he said *"In all the fighting in which the Division has taken part, you have always figured prominently. I am paying you no idle compliment in saying this, that throughout the Division you have the name of hard and dogged fighters."*

After the failure of the Allied offensives of December, the weather became too bad for any further attacks, other than small local ones. The German advance had made a large salient between Rheims and Amiens which threatened the French lines of communication with the north. Joffre decided to attack early in March, using his own Tenth Army to capture the Vimy Heights and the British 1st Army to seize the Aubers Ridge. As a preliminary move, Haig captured Neuve Chapelle on 11 and 12 March and consolidated the move. The 2nd Welch were not in the battle but were moved into the village on 24 March, taking over trenches from the Munsters. These were supposed to be "quiet trenches" but ten days of inaction nonetheless cost 68 killed and wounded from snipers and hand grenades.

A Long Way from Tipperary

William, Nell and Edward - Early 1915 on Leave

The photograph of William in civilian clothes and his brother Edward dressed as a member of the Royal Horse Artillery standing behind their sister Nell was probably taken at the beginning of 1915 whilst William was home on leave from the war. William is looking fit and healthy so the enteric fever which laid him low and brought him out of the trenches in 1915 had not yet struck.

A Long Way from Tipperary

Chapter 8.

Aubers Ridge and Repatriation

The 2nd Battalion stayed in the trenches at Neuve Chapelle for much of March and April, as the offensive was delayed. The reason for this was the Second battle of Ypres in which the First but not the Second battalion was involved. This battle saw the first use of gas by the Germans, aided by massive use of heavy artillery. The losses were as heavy as in the first battle, (2,000 officers and 57,000 men) and it has been commented that

"Ypres 1915 was the first battle of the new era of military science in a war of masses. The destruction of defences by weight of explosive shell, the incapacitating of defenders by gas, the advance to the limit of the destroyed defences, the barrage of gunfire to prevent reinforcements and the consolidation of captured ground by barbed wire and machine guns. This remained the model until the invention of the tank and the creeping barrage."

The Germans lost 35,000 men and the British did well just to hang on until their own supply of materiel could be brought into play. By the first week of May Sir John French decided that he was strong enough to continue the attack on Aubers Ridge whilst holding the enemy at bay in Ypres. The First Division, of which the Welch were a part, and the Meerut Division held a 2000 yard front just south of the Estaires-La Bassee Road and East of Richebourg. The 6000 yards

A Long Way from Tipperary

further north was held by IV Corps, whose task it was to advance on a 1500 yard front south towards Aubers and Fromelles, thereby pinching out, if successful, the intervening enemy. The attack on 9 May was to be preceded by heavy shelling from 516 field guns and 121 heavy guns . It was thought that the first assault would prove to be an easy and bloodless task – wrong again. In the First Division, the Second Brigade attacked on a 650 yards front on the right of the 1st Army. The Third Brigade attacked on the left across a similar footage. The Ist Guards were held in reserve and the Munsters were on the right of the Third Brigade. The Welch on the far left of the Third Brigade attacked with two companies in the first line. C Company on the right, B Company on the left; D and A Company were in support. The SWB were behind the Welch, the Gloucesters behind the Munsters and the 4th RWF were there to mop up.

Facing the Welch was 150 yards to the enemy line. 20 yards in front of the Welch trench was an old, half full trench. 25 yards beyond that was a stream that was 9 ft across, and 2 to 4 feet deep with banks about 2 ft above water level. 80 yards beyond that was the enemy wire behind which the Germans raised parapet could be seen. The Germans were obviously expecting the attack after the relatively brief period of artillery fire. During the night the Royal Engineers had laid duckboard bridges for the Welch across the stream. The plan was that two platoons would cross the stream and lie down, awaiting the other two platoons. The reserve would then advance across the open fields to occupy the jump - off trenches. A good plan but what actually happened is briefly told and best described from the diary of Lieutenant Cripps

A Long Way from Tipperary

M.C. At 5 am the bombardment commenced, intended to cut wire, destroy trenches and enemy guns. As the bombardment died down, Cripps observed;

"The shooting was erratic, many casualties occurred from short rounds. Few shells appeared to be going anywhere near the German wire or parapet and the tops of their bayonets could be clearly seen. As the first wave mounted the parapet, it was met by a hail of bullets, and many men fell back dead or wounded into the trench. At the end of a minute, I blew my whistle, and the second wave went over the top. There were no troops visible. Every man was down and there were heaps of dead and wounded by every bridge. I ran between the bridges and reached the stream by which time few were left standing. What remained got into the water, with the Germans standing up and firing at us. Many wounded were drowned. No other troops appeared, and the fire died down... I was the only officer in B Company left unwounded.....A message was thrown in a tin, saying that the attack would recommence at 7 am and that the remnants of the leading companies were to join in the attack. It never materialised as the reserve companies were shot to pieces getting to the front trench. Collecting about 30 wounded and unwounded men I set to work to dig a shallow communications trench back to our original line. This was completed by midday and crawling along, we all got back safely. The survivors had been in water since 0500 am and were very cold"

All along the front of 1 Corps, the attack had fared equally badly and a heavy bombardment had to be put down to

A Long Way from Tipperary

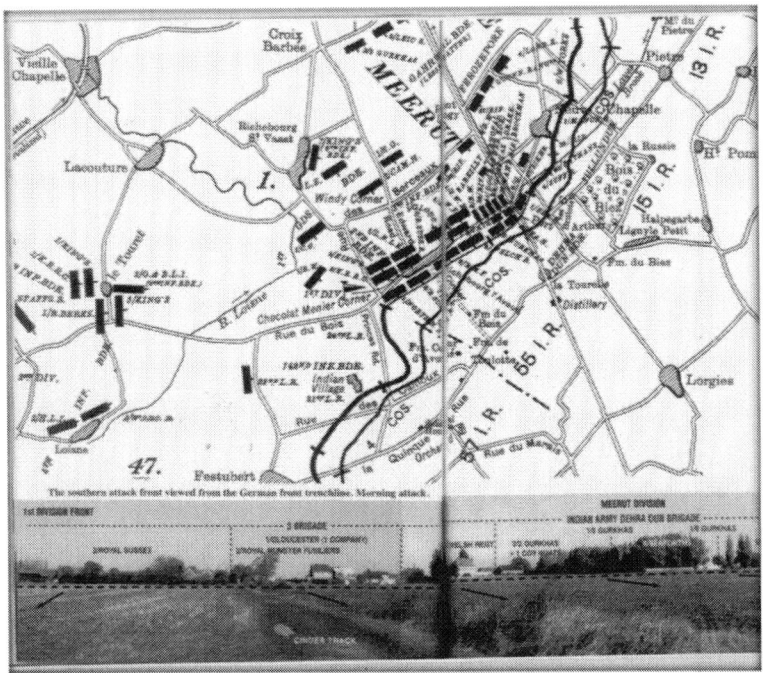

Aubers Ridge from the German Perspective; Welch Line of Attack in the Centre

enable the shattered remnants of the lead Battalions to withdraw. In the evening under cover of dark, the 2nd Welch, or what remained of them were withdrawn 8 miles to Hinges into billets to recuperate. It had been a disastrous day, the only redeeming feature being the bravery shown in bringing wounded back under fire. The battalion lost 11 officers and 245 other ranks at Aubers out of 24 and 830. The regimental diary records that *"among the killed was CSM Murphy (Spud) a powerful 6ft Irishman hailing from Merthyr.*

A Long Way from Tipperary

He was a rugby forward having played for Newport, Cardiff and the Army and scored many a try. But this, his last, was his best" (sic).

CS M William Murphy was born in Merthyr Tydfal in 1881, the son of a coal miner. Eleven other Murphys from South Wales died during the War with the Welch Regiment, falling in Flanders, Loos, Merville, Mericourt in the Dardanelles, in Greece, in Allenby's campaign in Palestine and at home from wounds receive on the Western Front. Those bearing the Murphy name certainly paid their dues in blood in the war; over 1050 members of the clan died overall, many from Australia, representing something under 0.01% of British fatalities.

The failure of the attack can be attributed to the strength of the German position and the weakness of the artillery preparation. The Germans after Nueve Chapelle were not going to be taken by surprise and made fortification their principal asset. The scene of the action was flat meadowland and marsh which had a fair scattering of trees with water two to three feet below the surface. German breastworks were built 6 feet high and 15 to 20 feet across, parados were constructed, and boxes used to make dugouts. At ground level, shaped structures were placed at angles, protected by steel plates into which were inserted loopholes to provide machine guns for enfilade fire. Nothing but a direct hit would knock out these guns. In the depressions, the Germans had laid barbed wire in addition to that above ground. There was nothing new in all of this – it was merely siege warfare but it made breastworks immune

A Long Way from Tipperary

to anything but the heaviest artillery and at that time the British had too little of this and what they had was worn.

In a critique of the Aubers attack written by Lieutenant Colonel Kearsey formerly of the General Staff in 1929 he noted " Though we had a superiority in numbers of possibly some 500 men, we could not counterbalance the advantage which the enemy had in strength of position and in numbers of machine guns. To support the 7th Division , 109 guns and howitzers were available to cut wire and deal with communication trenches but the advance of our infantry was met with such heavy fire that 40 minutes after zero the attacking troops were definitely checked in " No Man's Land". The plan had been ambitious and not in accordance with the relative armament, training and morale of the opposing forces." Kearsey also referred to defective ammunition and worn guns.

To the right of the line, the French after 6 days of continuous bombardment, advanced 2 and a half miles on a front of 4 miles. This was the first attack of its kind and was the prototype of the battles that were fought for the next four years. The 2nd, 7th and Meerut Divisions between 15-27 May succeeded in penetrating the enemy on the Festubert front to an average depth of 600 yards but fresh troops were not available to consolidate this success. The ground gained in these battles had been purchased at an enormous cost in lives.

The jumping off position for the Welch at Richebourg is clearly identifiable today to the right of the Indian memorial to

A Long Way from Tipperary

the Meerut Division; when William's grandchildren visited the location in 2007 it was impossible to imagine the carnage that took place over the first 50 yards of the ploughed field before us between the road and the stream. The distance involved on a sunny day could be covered in 25 seconds at a fast walk. A sleepy village made of red brick cottages, children playing on swings and the quite rumble of tractors in the fields give no inkling of the bloody history that was enacted here .It was difficult to conceive of what would have passed through William's mind as he contemplated yet another suicidal operation after having survived thus far.

Richebourg –Welch to the left of the line, Germans to the right

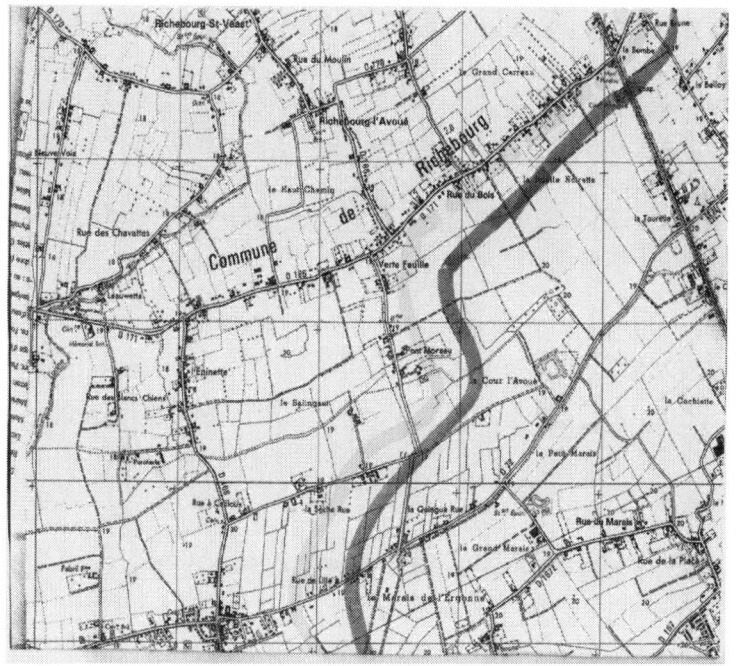

A Long Way from Tipperary

Robert Graves, whose book "Goodbye to All That" became a classic of the First World War and who was a Royal Welsh Fusilier, joined the 2nd Battalion of the Welch in May. He was fresh from home and found them "an unbelligerant lot", his remarks in his book drawing unfavourable comment in the Regimental History as they suggested that he did not realise what the Welch had been through. In fact he records that the Battalion had been in constant hard fighting since the previous August and had lost its full fighting strength 5 times over. On Aubers, he says "the last occasion was at Richebourg (Aubers Ridge) on 9 May, one of the worst disasters hitherto. The Divisions epitaph in the final communiqué read "Meeting with considerable opposition in the direction of Rue du Bois, our attacks were not pressed." Almost all the officers sent in replacement at this point were from other regiments, most as callow as Graves. Only four NCOs were originals. The First Battalion had also suffered badly. In Cardiff the Regiment advertised without apparent irony, *"Enlist at the Depot and get to France quick".* The result was a mixed bag.....Graves platoon of 40 men consisted of 14 over forty, including one of 63, and 5 under 18, one of whom was only 15.

Graves was briefed on arrival in the trenches at about a mile from Cambrin village by Captain Dunn his new company Commander. Dunn. Dunn wrote another first world war classic called " The War the Infantry Knew". Dunn said *"These Welshmen are peculiar. They won't stand being shouted at. They'll do anything if you explain the reason for it - do and die, but they have to know the reason why. The best way to make them behave is not to give them too much*

A Long Way from Tipperary

time to think. Work them off their feet. They are good workmen too. But officers must work with them, not only direct the work."

Graves witnessed evidence at first hand of the obstinate nature of the troops under his command. He records how two young miners felt that their Sergeant had a down on them and gave them all the dirty and dangerous jobs. So they decided to kill him. Later, they reported themselves to the Battalion Adjutant. The exchange went as follows, smartly slapping the butt of their sloped rifles, they said "*We have come to report sir, that we're very sorry Sir, but we have shot our Company Sergeant - Major*"..." *Good heavens!*" replied the adjutant, "*how did it happen?*".... "*It was an accident sir*"..." *What do you mean an accident, did you mistake him for a spy?*"....." *No,*" they replied, we mistook him for our <u>Platoon Sergeant</u> ".

Their naïveté cost them their lives, They were court - martialed and shot against the wall of a convent in Bethune by their own comrades, their last recorded words being inevitably "Stick it the Welch!"

Graves does not identify the two soldiers from the 2nd Battalion who were shot on 15th February 1915 but they are known now to be Lance Corporal William Price and Private Richard Morgan; they were executed for the murder of Company Sergeant Major Hayes and they are buried in Bethune Town Cemetery. These were the only soldiers from the Battalion shot during William's time at the front but Private J Carr was shot for desertion on 7 February 1916, as

A Long Way from Tipperary

was Private J Thomas for the same offence three months later. The last to be executed from the 2nd Battalion was Private James Skone for murder on 10 May 1918. 35 British soldiers in total were executed during the war for murder and 306 for military offences of which 18 were convicted of cowardice, 263 for desertion and the remainder for mutiny and other serious offences.

These executions represented only 10% of those sentenced to death as 90% of those convicted during the war had their sentences commuted. The whole subject is very controversial but a close examination of the individual cases, with one or two tragic exceptions, suggests that in the context of the time, the decisions made were not unreasonable. It is interesting that the Labour Government reviewed the whole issue in 1998 and decided against individual or blanket pardons.

It is impossible to say what William Murphy would have felt about these matters. I doubt that he would have admitted playing a part. In the case of Price and Morgan, it could well be that he formed part of the firing squad as soldiers were always shot by their own comrades. As one of the original members of the Battalion who had survived thus far, he may have been considered steadier than most and therefore suitable for the task. The penalty for murder in the civilian courts at that time was hanging, so perhaps in this example, there may have been less soul searching in the Battalion about these executions than would have been the case for desertion or a purely military offence. It is also worth noting that the British Army at the time was losing 400 soldiers per

A Long Way from Tipperary

day to casual fire and that many of those shot for military offences had poor records, sometimes including previous serious offences of the same type and were generally considered to have betrayed their comrades who risked death every day.

After Aubers, the Battalion went for a short time into quiet trenches which had been held by the French for six months and which contained dug-outs described in the Battalion Diary as " almost works of art as well as nearly shell proof since some were lined with steel girders". It was here that Graves and others from the 3rd RWF joined it. The peaceful period did not last long. On 20 May, the Battalion was moved to the Cuinchy area where there was a good deal of bombing and rifle - grenading. At the latter end of June the Battalion moved to the Vermelles area in preparation for the battle of Loos. Except for aerial torpedoes and the occasional orgy of shelling, it was a peaceful sector. Both sides were improving their defences and the Battalion was busy digging in at night. In August aggressive patrolling occurred to recce the enemy defences. Graves met the Battalions of the New Army during this period and felt like a scarecrow by comparison. By this time he claims to have caught the pessimism of the First Division. He saw ghosts of dead comrades and had some narrow escapes. Constant mining went on as well as counter-mining, which contributed to the atmosphere of anxiety. (The novel "Birdsong" gives a good understanding of what was involved). At the end of July, Graves was transferred back again to the Second Battalion of the Royal Welsh Fusiliers, where the usual peacetime insufferable behaviour prevailed in the officers mess.

A Long Way from Tipperary

The condition of the RWF at this time testified to the caprice of war. Although an original component of the BEF, it belonged to 19 Brigade which had experienced the good fortune to have been deployed as an Army Reserve rather than attached to any division for the period since Mons. As a result its casualties had been light and most of its company commanders and NCOs were the original regulars. They maintained the custom in the mess of not speaking to newly joined officers for their first six months and addressing subalterns as "warts". Graves was sufficiently disgusted with his treatment to vow that he would survive them all, which he accomplished.

The experience of another less well known Welch subaltern was rather different. Charles Pritchard Clayton was sent as a young subaltern to join the First Battalion in March 1915. He fought initially around Messines Ridge and Cookers Farm and his account of trench warfare is worth reading. He was soon sent to the Ypres salient where he was put into trenches at Zonnebeke. His impressions of Ypres were as follows

"About 4 o'clock we enter the streets of Ypres. The town shows little sign of enemy shelling and many of the inhabitants stand on their doorsteps as we pass by. Our men hail them with the usual cheery remarks and rough and ready jokes, half in English and half in something which is their version of French. But they do not respond like the people that we pass in the back areas. It seems that they are anxious for their homes. Turning a corner we come to the famous Clothe Hall. It is a building of striking beauty. Its

A Long Way from Tipperary

fretted pinnacles shine in the sun and it seems like an enormous fairy palace."

Clayton was then involved in three weeks of bloody fighting and horror in which he observed death in many forms including from German gas attack. He was pinned down in an apparently hopeless situation in trenches in front of Zonnebeke, when relief appeared at hand. His account of what happened is a simple but poignant description of the kind of experience that destroyed the veterans of the Second Battalion at the earlier battles in the salient.

"Hearing the German field guns open out vigorously, we see that their shells are bursting thickly above the slightly higher ground behind and to the north of the village. Then we see why they are shelling. Lines of British skirmishers are coming over the rise to support us and to try to throw back the enemy from his advanced positions on our left. In long regular lines they come with two and three yards between each man, and a hundred or two hundred between each line. As they top the ridge and the shelling opens, the bursts do them little harm. As they advance down the slope, the shelling becomes more accurate; here and there we see men blown down, and some do not get up again, but still the skirmishers keep their line in advance as if drilling on a parade ground. But now they are met by machine gun fire from some points to the north of us and parts of the line begin advancing on the run and lying down to fire while another section rushes forward....Now comes the real tragedy. The enemy seems to get their range and down go several of the gallant skirmishers almost simultaneously in

A Long Way from Tipperary

the middle of their rush. At the same time the guns seem to both quicken their fire and to become more effective. It is becoming a slaughter. It is terrible to watch and to be helpless to do anything .The lines are broken and there is a tendency to crowd left. The shrapnel is murderously effective now. It seems to sweep down whole sections of them. Some struggle helplessly after they fall. Nothing can help them now. Only one or two reach the shelter of the village...We cannot help wondering why they were sent over that ridge in broad daylight."

After three weeks Clayton re-enters Ypres on foot.

"The shelling has ceased and the city is very still. Our footsteps echo on the stones. One of my companions kicks open a door and we see the remains of a meal and traces of hasty flight. As we get near the square, the houses are more broken. The square itself is a miniature desert in which there is no movement. In the silence it is almost uncanny. A solitary horse appears from behind a block of ruins and leisurely strays across, picking his way between numerous shell holes. The Clothe Hall is now a gaunt skeleton. Gone are the fretted spires which shone in the sun three weeks ago. On the south side of the square is a monotonous stretch of flattened masonry, broken only by one huge piece of wall critically balanced on a single steel girder, and on the point of collapse. At several points from this stretch of ruins, spirals of smoke rise into the calm air."

Clayton was a tough operator and as a consequence he survived four years at the front, rising temporarily in

A Long Way from Tipperary

November - December of 1916 to Acting Lieutenant Colonel, commanding the Second Battalion, which he joined in September 1915 after a brief visit home, just before the battle of Loos.

It seems clear from the timing of William hospitalisation in early September that he did not participate in Loos which opened 15 days later on 25 September. Clayton had already taken over as Company Commander of B Company by this time so his view of the Welch is worth noting. He wrote in his diary published as "The Hungry One", the following description:

"The French and the Welsh become very friendly. It is a hard job to prevent the exchange of helmets, bayonets, caps puttees and whatnot, to such an extent as to have our men taken for French troops on the way back to the line. In temperament the Welsh and the French seem to have much in common. The English worship the idea of the unbroken square, the unbroken line, at any rate, some outward sign of conformity. Not so the French and the Welsh. In the calm self reliance and disregard of danger, and equal disregard of external discipline in a crisis, in their impatience with what they regard as the mere formalities of soldiering, the Welshmen, especially the miners of whom there are so many in the Battalion, and the French seem to see eye to eye. The English officer fails, I think to do justice in his own mind to the Welsh miner - soldier, who has no use for the martinet officer, for clean buttons in the trenches, for arms drill and sentry-go, but who, when it comes to fighting, is absolutely imperturbable. In virtue of the very independence of spirit

A Long Way from Tipperary

that makes him unhappy on the parade ground, he can be depended upon to take initiative when there is no one at hand to command. "

It was probably just as well that William left the Battalion before Loos. It was engaged on the opening day in an attack on the German lines which resulted in the capture of 5 German officers and 160 men in one spot, and the surrender of 400 Germans holding up the attack from Lone Tree Redoubt. But on the next day due to a misinterpretation of orders by the Forces on its right, the enemy was able to outflank the Battalion and capture its HQ and Colonel Prothero. The eventual losses of the Battalion were 12 officers and 224 other ranks. The First Battalion lost 15 officers and 350 men in a failed attempt to hold the Hohenzollern Redoubt after an initially successful assault.

Perhaps the last word on Loos should be left with the albeit controversial historian AJP Taylor. Loos, was, it will be recalled, the post dated cheque that Joffre extracted from the British for an autumn offensive if the effort in the Dardanelles failed, which it did. He specified that the attack should be made at Loos so as to support the French in Champagne, whose own attack was called off after 3 days. When the fighting in the Loos area petered out early in November, the balance sheet was grim. The Allies had made no strategic gain but had experienced useless slaughter. The British lost over 50,000 men as against 20,000 Germans. The French lost 190,000 men against 120,000 Germans. Taylor commented; -

A Long Way from Tipperary

"Yet Joffre was still cheerful. Even if he had not defeated the Germans, he was confident that he was wearing them down. One of these days all the Germans would be killed, even if far more British and French were killed in the process".

William was withdrawn from the front line and eventually sent back to the UK because he contracted enteric fever which was a killer disease from which many did not survive. It was contracted from ingesting trench water which contained all kinds of human and animal waste, from faecal matter to the detritus from human remains, chemicals and rusting metal and soil microbes. About 6% of those who contracted the disease died even after receiving medical attention and the long term effects were very debilitating.

Addington Palace Hospital

In London he was treated at Addington Palace Hospital in London and it appears from the photo that we have of him

A Long Way from Tipperary

there (he is marked "x") that it must have taken him a long time to regain his strength. Addington Palace near Croydon was the official home of the Archbishop of Canterbury until he moved to Lambeth Palace. During the Great War, huts were constructed in the grounds so as to accommodate the war wounded and the larger picture from which the extract was taken, indicates that the ward is in a hut. The Palace still exists as a leisure centre and apartment complex.

Addington Palace Hospital

William at Addington Palace Hospital

A Long Way from Tipperary

William's brother Edward did not escape unscathed. He was a victim of Mustard gas, whose effects he fought all of his life, but he lived until 1978 reaching his 84th year

When William Murphy joined the Reserves in 1908 (It is probable that he worked for North Navigation Ltd, the main coal company in Maesteg which owned the Garth and Caerau collieries), mining was a dangerous business which in the last three years of peace killed an average of 1430 coal miners per year, and injured a further 165,000 (about 10% of the work force but lower than the French, German and US colliery figures). Indeed pit tragedy had already struck in his own family when his brother James had been buried alive in Maesteg Deep. It might have appeared to William in the pre war years that soldiering was a healthier occupation, if so, the war changed that idea forever.

By the time of the Armistice in November 1918, all the belligerent nations bore lasting scars. Russia had lost 2 million men, Germany nearly 2 million, France and her colonies nearly 1 million, Austria Hungary around 1 million and the British Empire almost one 875,000. The US incurred 115,000 deaths of which a half resulted from the great influenza epidemic that followed the Armistice (and from Pershing's futile and costly attacks on the last day of the war). In total more that 10 million men of all nations lost their lives, and most were under 40 years old. More than twice that number were wounded and a considerable proportion maimed for life. Casualties on this scale were unprecedented and the post war social dislocation was profound.

A Long Way from Tipperary

William did not keep a diary of his experiences in the First World War, as he was not much of a writing man. Neither did he talk very much about it. When his four sons visited the battlefields in October 1990 and followed in his footsteps, none could recall many significant tales of war beyond the one or two anecdotes that I have recorded. William did show his sons however when they were eventually called up for national service over thirty years later how to present arms, using a broom rather than a Lee Enfield 303, but my father did not stray further. I believe however that the war did have a long term effect on him and that he suffered all throughout his life from a susceptibility to melancholia that he passed on to us all. Certainly, we were profoundly affected by attempting to re-imagine what he had experienced in the first year of war and this is a feeling that does not diminish with time.

<u>Linen Postcard sent from the Front by Edward to William in 1916</u>

A Long Way from Tipperary

William rejoined the Armed Forces in May 1918 when the outcome of the war was still very much uncertain. He enlisted in the Royal Air Force. We do not know whether he was medically discharged between 1915 and 18 or if he was engaged in non combatant duties. He may have taken some considerable time to recover his health as it was clear that he was not automatically reenlisted in his old Regiment which would have been the case if he had been considered fit for combat duty. Following his enlistment as Private Second Class on 8 May in the Royal Air Force, he was promoted Private First Class on the following day and Corporal on the day after that! The records do not show where he served with the RAF but there are indications that he was a drill instructor who would have been deployed training new recruits. As the BAC at Filton trained the bulk of British pilots, it is even conceivable that was given his first introduction to Bristol in this role. He transferred to the Air Force reserve on 6 February 1919 and finally left the Colours on 20 April 1920. His next of kin was given as Thomas Murphy of Philip Street, Sengennydd, brother.

After the war he did not return to Maesteg – his parents were now dead and in any event, he had not had a good relationship with his mother and his sisters. His address according to the linen Christmas card sent to him by his brother Edward in 1916 was 35 Deslwyn Street, Phillips Town New Tredegar in a row of houses that were built in 1905 for mining management. There were Murphys living in the Street at no 55 in 2010 so he could have been staying with a relative There was no question of William choosing to return underground if alternative choices were available.

A Long Way from Tipperary

His first post war job appears to have been as an orderly in a psychiatric hospital in Newport, bluntly called a "lunatic asylum". He found the work less than congenial and indeed began to doubt his own sanity. It seems likely that he was working at St Cadoc's Hospital Caerleon founded in 1906. He then lost his pay packet at some point which was the final straw which triggered a decision to leave Newport and go to Bristol. It is worth remembering that there were close connections between Maesteg and Bristol dating back to the beginnings of industry in the Llynfi valley. He then came to Bristol and worked in a confectionary factory near the old Horsefair in Bristol called Champion and Davis, where he met his wife, Alice Turner.

William's records with the Regiment, like those of millions of other soldiers were lost in the Second World War when the Germans blitzed Army archives. The first positive proof of his affiliation with the Welch derived, ironically not from the Army at all but from the RAF Personnel Management Centre at Innsworth in Gloucester who retained a statement of his service, including his period in the Welch Regiment. The RAF also provided the information of his enlistment in 1918 in their service. The Army Medal Office at Droitwich, were able to confirm his service and provide his original military number of 260 which is engraved on the only souvenir of the War that he left behind, his brass button stick, used to protect his uniform from Brasso when he was cleaning his buttons. They confirmed that he entered the Theatre of Operations in France in 1914 and was awarded the 1914 Star, the British War Medal and the Victory Medal. Their records show that these medals were returned to the

A Long Way from Tipperary

Branch, the reason not being clear. It could be that he never signed and received them, or (less likely), he returned them himself for some reason.

William spoke well of the French (although not of their cleanliness in the trenches!), particularly the Bretons with whom he was able to converse, speaking Welsh on his part, and Breton on theirs – the languages have common roots. This memory came to mind on Armistice Day in November 2008 when I attended a Commemoration ceremony in the small Pyrenean village of St Lizier d'Ustou. Like many French villages, St Lizier and the area around suffered grievously from its heavy losses during the First World War which impacted on the relatively small number of families in the community. I was the only foreigner present amongst a cluster of elderly villagers and they were not aware of the presence of an outsider. It was very touching therefore to hear the Mayor in this tiny village pay tribute in his speech to the British soldiers who came to the aid of France both in the First and Second World Wars. I am sure that similar sentiments were expressed that day all over France. My father would have appreciated the recognition.

Many of the myths that dogged the history of the First World War were dispelled in the lead up to 100th Anniversary of the War in 2014, particularly those promoted by the liberalism of the 1960s in which war poetry was treated as history and left wing notions of class conflict were behind such popular and influential musicals as "Oh What a Lovely War". The "Blackadder" series was still at it in the 1990s however, feeding off the invention of Alan Clarke's wholly fabricated quote

A Long Way from Tipperary

attributed by him to a German General that the British Army consisted of "Lions led by Donkeys". The myth of "Chateau Generals", busy quaffing fine wine whilst the working classes died in the mud was useful to class warfare. Although the great majority of casualties in WW1 were from the working class, the social and political elite were hit disproportionately hard by the War. Their sons provided the junior officers whose job it was to lead the way over the top and expose themselves to the greatest danger as an example to their men. Some 12% of the British army's ordinary soldiers were killed during the war, compared with 17% of its officers. Eton alone lost more than 1,000 former pupils - 20% of those who served. UK wartime Prime Minister Herbert Asquith lost a son, while future Prime Minister Andrew Bonar Law lost two. Anthony Eden lost two brothers, another brother of his was terribly wounded, and an uncle was captured. Over 200 British Generals were killed or captured.

On the competence issue, it is the case that none of the combatants knew how to deal with the new form of industrialised warfare that erupted in 1914 and that all those in the field suffered as a consequence. Before 1914, the British army had been primarily a colonial army, small but efficient. The generals, used to handling small-scale forces in colonial warfare, had much to learn about a type of war for which they were almost entirely unprepared. It is not surprising that in the course of its apprenticeship the BEF had a number of bloody setbacks. It is a feature of William's story that he was right in the middle of this learning and part of what was a bad beginning in which a relatively small British Force was a junior partner never entirely in control of its destiny and subject to pressures from France, its principal practical ally

A Long Way from Tipperary

In 1914-17 the defence had a temporary dominance over the offense. A combination of quick-firing artillery and machine guns and trenches and barbed wire made the attacker's job formidably difficult. Communications were poor. Armies were too big and dispersed to be commanded by a general in person and radio was in its infancy. Even if the infantry and artillery did manage to punch a hole in the enemy position, generals lacked a fast-moving force to exploit the situation, to get among the enemy and turn a retreat into a rout.

In previous wars, cavalry had performed such a role, but cavalry were generally of little use in the trenches of the Western Front. And the early tanks were not up to the job. With commanders mute and an instrument of exploitation lacking, World War One generals were faced with a tactical dilemma unique in military history.

It is not true, as some think, that British generals and troops simply stared uncomprehendingly at the barbed wire and trenches, incapable of anything more imaginative than repeating the failed formula of frontal assaults by infantry. In reality, the Western Front was a hotbed of innovation as the British and their allies and enemies experimented with new approaches. Even on the notorious first day on the Somme, the French and 13th British Corps succeeded in capturing all of their objectives through the use of effective artillery and infantry tactics; the absence of such methods helps to explain the disaster along much of the rest of the British position.

A Long Way from Tipperary

From 1915 to 1918 the BEF learned, in the hardest possible way, how to fight a modern high-intensity war against an extremely tough opponent. By 1916 it had expanded enormously, taking in a mass of inexperienced civilian volunteers. Later still, it relied on conscripts. Either way, it was a citizen army rather than a professional force. . What was extraordinary was that, despite this unpromising beginning, by 1918 this army of bank clerks and shop assistants, businessmen and miners should have emerged as a formidable fighting force. Within three years the British had effectively invented a method of warfare still recognisable today. By the summer of 1918 the British army was probably at its best ever and it inflicted crushing defeats on the Germans by combining improved artillery, better infantry weapons, tanks and even aeroplanes to pursue an effective strategy. Germany's army collapsed as a series of mighty allied blows scythed through supposedly impregnable defences.

By late September 1918 the Kaiser and his military mastermind Ludendorff admitted that there was no hope and that Germany must beg for peace. The 11 November Armistice was essentially a German surrender. Britain had played a major part in saving Europe from the consequences of German victory in a war started by German aggression. The price was heavy but no one at the time, not even the surviving poets, believed that it had not been worthwhile.

I leave the last words on the War to John McCrae whose poem seems particularly apt for William in view of his service at Ypres and the surrounding battlefields..

A Long Way from Tipperary

In Flanders Fields.

In Flanders fields the poppies blow

Between the crosses, row on row

That mark our place; and in the sky

The larks, still bravely singing, fly

Scarce heard amid the guns below

We are the Dead. Short days ago

We lived, felt dawn, saw sunset glow,

Loved and were loved, and now we lie

In Flanders fields.

Take up the quarrel with the foe:

To you from failing hands we throw

The torch; be yours to hold it high.

If ye break faith with us who die

We shall not sleep, though poppies grow

In Flanders fields.

A Long Way from Tipperary

Chapter 9

Rescuing the Turners

Alice Turner was much younger than William and was a very live wire who loved dancing and had a real spirit of adventure. But William was a very good singer and dancer himself appearing at one point with an amateur group of troubadours called "The Magnets". The Turner family were living in straitened circumstances at No 47 Cattybrook Street, Easton Bristol, in a house containing far too many people and where the principal breadwinner, Alice's father William Albert Turner, was institutionalised in a psychiatric hospital after a spell in prison. William became the main pillar and support of the family as his father in law, William had long since left the family. William Turner was a victim of war in that he was badly destabilised by his experiences with the Gloucester Regiment during the Boer War where he fought at the Cape and in the Orange Free State. Private The record shows that William Albert Turner of the 2nd Battalion Gloucesters was born in Ashley Hill in, Bristol in 1873 and came from agricultural stock from around the village of Frampton Cottrell in Gloucestershire.

William is in some respects something of Victorian caricature in that he conforms to the stereotype of the hard working man brought low by drink. He was the kind of man who gave life to the temperance movement, which was still going strong in Bristol even in the nineteen fifties. I remember winning a

A Long Way from Tipperary

William Seated Third from the Right

"Temperance Badge" as an eight year old when I was in the Life Boys by answering a series of difficult questions about how I would resist the blandishments of well meaning friends pressing drinks upon me should I ever find myself in the presence of alcohol later in life. Parables of the evil wrought by the demon drink livened up most non-conformist sermons at that time but seemed a little remote from the preoccupations of a child wrapped up in train numbers and street marbles.

Alice's mother, Alice Baxter met the handsome young William Albert at some point in the mid 1890s. The couple were married in 1898 from 3 Henry Street, Totterdown. George Baxter was given as Alice's father on the wedding certificate. Rose Caple was a witness. The ceremony took place in St Luke's Church in Barton Regis Bristol. St Luke's was built in 1842 with the help of a donation from the Cotton Factory of

A Long Way from Tipperary

£1,000. William was living at 9 Corbett Street. Alice rapidly conceived a child and Rosina May was born in 1899. William Albert however was soon off to the Anglo South African war departing in early 1900. Albert's father Aaron at the time of the wedding was a car man, which meant that he worked on the horse driven trams that preceded the motorised bus. Research going back into the mid 18th century reveals a history in the Turner family of masons, blacksmiths, agricultural labourers and an excursion into hat making at Frampton where a small local industry had a brief florescence under the famous hat making company Christy who were trying to break the unions at Salford in the mid 19th century. As soon as they had done so, they went back to Lancashire.

It is rather sad that the best remembered detail about William is that he drank a lot and that he beat up his wife. There may well have been lots of good things to say about a man who fathered four children, but if so, the record is largely silent. He could not have been all bad however as I recall that William in old age still spoke with a certain affection of him and his daughter tended to attribute his problems to a hard life (which for his wife was considerably harder). His alcoholism and violence eventually caused him to be hospitalised in a psychiatric institution from which he never emerged. His daughter Ada believed that the root of William's drinking had been his experiences in the South African war and what he had seen in that conflict.

No photographs of him remain from this period, indeed we have none at all today but Aunt Ada recalls seeing him in a

A Long Way from Tipperary

Hat Factory at Frampton Cottrell

khaki uniform wearing a slouch hat, which was not headgear typical of that time. By all accounts he was a tall (for the time), strapping moustachioed figure who must have cut a dash. As he only married in 1898 we must assume that William was a reservist called up to fill gaps in the regular Battalion having either served before with the Colours or been in the Volunteer Service Company which joined the Battalion in May and June 1900. The Army was always under strength. By the end of the Century regular soldiers normally did 7 years with the colours and 5 in the reserve.

Williams Army Attestation papers describe him as Private Soldier No 2897 of the 2nd Battalion of the Gloucesters. He was 5 feet 9 inches tall, had a fresh complexion, grey eyes and brown hair. According to the Medal Rolls, he served in South Africa from 1900 and was entitled to the Queens South Medal and clasps for service in the Cape Colony and Orange Free State and the Kings South Africa Medal 1901/02. He

A Long Way from Tipperary

went out with the 2nd Battalion to South Africa in January 1900. The Battalion numbered 26 officers, 930 men, 119 horses and their Maxim gun. The horse were mostly those of the mounted infantry company who travelled separately on the SS British Prince. The Battalion had 8 companies commanded by either a major or a captain; each company had a colour sergeant as its senior NCO.

The First Battalion of the Gloucesters had been one of four sent from India between the 16th and 30th September 1899. They were first engaged at Riefontein and then in the Defence of Ladysmith. It was there in probing the Boers encirclement on 20 October that they became victims under Colonel Carleton of the disastrous action at Nicholson's Nek (or Tchrengula Hill). Their mission was to find their way through the encircling Boer lines but after losing their way at night, when dawn rose they were surrounded by Boers who commanded the protected high ground above them and were able to bring converging fire to bear. By mid afternoon they had lost 33 men killed, 6 officers and 75 wounded. The remainder of the Battalion fought and suffered in Ladysmith until the Siege was lifted.

A further coincidence arises from this disaster as John Norwood was ordered to take out a patrol from Ladysmith to find out what had happened to the Gloucesters. He could not penetrate the Boer lines but in the course of searching for them, his squadron of the 5th Dragoon Guards came under fire, one trooper fell and by galloping back to save the soldier concerned, he won his Victoria Cross .

A Long Way from Tipperary

Gloucesters Preparing for War 1899

William sailed with the 2nd Battalion on the Cymric on 1 January 1900 and arrived at Capetown on the 21st ; the Battalion formed the 13th Brigade along with the East Kents, the West Ridings and the Oxford Light Infantry in the VI th Division and soon entrained for De Aar, inland to the north east on the borders of the Orange Free State. Here the Army was deployed in great force for a drive against the enemy, to relieve the besieged towns and to capture Bloemfontein, the capital of the Free State and then Pretoria, in the Transvaal. The plan was a wide encircling movement, to herd the Boer Army under Cronje together and to bring them to one final action. It was to be a whirlwind campaign with the cavalry sweeping the country

A Long Way from Tipperary

ahead of columns of infantry. For the Infantry it meant hard forced marches over enemy territory with a minimum of rest and with scanty rations as the Boers kept interdicting their supplies. Marching was done under quarter rations of I hard biscuit and a quarter a day until they reached Bloemfontein. They reached the Modder River in a state of exhaustion but in high spirits.

The Gloucesters gave a good account of themselves in the advance from the Modder River to Bloemfontein. At Klip Kraal they had sharp fighting with Cronje's rear guard and whilst they were not so seriously engaged at Paardeberg as other Battalions, they did good work between the 18th and 28th of January 1900.

We have an account of one of the many days fighting by the Battalion around Paardeberg by Lieutenant Gardner.

"The whole regiment went out on outpost, and we entrenched ourselves a little during the night. On the morning of 19 February, we came under heavy fire, were parched with thirst and we could get hardly a drop of water. In the afternoon, the Artillery shelled the kopje we faced, and we and some other regiments were ordered to advance." The Gloucesters advanced in grand style and were soon under a very heavy fire at 800 yards from our position; we had to advance across a plain without a scrap of cover. The Regiment ordered to support us said that they thought we were going to retire and they retired,...the left of the Gloucesters had to fall back , but the rest of us went on, about 85 all told, 26 of whom belonged to my company, though all companies were" represented, if not by their men, then by some of their officers. We came under

A Long Way from Tipperary

heavy cross fire and found ourselves short of ammunition; it was now getting very dark and the bullets must have gone over our heads, although they seemed to strike the ground all around. At about 400 yards, we fixed bayonets, advanced

Gloucesters in South Africa

steadily without another halt, gave a huge cheer and took the position."

They put the Boers to flight, losing 6 killed and 20 wounded including Colonel RF Lindsell who was shot in the lungs but recovered and stayed with his command until the end of the war. He subsequently drowned off the Island of Jersey in 1914.

A Long Way from Tipperary

This campaign resulted in a major reverse for the Boers in that after 9 days fighting, the then Orange Free State President, Cronje (subsequently replaced by Jan Steyn) and his family were captured and taken down to the Cape and thence to exile in St Helena until the end of the war. The Gloucesters provided part of their escort before returning to the main force in the Orange Free State. 4,000 Boers had surrendered with him.

At Driefontein, on 10 March the Battalion performed well even though it was not in the first line, losing 5 killed and 20 wounded. On 15 March they entered Bloemfontein in triumph. Their uniforms were ragged and torn, they were deeply sun burned and lean from short rations and hard living. They were to stay in Bloemfontein and the Orange Free State for four years until they returned to the UK in May 1904. There is a rare photograph of a section of A Company of the Battalion at Bloemfontein which could contain William - we shall never know.

By the autumn of 1900, the war had moved on from fixed piece battles as the British moved out of Natal and the Orange Free State towards the occupation and annexation of the Transvaal on the 25th of October 1900. The war now entered its guerrilla phase in which the Boers operating in bands from horseback sought to wear down the 200,000 British troops in South Africa, hoping at the same time that one of the great powers would intervene on their side and that the British Government would tire of war. The war took an even crueller turn as the Army found itself thinly stretched, the Infantry guarding fixed installations and the Cavalry and Mounted Infantry chasing Boer chimera across the veldt. Gradually, over time, the British

A Long Way from Tipperary

would grind out a victory of sorts, seeking to establish small garrisons across the country to keep the Boers on the run and force their surrender, but the war was not without controversy, particularly the policy of herding Boer families into "Concentration Camps", which did not have the connotations then which they have now. Many women and children died from disease and malnutrition leaving a bitter legacy. Disease was of course the principal cause of death amongst the British forces amongst whom knowledge of the importance of effective sanitation and personal hygiene was poorly developed.

Apart from garrison duty in Bloemfontein, the Battalion were engaged in extended operations throughout the Orange Free State to deal with the threat from Boer guerrillas amongst whom Christian de Wet, a Free Stater was one of the most outstanding. De Wet decided in autumn 1900 in order to take the war to the British, to cross the Orange River (with the itinerant President Steyn of the Orange Free State in tow) into the Cape Colony which had Boers amongst the population but which was regarded as "home territory" by the British (to such a degree that it was later declared that anyone collaborating with the Boers in the Cape would be tried for treason). In order to impede this kind of movement, the British had built a line of forts in the southern Free State about two miles apart from Bloemfontein to Thaba'Nchu in Basutoland (now Lesotho) and Ladybrand and also in some of the larger settlements. De Wet managed to get through across this line and headed for Dewetsdorp, which had been named after his father and which had a British garrison.

A Long Way from Tipperary

Major Massey commanded the British force at Dewetsdorp of around 500, consisting of the 68th Field Battery and detachments of the Gloucesters (A, B and F companies lead by Major Tufnel), the Highland Light Infantry and the Irish Rifles. The garrison was divided into two sections which primarily occupied two positions on the high ground overlooking the town. These were separated by a deep kloof which led into the

Gloucesters Marching to Pretoria

town. The British placed simple strong points made of low stone walls and trenches on top of these hills; smaller posts were also placed on some of the prominent features within rifle range of the main camp, called "Cossack Posts".

A Long Way from Tipperary

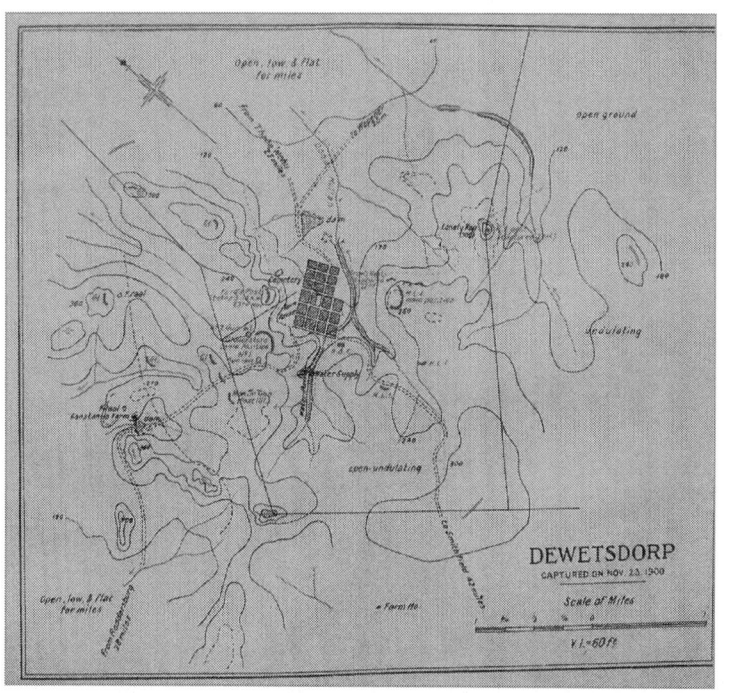

In general, the British held the ground to the south east, south west and north west of the town. The names of these positions are very evocative –"Lonely Kop" and "Gun Hill" especially. De Wet had around 1700 men at his disposal and beginning 18 November took each of the ridge top "Cossak Post" points one by one, as a prelude to the main attack whilst receiving artillery fire from the two British guns. The first to fall was the small post on Lonely Hill then Gun Hill was taken. The pattern in each case appears to have been the same, according to De Wet's account; the burgers worked their way in close, often under cover of dark, and launched brief attacks during the day and night keeping up steady fire from sharpshooters on the British

A Long Way from Tipperary

lines in the meantime. On the 20th of November the water supply was cut off to the main strong points and whilst volunteers brought in limited supplies, it could do no more than moisten the throats of the parched defenders. On the 21st November, De Wet was reinforced by another Boer Commando coming up from Rietport.

The Boer plan of attack appeared to be to push steadily up the nullah leading to the town, covered by rifle fire from all sides and by their own gun which had been placed on Lonely Kop. Another outlying post was captured on the 21st and the Boers then tried to rush one of the remaining key positions but were beaten off initially. The officer commanding No 2 Section of the Highlanders reported that he could not hold his ground, however, so was instructed to fall back on the second section. His position was untenable; the Boers sensing this, charged the line. This attack was foiled by ten privates with fixed bayonets who ensured an orderly withdrawal. The British fell back onto their main garrison.

With daylight, the position of the garrison became desperate; they were under crossfire, without water and running low on ammunition; of the two field guns, one had become unserviceable and such a hail of bullets was directed against the second that it could only be fired with difficulty. 16 of the 18 gunners were killed or wounded at the guns and for some time a sergeant - farrier worked the gun alone. What added to the suffering was that November 23rd was an exceptionally hot day. There was no sign of a relief force on the veldt even though help had been sought. In the meantime, the Boers were being supplied by their fellow burgers from Dewetsdorp who naturally

A Long Way from Tipperary

supported their cause. The final action began at 2.30 am when the Boers attacked the line held by 30 men of the Gloucesters under 2nd Lieutenant Ford. They held out for an hour until nearly all were killed or wounded, at which point they were compelled to surrender. From the position thus gained, the Boers were able to command most of the trenches at close range and at dawn, a heavy cross fire was opened, putting the last gun out of action.

The final surrender came as a result of a misunderstanding. Late in the afternoon it was reported to Massey that a white flag had been hoisted from an isolated position; he replied that it was to be put down at once, and that anyone hoisting another would be shot. This message never got to its destination and soon afterwards, cries were heard that the enemy were murdering the wounded because the garrison was continuing to fire after the flag was up. This proved not to be true but Massey believed it and was compelled to anticipate the inevitable result, so he surrendered the garrison. This was probably just as well for the Gloucesters because Tufnell had ordered his men to fix bayonets and be ready to follow him in a final charge to try and save the situation. It is not surprising in the circumstances that Massey subsequently wrote to the Colonel of the Gloucesters to say that his men had behaved splendidly and were in no way to blame for the ultimate result.

The same could not be said of the Highland Light Infantry who were in a stronger position than the Gloucesters. Owing to a lack of water, mounting casualties, and himself wounded, their officer in charge, Lieutenant Milne-Home surrendered his position to the Boers. He was Court Martialed in Bloemfontein

A Long Way from Tipperary

on 29 January 1901, for surrendering his post at Dewetsdorp, and "Dismissed the Service". Having family and friends of some influence, however, his case was reopened by order of King Edward in March 1901 and Milne-Home was exonerated and reinstated. On 1 April 1901 (April Fools Day!) Milne-Home was promoted Captain. There may well have been a political element to the original court martial, as it is certainly the case that de Wets success gave a boost to Boer recruitment.

In the end, the Boers took 451 prisoners, amongst whom was Massey and 7 Gloucester officers, Tufnell, Ford, Menzies, Fyffe and Walshe. Two Armstrong Guns with three hundred shells, and lots of Lee Metford cartridges were also seized. The record shows that William Turner who was wounded was also taken prisoner. The outcome was like many such engagements in the war where the Boers, knowing the countryside, being much better shots and having more determination in battle, triumphed over their enemy who often lacked sound tactical judgement (in this case, occupying positions without access to water).

The Boers then heard that a British force was en route to relieve Massey and withdrew with their prisoners whom they planned to release due south on the other side of the Orange River should they succeed in crossing into the Cape. It was often the custom of the Boers, who had of course no means of keeping their captives prisoner permanently, to strip them of clothing and shoes as well as food and weaponry as they were always operating with reduced supplies and to leave them thus on the veldt. On this occasion, there appears to be an element of hostage taking about the operation, although undoubtedly the prisoners were going to be released in due course. It is also

A Long Way from Tipperary

clear that the Boers handed out some pretty rough treatment to their captives. But let one of the prisoners speak for them about an experience that was quite traumatic.

The following account comes from one of the officers who later wrote the following in the London Times;

"De Wet's men stripped and looted the prisoners, compelling them to hand over great coats (which were placed on the Boers horses) under threat of violence". On the night of the 23rd, the prisoners were driven into a filthy cattle kraal and the following day, after only a cup of coffee and some bread, were taken to a hidden farm known as Blessbokfontein where their only source of water was already sullied by mules and horses. On the 26th De Wet moved to Vaalbank and at 08 30 am on the 27th, the advanced guard of one of the pursuing British columns under Colonel Pilcher caught up with the Boers, leading to a rapid evacuation -"we wretched prisoners marched until 2am the next day – nearly 18 hours – and this began to tell horribly upon the men, who were getting weak, especially the 20 wounded men, (of whom we know that William was one) some still having more than one bullet in them". De Wet outdistanced his pursuers as he headed south in the direction of Bethulie but the British succeeded in getting between him and the Orange River and on December 2nd the British were in contact with him again as he headed for the Odendal drift on the Orange River. The two forces engaged along a front of 15 miles from Sterkspruit to Willoughby but when darkness fell, De Wet succeed in passing clean around the British right, heading for the Caledon fords. The British wheeled and followed. It began to rain heavily and a bitterly cold wind blew.

A Long Way from Tipperary

At 4 pm on December 3rd, De Wet started a march which went on without remission for 27 hours, the longest halt being of one hour and pushed on to the River Caledon which he forded at 7 pm on the 4th. The British officer quoted before wrote " It is almost impossible to make anyone appreciate the appalling times we had; it rained the whole of the 27 hours; we were all drenched to the skin by day and night; we had no food whatever and no sleep; at the end De Wet ordered the men to wade across the Caledon River which had swollen enormously; our Commanding officer protested against this, but without avail, and our men had to strip and wade across , carrying their clothes on their heads, the water being up to some men's armpits – one poor fellow lost all of his clothes and had to continue the journey wrapped in a blanket. Towards the end of this unique march, the Boer corporal in charge of the escort, said that the General had ordered the men who lagged behind to be sjamboked, and if it had not been for the officers marching behind the men, this would have been done systematically; there were a few instances of it and one soldier had a piece of flesh cut right out of his cheek…. Well by this time, both officers and men were getting depressed, footsore, weary and half starved and with a feeling that after the extraordinary distance that we had travelled, the British columns must be in touch with us. The way that the men were treated during the March was simply monstrous; the Boers rode their horses into them, prodded them with the butts of their rifles, and, if they got a chance away from an officer, used the sjambok freely".

A Long Way from Tipperary

On 5 December De Wet succeeded in joining other Boer forces and his commando swelled to 5,000. That same day, he released the NCOs and the men who were so exhausted by the hard marching and want of food, that they could not have gone further. He was now in triangle enclosed by the Caledon and Orange River both of which were in flood and he therefore decided to give up his attempt to get into Cape Colony. However, true to form, he evaded his pursuers and eventually managed with a much reduced force following a number of skirmishes, to get back into the northern Orange Free State to continue the guerrilla war. In the course of those skirmishes, four of the British officers whom he held escaped, I believe that the rest were released later.

De Wet says nothing in his memoirs about the way in which his prisoners were treated after Dewetsdorp, or indeed anywhere else. But he does comment of Dewetsdorp that "Of Major Massey, who was in command, and his force, I have only to say that both commanding officer and men displayed great valour" From his perspective, the privations of the British prisoners were probably measured from a different perspective than our own, bearing in mind the hand to mouth existence of a guerrilla army forced to live from the land, harassed from pillar to post and in forced separation from their families. De Wet of course was a reluctant adherent to the eventual peace that brought war to a close and seized the opportunity to rise against the Union in 1914 with other malcontents when the Great War began. But he was captured by a South African Force containing many of his old colleagues, sentenced to 6 years in prison but released after one year having accepted a lifetime ban on any further political activity.

A Long Way from Tipperary

Is the case that no British war since 1815 had been so prodigal of money and lives. There were over 100,000 casualties of all kinds among the 350,000 imperial troops (only 200,000 of course at any one time) and 80,000 colonials who fought on the British side during the course of the war. 22,000 died, of which 5,700 were killed by enemy action and were shovelled into the veldt where they fell and over 16,000 expired from wounds or disease. The cost proportionately to the Boers was also very

Contemporary Print of The Dewetsdorp Affair

high, when their families are included. However although the agonies suffered by the British troops were only a harbinger of what was to come in the First World War, the Army suffered

A Long Way from Tipperary

humiliating reverses and high casualties in a number of battles which must have been traumatic for those involved. Some of this was due to poor British General ship and bad tactics but much was also owed to the determination and superior marksmanship of the enemy matched with an iron resolve to continue fighting, until this eventually leached away. Some of it can be accounted for by weaponry, the advent of smokeless, long range high velocity bullets which the Boers were adept at using and which favoured their tactics. But this was the first war since the Napoleonic period in which the British had faced a determined European enemy whose warlike skills, particularly in bush warfare, exceeded their own.

I have walked in the footsteps of William Turner, from the Modder River through Belmont and Paaderberg to Bloemfontein. The battlefields are still marked by the detritus of war, especially remnants of rusted cans and bullets (I picked up an unused Lee Metford bullet at Paardeberg which had fallen from a soldier's pouch no doubt in the heat of battle). The veldt has a parched, harsh and forbidding quality which must have made an awesome contrast to the lush green fields of Gloucestershire from which the Battalion had been drawn. It is striking in reading military records of the first phase of the Battalion's war to find how often the Infantry were required to fix bayonets and march to the attack over open ground – this defies belief when you gaze across this terrain to flat and distant horizons and understand the quality of Boer marksmanship.

In the campaign, the two Gloucester Battalions lost 2 officers and 94 other ranks killed and 13 officers and 201 men

A Long Way from Tipperary

wounded. 250 men died from sickness in South Africa making a total of 350 men dead and 214 wounded - a sorry tally, representing a mortality rate of almost 20% and an overall casualty rate of closer to 30%. The 2nd Battalion logged 1270 miles of hard marching in the course of the war. Five officers received the DSO and twelve men received the DCM.

William obviously recovered from his wounds and remained in the Orange Free State until the end of his service. But I believe that Dewetsdorp and its aftermath was the traumatic experience that marked out his life. The term "Post Traumatic Stress Disorder" was not of course recognised at the turn of the 19th century – it was probably regarded as tantamount to malingering, so we shall never know for certain if this condition had anything to do with William's psychiatric disorder. But there was nothing else in the Battalion's campaign quite like Dewetsdorp and it must have played some part in changing his character and causing him to behave on his return to Bristol in a way that lead to Horfield prison and his subsequent incarceration in Fishponds Hospital.

William left his first child, Rosina May Turner , who was born in early 1899, behind him when he embarked with the Battalion. His second. Alice Maud, was born in mid 1903 suggesting that he returned on leave or ended his tour early in autumn 1902. Documents show that he left the active list on 10 March 1903 and that he was required to do a further 4 years with the Reserve. The Regiment was then based at Horfield Barracks, Bristol. It may well be that whilst on the Reserve he was part of the Third Volunteer Battalion of the Regiment formed in Bristol. This would solve the mystery of the slouch hat that he wore in

A Long Way from Tipperary

the photograph that the family remembers which is unusual headgear for the British Army. The Volunteer Battalion wore khaki jackets with red facings, khaki breeches brown leggings and khaki slouch hats with green feathers, just the sort of kit that would look well in a photograph. It was replaced in 1908 for something more conventional.

When William was finally discharged from the Reserve on 9 March 1907, he was 34. His place of residence was given as 47 Cattybrook Street and his trade was "carman", which is presumably means that he followed his father on the trams or buses. William and Alice had two further children over the following years; Charles was born in 1907 and Ada in 1913. In April 1913 William was sentenced to three months imprisonment for failing to maintain his wife and children. It appears that he had been in trouble before for disorderly behaviour and according to family lore, it took 7 policemen to arrest him. His arrest came after he had moved out of 47 Cattybrook Street and was living with another woman not far away in Brougham Street. He had rejected the entreaties of his wife to support the family and therefore paid the penalty. Having served his time, he was rearrested in July for the same offence and whilst in custody began to behave oddly and violently leading to his transfer from goal to the Asylum.

Fishponds (now Glenside Hospital) records show that William Albert Turner, Register Number 8366, was admitted on 27 August 1913; his age at the time of his last attack of mental illness was 40 (i.e. in 1913) and he died on 20 December 1939 at the age of 66 from myocardial degeneration, Some of the details of his state of mind and the delusions from which he

A Long Way from Tipperary

suffered could not be released even in 2001 (but will be open in 2015) but the following notes were recorded "... His wife Alice, was married for 16 years and for 9 years of these he was an exemplary husband. He went to South Africa as a reservist and on returning after 2 years was completely changed...he was never a drinker, but a teetotaller" Clearly, no more. . As the couple married in 1898, this suggests that William's behaviour began to deteriorate in 1908.

In the twenties when life began to look up a little for my parents and in spite of children arriving at regular intervals- my father by this time had moved into 47 Cattybrook Street- he was invited by William to return home from Fishponds Asylum, as age had brought tranquillity, but he refused on the grounds that he was comfortable there and was satisfied with the small pleasures that he was given, tobacco etc. He died in 1939 after 27 years in the hospital. Williams's status at the time of his death is recorded as "voluntary" which is not surprising if his last mental attack was effectively just at the moment when he was transferred to Fishponds from prison. He is buried in Greenbank Cemetery Bristol with his wife and eldest daughter, Rose.

Long before then he achieved a level of peace of mind and was no longer a threat. He was regularly visited by the family in the Asylum and his status changed to that of "voluntary inmate". In spite of children arriving at regular intervals William, conceived the idea of bringing William Albert back to the family home. He declined the invitation, on the grounds that he had peace of mind at Fishponds, his needs were being met, even to the extent of being given tobacco, and that back at No 47 he would be only a burden.

A Long Way from Tipperary

Chapter 10.

The Baxter Connection

Alice Baxter, my grandmother, had a difficult upbringing. She was born to a single mother in Burnham on Sea in 1875 and although the family story has it that she was left in a basket on a doorstep in Love Lane, it seems evident that she was in fact given over to a family called Caple or Capel who lived there. The birth was properly registered and although we have no idea what drew Alice's mother, Emily Julia Baxter to Burnham from London, her family home, Burnham in those days was a fashionable seaside resort and it could be that she either went there for seasonal work or as a domestic servant. She was only 17. The birth certificate of Alice Maud Baxter shows that her mother was living in Princess Street, Burnham Somerset at the time of the birth. This is around the corner from Love Lane which is the site of her apocryphal abandonment. Also in Princes Street in the 1871 census was Frederick Caple, profession tiler, then aged 47 and his wife Anne born 1845 plus their sons Joseph,12 Henry 8 and Jas 5.

Alice was fortunate in that the childless couple who became her adoptive parents, George Marshall May and his wife Mary Jane nee Caple were kindly and responsible people who regarded themselves as her true parents. Mary Jane was Frederick's sister. There is evidence from Alice's wedding certificate that her father was a man called George Baxter, a boilermaker, who could have been related to her mother but was not in her mother's immediate family notwithstanding sharing the same

A Long Way from Tipperary

George and Mary May seated

surname. Although later in life my grandmother Alice fantasised that her mother had married well and acquired wealth, she never met her mother and the sad truth is that after the birth Emily Julia Baxter returned to London. There she spent her life working as a machinist in the shoe industry and later as a domestic. She died in 1927 in East London. The Baxters were a long line of shoemakers who had migrated from Bury St Edmunds to the East End in the course of the 19th century; Emily's mother's side, the Archers were toymakers. The Baxter line goes back to the mid 1750s and some of our ancestors are buried in the cathedral graveyard at Bury St Edmunds.

A Long Way from Tipperary

Alice my grandmother moved with George and Mary Jane May from Burnham to Western Super Mare by the time of the 1881 census. George was working as an engine driver and Alice was at a local boarding house with the Caples when the census took place. In the 1891 census, Alice is registered as living at 11 Cattybrook Street under the name of May. George May is now aged 50 and is working as a boilermaker. He is recorded as born in St George, Gloucestershire; his wife Jane, is now 43 and she was born in Cross, Axbridge in Somerset. Alice is listed as the May's daughter and is employed as a weaver. In the house is another young woman identified as Rose, described as another daughter, aged 13 and a scholar born in Burnham. It is clear that Rose is the sister of Frederick Caple (born 1878 Burnham).

The Mays were the responsible adults completing the census and they allowed the census taker to believe that both Alice and Rose, their niece, were their natural, rather than adopted children. I believe that because of the construction of the Pinnell boiler works in Cattybrook Street, the houses were renumbered and that 11 became 47. These were poor houses built in the 1880s and we have an interesting insight into No 47 through a rating document from about 1900. This gave the gross value of 47 Cattybrook Street as £910 and the rateable value of land and buildings as £710. The occupier is identified as George May and the owner is "A. Deacon of Rosemary Street Bristol". The rent appears to be £5/3. The building is described as having three bedrooms, a front room, kitchen and scullery. It is said to be in poor condition. Later, Pinnell took over ownership. Alice worked as a weaver at the Cotton Factory that was constructed along the Netham Canal to take advantage of the

A Long Way from Tipperary

captive work force in East Bristol. The Great Western Cotton Factory was one of the industries to crop up in Barton Hill at around 1838. The Factory and Cotton Works extended from the canal up to the beginning of Aiken Street. It was the largest in the south of England. Men, women and children (as young as 10) worked at the Cotton Factory for very long hours and very

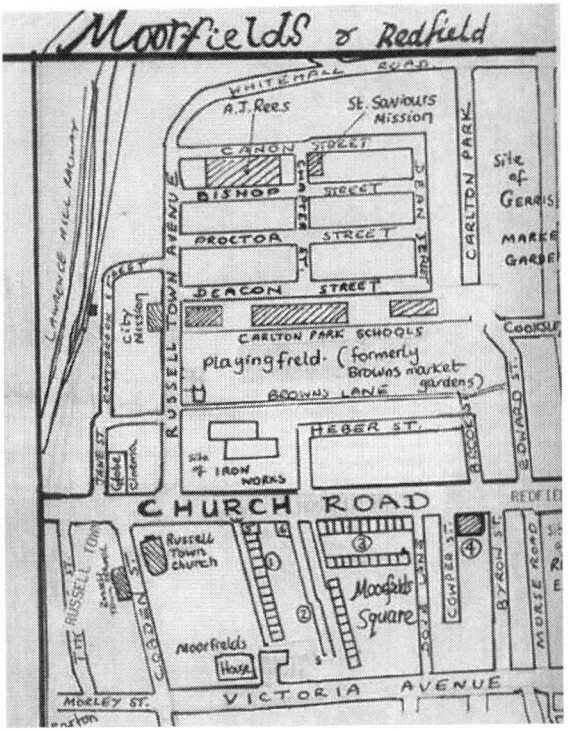

A Sketch of the Neighbourhood

little pay. The working conditions there were very noisy, as the sheds contained up to 1600 looms. It was very dusty, extremely unpleasant and could be dangerous. The workers,

A Long Way from Tipperary

who were mainly women, became quite proficient at reading lips. People could become deaf if they worked there for a long time and cotton weavers quite often lost a finger if they didn't catch their shuttle correctly, as the shuttle travelled at very high speed. The day started off very early at 06.00am and there was a break for breakfast, sometimes consisting of cockles (brought from Wales) and pickled cabbage which could be bought for a penny ha'penny each. Lunch was for an hour and the machines were turned off.

The Cotton Factory at Barton Hill

During this break, the workers had to clean their looms and sweep the floor as they couldn't clean whilst the machinery was working, as it would have been a very risky thing to do. Each person was responsible for 4 looms so the hour break wasn't really for the full hour. They then worked through until 05.30 pm. All this time was spent standing as there was nowhere to sit. In 1889, 1500 women employees of the Great Western Cotton Factory went on strike. It is believed they were

A Long Way from Tipperary

encouraged by the successful outcome of the London Dockers strike.

They were on strike over their working conditions and pay. Ben Tillet a London union leader who had been born at 8 John Street, Easton, Bristol and who had led the Great London Dock Strike earlier that year was invited with two other union leaders to consult on the GWCF strike and another that was taking place at the time, a dispute between the gas stokers of three gas works. A large gathering of people met them at Temple Meads and then the crowd of 15,000 marched on to the Downs. The GWCF "Cotton Girls" were at the head of the

Weavers Holding Bobbins

A Long Way from Tipperary

march. The Great Western Cotton Factory changed hands in 1925 and became the Western Viscose Silk Company until 1929 when they closed. The building was demolished in 1968 but there are still some stone remains to been seen there today. Tillet was a hero to William and other working class men of his time.

Throughout the troubled marriage of William Turner and Alice, the Mays remained stout supporters of Alice. They had advised her earlier before she married against moving out to live with her father - advice that she had accepted. There is a suggestion however that when William departed for South Africa in 1900, Alice stayed briefly with her father George in Deacon Street. But at the time of the 1901 census, Alice and daughter Rosina are at 57 Francis Street, Battersea staying as visitors with the family of Henry Caple, Jane's brother (who appears in the centre of the photograph of the Mays.) Henry aged 38 was making a living as a chemical worker in St Marys, Battersea. He was married to Ada and had three children, Rose Maud, Alfred and Olive Alice. At Number 47 are George May, who is now described as a night watchman at the Port of Bristol and Jane. They have as lodgers Bessie Herridge, aged 23, a domestic servant and Alice her daughter aged 4 months; Emily Talbot and her son Samuel aged 3, and daughter Florence Talbot, aged 1.

There must have been some rearrangement of the accommodation when William came back from the war in 1902 (I assume that the Herridge and Talbot families departed) and moved into Number 47 with Alice, particularly as the family began to grow. By 1911 no 47 must have been quite full

A Long Way from Tipperary

because in addition to George and Jane, William and Alice and their four children, the front room of the house had been let to a couple called Cross. Elizabeth and husband Alfred Cross (born 1855 in Thornbury, Gloucestershire) were living at No 3 Roaches Buildings, Croydon Street in the 1901 census. This tenement was behind the Off Licence on the corner of Leadhouse Road and Croydon Street. He was described as a mason's labourer. Her mother, Mary Thomas, aged 79 was present in Croydon Street in 1901 as was a brother.

The Moorfields estate which included Cattybrook Street was developed in the 1870s as a tight knit working class community with its own corner shops, school, off licences and mission halls. Work was available as East Bristol's industrial base grew, from coal mines in Easton (the site of the present Pit Pony Pub marks the principal entrance) to the railways and the Cotton Factory which was located in the area to take advantage of the labour pool. The other side of the street from no 47, which was occupied by a long wall, was not fully defined until two events took place. Lawrence Hill station on the other side of the wall opened in 1863, doubled in size in 1874 and then doubled again to 4 lines in 1891. The big signal box which loomed over the wall opposite 47 was not installed until almost the turn of the century. The second big change in the landscape took place in 1903 when Joseph Pugsley bought land at Cattybrook Street for his engine business and scrap yard which occupied a space between the street and the railway station. Pugsley also constructed the Globe Cinema in 1903 at the end of the road in Jane Street. He owned an Ironworks in Dean Lane as well.

A Long Way from Tipperary

The junction between Cattybrook Street and Dean Lane (renamed Russell Town Avenue in the 1920s) was occupied by an off - licence called the Prince of Wales; next to this was the firm of AH Pinnell, boiler makers and electrical welders and immediately after that was No 47. The houses in the Street were oddly numbered from 47 to 65, although there may have been some re - ordering at one point. The presence of Pinnells in a residential area was not odd at the time – the idea appeared to be to mix industry and homes; the grandly named Beaufort Works in Bishops Street across Dean Lane had been a glue, gum and size works; it turned into Rees Coachworks in 1900 and later did car body repairs for the British Motor Corporation. Across the wall that divided the Street from the railway station and behind the station was a big good yards that specialised in coal.

The 1901 census is useful for identifying the kind of people who lived in Cattybrook Street at this time. Apart from general labourers, there is a boot machinist, a shopkeeper, a coal miner, a letter carrier, a haulier of ginger beer, an unemployed sugar house labourer, a drawer at the Cotton works, and a labourer at the saw mills. Most houses had only 4 to 6 occupants. Indeed we know the street was considered to be somewhat superior in the neighbourhood because it had so many people in work.

The quality of the back to back housing in Moorfields was pretty substandard and the proximity to the railway of No 47 ensured that the air was always full of noise, dirt and vibration from the steam engines. But the scrap yard, whose most prominent feature was a primitive crane, contained bits of old boilers and

A Long Way from Tipperary

engines which made a perfect, if dangerous playground for the children, once they had become big enough to scale the wall and drop down the other side. Playing in the yard made a change from train spotting, sitting on the wall.

The houses formed a terrace on one side of the street, their front doors giving straight out on to the pavement. The front door of No 47 was on the left side of the building and opened inward into a passageway that lead straight through the house to a scullery at the rear. The first door on the right opened into a room with a fireplace and a window onto the street; this was followed by a staircase that ascended to the bedrooms and then by another door that opened into another room that had a fireplace and a window that gave onto a back yard. Upstairs, there was a front bedroom, a back bedroom and a small bedroom with a tilted roof that sat above the scullery. There was no bathroom and just one lavatory which was a lean - to in the garden built beyond the scullery. There was only one sink and that was used for all purposes. When the house was only occupied later

A Long Way from Tipperary

by the Murphys, bathing involved dragging a zinc tub in from hanging from a nail in the yard into the back room and filling it with water from the boiler in the scullery. Under a lean - to in the yard was an ancient mangle into which my brother Graham later incautiously placed his fingers at the urging of one his brothers. He had flat nails thereafter.

It is difficult to imagine how bathing worked when the house was filled with three different families. As for sleeping, one assumes that the Cross couple lived and slept in their room, that the two bedrooms were occupied by the Turners and the Mays and that the children were distributed between the back bedroom and their parents room. Mary Jane and George May lived a long life together; Mary died in November 1922 aged 72 and George died April 1923 in Bristol aged 82; they are buried in unmarked paupers graves in Avon View cemetery. The photograph that we have of them is undated but it is clearly taken in a studio with Henry Capel, Jane's brother standing behind. They are both wearing their best finery and there is an indomitable twinkle in George's eyes. At some point in his life, probably on the railway or at the Port, he lost a leg in an accident and had it replaced by a wooden one. But you would guess that he is not the sort of man to let this bother him.

William's decision to start a new life in Bristol at the end of the war was not surprising as the city had a greater variety of employment to offer than the South Wales coalfields. The construction of the King Edward Docks in 1908 at the mouth of the Avon had revitalised the shipping industry and liberated the city from the constraints of the winding and tidal River. This was

A Long Way from Tipperary

just in time to turn the city into a major transatlantic hub again for vital imports from the US during the war and eventually, the

Lawrence Hill Signal Box Opposite No 47

port of disembarkation for American troops when the US entered the war. In fact Bristol was a strategic hub from as early as 1914 and its hospitals were a vital support to the Army. Avonmouth handled around 2300 ships and 1.8 million tons of cargo between 1914 and 18 and treated 70,000 wounded soldiers. It was already a Garrison town for the Gloucestershire Regiment. Whilst the coal industry in East Bristol (Easton) and North Somerset (Ashton) was in decline and with it the festering districts of closely packed houses like ours that were the homes of the influx of workers drawn into the city from the rural areas in the 19th century, new industries had been started.

At Filton pioneering work was carried out by, George White, who founded the British and Colonial Aeroplane Company,

A Long Way from Tipperary

which eventually produced one of the outstanding fighters of the Great War, the Bristol Fighter, and became the largest 'plane manufacturing entity in Britain for a period. It made 4,000 military aircraft and was the most important trainer of Military Pilots. At the outbreak of war, Bristol was manufacturing everything from cotton, tobacco, leather and soap to paper bags, chocolate and boots. This soon expanded to shells and other munitions, including mustard gas and gas shells, as well as footwear and clothing for the Army. At Kingswood, 25,000 Douglas motor cycles were supplied to the Armed Forces. Parnalls produced seaplanes for the Admiralty and Portishead on the other side of the Avon from Avonmouth was a major supplier of petrol for aviation and transport. The War also gave rise to the zinc smelting works at Avonmouth where William was to work. The smelter was opened in 1917 and processed lead and zinc from ore mined in Australia. Previously, this ore had been processed in Germany but then exported to Britain so the war gave rise to a new industry which lasted well into the mid 20th century when the site was called confusingly the "Spelter Works.".

The end of the war was marked by the devastating influenza epidemic of 1918-19 which had found an ideal breeding ground in the trenches and was spread by returning soldiers. By January 1919 over a thousand Bristolians had died. This was just under a quarter of the 4,400 local men who had been killed in the war out of 60,000 recruited from the city. Officers fared the worst – Clifton College, the school of Field Marshalls Haig and Birdwood, supplied 3,100 officers to all branches of the Services of which 578 were killed. The gloom was deepened by a return of unemployment caused by the closure of war

A Long Way from Tipperary

industries. Many vital jobs had been taken by women in the war, from fire fighting to running the buses and after ugly protests; they were fired to be replaced by veterans. One legacy of the War was that the hospital which housed William Albert Turner, William Murphy's future father in law, became a specialist in shell shock where the eminent neuro - psychiatrist Professor Frederick Golla did much to refute the idea that sufferers were malingerers.

A Long Way from Tipperary

Chapter 11.

William and Alice

William's job at Champion Davies, a confectionary factory at Lewin's Mead near the Horsefair was as a delivery driver (in those days neither driving tests nor licences were required - in later life, William never drove). This was where he met Alice; we have a photo of them with Aunt Ada, Alice's sister, dated 1923. It is clear from the tent in the background that William was still involved with the Army Reserve. At his point William was lodging in a sweet shop in Gloucester Lane (now Lamb Street), New Town also known as St Judes.

William and Alice in the Centre at a Dance

A Long Way from Tipperary

Alice, William and Ada c 1924

The company was founded in the 1860s by a Mr Jerman. At first the mixture was boiled in pans on open fires, but in 1892 the company, along with others bought up the revolutionary new vacuum pan patent. As well as boiled sweets, Champions produced a range of toffees, caramels, gums, jellies, creams and marzipan.

Early Advert for Champion's

A Long Way from Tipperary

Whilst William was right to see opportunities in Bristol, certainly more than he could expect to find in Maesteg, life was not going to be easy and the history of his working life shows in its variety a relentless commitment to doing the best that he could for his family.

Alice was 12 years younger than William and evidently something of a handful; she had a real zest for life. The photographs of the time suggest that William was still quite lean from his battle with enteric fever which in the absence of antibiotics tended to have a long term effect. However he was a very lively man, an accomplished dancer himself and good company. He continued to be involved with the Army in a reserve capacity. He also liked old time dancing, the Valeta, the Dashing White Sergeant and other classical dances especially. He was light as a feather on his feet; Alice was more excited by American imports; the Foxtrot, Quickstep, Tango, Rumba etc i.e. modern dance.

Alice worked at Champion's in the canteen. Her closest friend there was Minnie Cainey who later married Harry, another veteran of the First World War who was In the Machine Gun Corps. Harry was a butler to the WD and HO Wills family (the tobacco barons whose business subsequently became Imperial Tobacco) at Will's Hall on the Downs. Minnie recalled to me in the 1970's that Alice was full of fun and mischief (Alice was born in 1903 and therefore scarcely 20 when she met William) and always getting into scrapes at work through practical jokes and tomfoolery. Mum and Minnie at 17 were climbing trees on the Downs on one occasion, and met up with two young medical students. Whilst they liked

A Long Way from Tipperary

the attention, nobody was going to take advantage of them so Alice walloped one of the students for putting his hands on her thigh whilst ostensibly "helping" her down. They would go to the "Old Gaff" a variety theatre in town and take pigs' trotters to eat during the performance. In the photograph of Alice and Minnie in an open topped bus about to depart for a day out on the coast, their eyes sparkle with anticipated adventure. Minnie recalled that Alice was not seeking to be married – life had far too much to offer. Moreover, William was considered by Alice to be "an old man". But he was a great dance partner and obviously fell for her in a big way; the photograph of them together in a Dance Hall brings out his longing and her unquenchable love of life. However, William Edgar their first child arrived in 1925 which settled matters. More were to follow. Before she met William, Alice was keen on a man called Leonard Whitehead who lived at Whitehouse Lane in Bedminster. The mild mannered William put his foot down however when she wanted to call her first born "Leonard"!

It is quiet clear that William and Alice did not marry in the early years of their relationship and indeed only got around to it in October 1943 after I was born in the March of that year. We puzzled over this as a family for many years as William was a Catholic with a strong sense of propriety (although he fell out with the Church in mid life) and Alice would have regarded marriage as essential to her standing as a respectable working class woman. Our speculation that the reason for this was that William was already married appears to be born out by their wedding certificate which states clearly that Alice was a Spinster but William was a <u>widower.</u> The marriage took place

A Long Way from Tipperary

Alice and Minnie

Alice

Charlie

A Long Way from Tipperary

at the Registry Office in Bristol on 23 October 1943; William's father Thomas was given as deceased and his profession listed as Colliery Platelayer; Alice's father, William Turner, also deceased, was described as a General labourer. William's profession was Hotel Cellar man.

Ada and Alice c 1922

It is unlikely that the marriage was prompted by the arrival of their latest child. It is more probably that William became aware in 1943 of the death of his first wife (which raises interesting questions as to her location) and took immediate steps to put his relationship with Alice on the proper footing. As to the identity of his William's first wife, it is obvious that William could not have married before his age of majority at 18 which occurred in 1909. The record indicates that he was still single when he was listed in the 1911 census at 1 Alma Road Maesteg as a Boarder at the home of David Owen, 54 widower and colliery worker; Owen had a daughter, Rachel Anne Owen

A Long Way from Tipperary

aged 20 (who married later), another daughter Ariamwen Owen aged 12 and a son, Norman Glendywer, aged 8. William is described as 20 and as having been born in Maesteg. He speaks English and Welsh and was an underground Colliery Labourer. Since this discovery, I have worked my way through a significant number of weddings consecrated by William's namesakes in Wales and Bristol during the period when he might have married, and so far, drawn a blank. None of the wedding certificates that I have acquired give the right name for the groom's father.

Undeterred by this failure, I decided to follow the theory that William could have married whilst he was in London during his period of convalescence or prior to joining the Air Force. So I have certificates for 1916 to 1918 covering Chelsea, West Ham, St Olave, Greenwich and Paddington... None are linked to William. There are certainly other marriages for William Murphy in other parts of the UK but these would be real shots in the dark without a viable connection. And there for the moment the mystery rests; it is at least interesting that William was sufficiently in touch with his ex wife in 1943 to be aware of her demise. It may also be relevant that William stayed away from visiting old haunts in South Wales until pressurized to do so in the late fifties to see his oldest sister before she died, so a Welsh connection is possible. His children consider William to be a man of honour however, so whatever caused his first marriage to fail, it is not thought credible that he would have abandoned children to their fate, so we assume that the marriage was childless. The one condition that could explain the short lived character of the marriage would be if his wife was institutionalised through mental instability.

A Long Way from Tipperary

William's arrival on the scene in around 1923 was rather timely as Alice Turner nee Baxter, my grandmother would have been struggling with the responsibility of bringing up a family with her husband institutionalised and the demise of the Mays, her effective parents. The care and support given to Alice by the Mays would have made her childhood and youth fairly comfortable for a young working class woman growing up in Victorian times. As we know, all that changed after her unfortunate marriage to William Albert Turner. Even an awareness of his tough time in South Africa makes it difficult to excuse his drinking and wife beating. Alice had become used to hard toil through supporting her children through her work at the Cotton factory. She did not sit back as she aged however as she began to earn additional money by taking a two wheeled handcart to the coal yard that was behind Lawrence Hill station and delivering coal to better off (but still modest) households; she was sometimes assisted by the children; (she had 9 children of which only 4 survived).

At some point, after William's arrival, Alfred Cross died of something truly horrible (a sealed coffin was required provided with copious quantities of sawdust etc) after the couple became lodgers at No 47. Mrs Cross managed to hang on at No 47 notwithstanding the death of the Mays. Whether or not her husband's death was the cause of her own deterioration is difficult to say. But she soon became a Miss Haversham figure, refusing to take care of herself and allowing the front room to become a fertile source of bedbugs and filth that permeated right throughout the house. She preferred to use a bucket rather than the outhouse, but this inevitably meant trailing its contents through the house to be emptied at regular intervals.

A Long Way from Tipperary

The smell from the room was of course compounded by cooking and body odours.

The public health authorities had to come to Number 47 on numerous occasions to fumigate the house as the bugs could be found everywhere and were a hazard to the children's health, penetrating into the bedrooms above and living behind the damp wallpaper. But any respite was purely temporary. Attempts were made over the years to have Mrs Cross taken into care but these failed. When in the thirties the case for doing so became overwhelming, a new obstacle presented itself in the form of the local Anglican vicar, the Reverend Mervyn Stockwood, a city councillor for Labour whose voice carried great weight. He was obviously an early advocate of "Care in the Community", provided of course that he did not have to provide the care. His behaviour earned him the undying enmity of Will and Alice. In the end however, not even he could stop the inevitable and in 1939, Mrs Cross was taken to a hospital, bathed for the first time in probably 20 years and promptly died from the shock.

Mervyn Stockwood's obituary makes enjoyable reading and I make no apology for singling out the parts that are in line with my own prejudices. He eventually rose of course to become the Bishop of Southwark, although he was in no doubt that that the Archbishopric of York was more his due. He was certainly the most colourful and controversial diocesan bishop of his generation. "Stockwood was born in 1913 in Bridgend, the younger son of a solicitor killed on the Somme. That same year, 1917, the family moved to Bristol where he was later to spend 19 years as Curate and Vicar at St Matthew, Moorfields. Stock

A Long Way from Tipperary

wood kept quiet about the fact that while an undergraduate he was a Young Conservative. His conversion to Socialism was said to have occurred through personal experience

Mr Pugsley's Iconic Crane

of deprivation at Moorfields, although, like many affluent middle class socialists, he enjoyed the fruits of capitalism. He served as a Labour councillor both in Bristol and Cambridge, and in Bristol he established the first health clinic in the country. One of Stockwood's suffragans used to say there was not much between his ears. "He thought he had a working relationship with God," one Chaplain said. His gravest flaw, his egotism, was almost impossible to exaggerate; it could take 40 minutes just to stop him talking about himself. He seldom bothered to

A Long Way from Tipperary

attend the Church Assembly or General Synod, and when he did, it was to make a speech and leave. The sound of his own voice was one of his especial pleasures and after 21 years as Bishop of Southwark he retired in 1980, to an elegant house in Bath lent to him indefinitely by a rich business friend."

Michael De-la-Noy's biography, "Mervyn Stockwood: A Lonely Life", paints him as a socialist who loved the trappings of wealth, privilege and royalty. Shortly before his death he was one of ten Church of England bishops 'outed' by the radical gay organisation OutRage! There is no doubt that Stockwood's "experience of deprivation at Moorfields" was vicarious and second hand; the life of an Anglican parish priest even in an inner city at this time was affluent and indeed, as the obituary makes clear, Stockwood would not have wanted it otherwise. He made much of his egalitarian ideas but always insisted on having a liveried servant and cordon bleu chef. His professed love for the poor sits uneasily with his pleasure in the company of the rich, including the Windsors whom he once numbered amongst his friends.

Will was able to bring some stability to the domestic situation at No 47 but everyone had to contribute. Rose, Alice's eldest sister, had curvature of the spine that resulted from being dropped at three weeks old and wore a brace with a neck support but that did not stop her collecting rent for a living. She was taken under the wing of Ada Vachell, a woman who was profoundly deaf and started at Broad Plain the Guild of the Handicapped to better the lives of the afflicted. The women did a lot of sewing and embroidery; visits were made to

A Long Way from Tipperary

housebound handicapped people etc and Rose received a strong sense of purpose from the Guild.

At some point, William left Champion Davies to work in the Spelter Works at Avonmouth which was physically demanding as it involved shovelling ore. He was fortunate however in that the line from Lawrence Hill station, just the other side of the wall, ran direct to Avonmouth, the location of the Spelter works. Later he became a ganger, laying track on the Great Western Railway. He worked all around the Bristol area including in the Severn Tunnel. Ironically, this was exactly the stuff of which most Irish immigrants were made as the legendary Irish "navvy" had constructed much of the track laid in Britain during the railway age as well as dug the canals.

The Great Western Railway originated from the desire of Bristol merchants to maintain their city as the second port of the country and the chief one for American trade. The increase in the size of ships and the gradual silting of the River Avon had made Liverpool an increasingly attractive port and, with a rail connection to London under construction in the 1830s, threatening Bristol's status. The answer for Bristol was, with the co-operation of London interests, to build a line of their own; a railway built to unprecedented standards of excellence to out-perform the lines being constructed to the north-west. This proved a mighty engine of growth for Bristol and the West during the 19th and early 20th century. Bristolians dubbed the GWR " God's Wonderful Railway", if local historians are to be believed.

At the outbreak of World War in 1914, the GWR was taken into government control, as were most major railways in Britain.

A Long Way from Tipperary

Lawrence Hill Station

Many of its staff joined the Armed Forces and it was more difficult to build and maintain equipment than in peacetime. After the war, the government considered permanent nationalization but decided instead on a compulsory amalgamation of the railways into four large groups. The GWR alone preserved its name through the "grouping", under which smaller companies were amalgamated into four main companies in 1922 and 1923.

Track lying was physically demanding but William was used to hard work and was comfortable in the railway environment. When I was a child in the 50's, I recall that we had a railway allotment alongside the track just outside of Stapleton Road station to which we gained access by walking along the rails from Lawrence Hill Station after climbing over the wall facing the house. I used to follow my father along the rails when I was

A Long Way from Tipperary

about 8, trying to stretch out my legs to reach the sleepers. We always walked facing the oncoming trains, and when they approached, we stepped down to the side of the track as they went by, turning our faces away from the enormous wheels and the steam that escaped from the pistons. The vegetables themselves on the allotment were frequent beneficiaries of mists of steam. William would bring a screw of sugar with him so that Paddie and I could enjoy a taste of fresh rhubarb.

The GWR was a source of great pride in the neighbourhood and the wall opposite no 47 was a terrific vantage point to collect train numbers as well as to offer a thrilling view of the enormous green liveried trains that steamed through Lawrence Hill, especially the famed Castle and Hall Classes that carried their names alongside the boiler. Our lives followed the rhythm of the trains; William was awoken in the morning by the noise of the milk train coming up from Wales and the time of day could be deduced by passenger and freight trains that hurried by on the other side of the sandstone wall. We knew when a big train was expected and this led to a scramble amongst the children to be the first up on the wall. The noise of the "matchbox" shunting engines in the yard on the other side of the station was a constant backdrop to our lives and the highpoint of my young childhood was when my father arranged for me to get up on the footplate of a shunter. The London Midlands and Southern line crossed the GWR line just out of Lawrence Hill Station before crossing Easton Arch and climbing the grade towards Staple Hill and so on north. As children, we held this line in great contempt; its trains carried only numbers and they lacked the elegant sweep of "our" locomotives.

A Long Way from Tipperary

Granma Alice once worked around 1900 as a general domestic for a woman called "Great Aunt Eva" who managed the Prince of Wales pub in the Centre and the General Draper in Hotwells between about 1918 and 1928. We considered that this lady could have been related to the Capels or the Mays or the Turners, although Aunt Ada was always sceptical that there was a blood connection. After lots of research, it is clear that she was not a relative of any sort and that the "Aunt" title was honorific. The location of the "General Draper" public house was on Hotwells Road in the small block currently shielded by a high wall that is between Hinton Lane and St Vincent's Parade on the Portway / Hotwells road. This was known as "Drapers Row " in 1901. The Pub itself was named after a General Draper name who was born in Bristol to a Customs Officer, went to Eton and served with distinction in the 7 years war, amongst other battles. He is buried in Bath Abbey. "Aunt Eva" probably lived in a house in St Vincent's Parade, probably No 11, which is just beyond the site of the pub, because there are no more houses after the entrance to Clifton Funicular Railway.

A Long Way from Tipperary

Chapter 12.

The Depression and the Thirties

In October 1929, the Stock Market Crash in New York heralded the Great Depression. The ensuing American economic collapse shook the World: World trade contracted, prices fell and governments faced financial crisis as the supply of American credit dried up. Many countries adopted an emergency response to the crisis by erecting trade barriers and tariffs, which worsened the crisis by further hindering global trade. The effects on the industrial areas of Britain were immediate and devastating, as demand for British products collapsed. By the end of 1930, unemployment had more than doubled from 1 million to 2.5 million (20% of the insured workforce), and exports had fallen in value by 50%. Government revenues contracted as national income fell, while the cost of assisting the jobless rose. The industrial areas were hardest hit, along with the coal mining districts.

Under pressure from its Liberal allies as well as the Conservative opposition, the Labour Government appointed a Committee to review the state of public finances. It urged public sector wage cuts and large cuts in public spending (notably in benefit payments to the unemployed) to avoid incurring a budget deficit. This proposal proved deeply unpopular within the Labour Party and the trade unions, which along with several government ministers refused to support any such measures. The dispute over spending and wage cuts split irrevocably the Labour government. The resulting political deadlock caused

A Long Way from Tipperary

investors to take fright, and a flight of capital and gold further de-stabilized the economy. In response, the labour leader Ramsay MacDonald, on the urging of King George V, decided to form a "National Government" with the Conservatives and the Liberals. On 24 August, MacDonald submitted the resignation of his ministers and led his senior colleagues in forming the new National Government. MacDonald and his supporters were expelled from the Labour Party and adopted the label "National Labour". The Labour Party and some Liberals, led by David Lloyd George, went into opposition. The Labour Party denounced MacDonald as a "traitor" and a "rat" for what they saw as his betrayal. Soon after this, a General Election was called. The election resulted in a Conservative landslide victory, with the now leaderless Labour Party winning only 46 seats in Parliament. After the 1931 election the National Government became Conservative-dominated, although MacDonald continued as Prime Minister until 1935.

In the 1920s and 1930s, Britain had a relatively advanced welfare system compared to many of the industrialized countries. In 1911, a compulsory national unemployment and health insurance scheme had been put in place by Asquith's Liberal government. This scheme had been funded through contributions from the government, the employers and the workers but it only paid out according to the level of contributions made rather than according to need, and was only payable for 15 weeks. Anyone unemployed for longer than that had to rely on poor law relief paid by their local authority. In effect, millions of workers who had been too poorly paid to make contributions, or who had been unemployed long term, were left destitute by the scheme. With the mass

A Long Way from Tipperary

unemployment of the 1930s, contributions to the insurance scheme dried up, resulting in a funding crisis. In August 1931, the 1911 scheme was replaced by a fully government-funded unemployment benefit system. This system, for the first time, paid out according to need rather than the level of contributions. This unemployment benefit was subject to a strict means test, and anyone applying for unemployment pay had to have an inspection by a government official to make sure that they had no hidden earnings or savings, undisclosed source(s) of income or other means of support. For many poor people, this was a humiliating experience and was much resented. William on one occasion took a job that offered less money than National Assistance.

Following Britain's withdrawal from the gold standard and the devaluation of the pound, interest rates were reduced from 6% to 1%. As a result, British exports became more competitive on world markets than those of countries that remained on the gold standard. This led to a modest economic recovery and a fall in unemployment from 1933 onwards. Although exports were still a fraction of their pre-depression levels, they recovered slightly. Unemployment began a modest fall in 1934 and fell further in 1935 and 1936, but the rise in employment levels occurred mostly in the south, where lower interest rates had spurred had spurred the house building boom, which in turn stimulated a recovery in domestic industry. In severely depressed parts of the country, the government enacted a number of policies to stimulate growth and reduce unemployment, including road building, loans to shipyards, and tariffs on steel imports. These policies helped but were not, however, on a sufficiently large

A Long Way from Tipperary

scale to make a huge impact on the unemployment levels. It was only rearmament and the war which reignited growth.

We can take it that William would have paid into the National Insurance scheme after the war like other manual workers but that any relief that he would have gained would be short lived. The unemployment benefit was subject to the hated means test which he found too humiliating to accept; like other working class people, he displayed a deep repugnance all of his life to means testing and what he considered "handouts". It was his proud boast in later life that he worked right throughout the depression for wages that were often below the level of benefits. He was a Labour man right through and would have shared the Party's characterization of Macdonald as a traitor. At the same time, he had no warmth for the Labour MP for South East Bristol who was Sir Stafford Cripps, a man who completely lacked the common touch. Cripps was elected in a by-election for Bristol East in 1931, During his time in parliament; he was a strong proponent of Marxist social and economic policies. He was the richest lawyer in Britain in the 20s and came from a wealthy background. Stalin regarded him as "a useful fool" because during his period as Ambassador to Moscow after the Labour victory of 1945, he supported the transfer of jet engine technology to Russia which was subsequently deployed against the UN, including British Airmen, in Mig 17 fighters during the Korean War.

Alice continued to work as a domestic when she could get it. Daughter Alice worked for a while as a cook general for a Mrs Pesach in Clifton/Westbury and also for a Mrs Ashman the sister in law of Jeffrey Farnol, the writer, where she was paid 2

A Long Way from Tipperary

shillings and sixpence per week with 6 pence docked for lunch. Farnol (1878 –1952), was an English author, known for his many romantic novels, some formulaic and set   in the English

Alice, Edward, Terry Graham and William

Granny Alice, Eddie and Terry

Terry and Eddie

A Long Way from Tipperary

Granny Alice (left) and Paddie

Alice and Graham

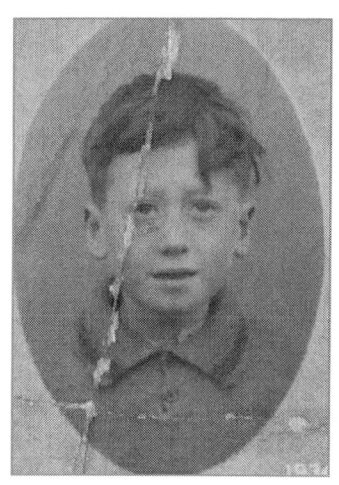
Terry

Paddie

A Long Way from Tipperary

period, and swashbucklers. He founded with Georgette Heyer the Regency romantic genre.

The pressure on all those occupying No 47 in the thirties was intense; I have mentioned already the incubus of Mrs Cross who could not be removed. Then there was Grandmother Turner and her four children, including Alice. My mother gave birth to William Edgar in 1924, Terence Bernard in 1926, Graham Clive in 1931 and Patricia Christine in 1935. Alice also lost two children in infancy, one a late miscarriage and another a stillbirth. The maximum period of occupancy was in 1938 when there were 11 people in the house. How these all fitted - in is a mystery. It seems that Granma Turner and Auntie Ada and the children slept in the front bedroom; William and Charles slept in the middle room and Alice and Rose slept in the back room. It is said that Rose was insistent on protecting her own space which had the effect of making it difficult for Will and Alice to sleep together (not wholly successfully and presumably save for Sunday afternoons!). Ada Turner married and moved out in 1939 as did Charles. Mrs Cross was finally removed in the same year (at around 82) and the front downstairs room was fumigated and recaptured. It turned into the best room. Aunt Rose died in 1939. By the forties, there was a further development; I was born in 1943 and Granma Turner died shortly afterwards. This lead to a reorganisation whereby Alice, William and Ralph slept in the centre bedroom; Paddie took the backroom and the older boys were in the front room until Terry joined the Army in 1944 and Eddie married in 1945.

It would not be unreasonable to assume that the tension generated by this level of humanity crammed into a small space

A Long Way from Tipperary

should have lead to a lot of argument and dissension. This seems not to have been the case at least between Will and Alice although Will's nickname for her was "TNT" in view of her capacity to explode in anger without much notice. She soon came down again however and did not bear grudges – after she clipped the boys around the ear, she would hug them and apologise. It appears that in spite of her temperament, she and William never seriously rowed – they seemed very much in love. William worshipped her. He however was inclined to sulk when offended and had a long memory for slights etc. Granma senior was a dear soul, but beaten down by life. She was thin as a rail and looked years older than her age as can be seen from the photographs. She was much loved by her grandchildren and had a very warm relationship with William and Alice; she doted on William – he could do no wrong and she sided with him in any spats with Alice.

Aunt Ada in old age and Alice Maud senior looked very much like each other. Alice probably followed after William Albert in looks. Rose was a discordant figure in the house - not very likeable and inclined to do spiteful things when given the opportunity. An egregious example was her delight at kicking coal dust and ash over the fireplace after Aunt Ada, her younger sister, had just blacked it as part of her chores. This behaviour could have resulted from her physical disability or psychological scars acquired from experiencing as the eldest the turbulent relationship of her parents. The large charcoal drawing of her shows that she was quite an attractive woman and she had a boyfriend with whom she enjoyed a full sex life, not allowing her disability (she had to wear a high corset to help her cope with her twisted spine) get in the way.

A Long Way from Tipperary

All the children started school at Whitehall Infants which is on Russell Town Avenue, just around the corner from Number 47; the building still stands at the entrance to the new Bristol Academy. Eddie would have been there in 1929 and Ralph in 1948. Afterwards, the family went to Whitehall Primary (now the site of a small housing estate opposite Chalks Road) and then on to Carleton Park Senior school, except Paddie who went to Redfield School for girls. It is certainly the case that teachers like Miss Badger in the infants and Miss Glide at the primary got to know all of the boys. By the time that I passed through the schools, they had clearly had enough of us! The senior school was a good one and had an inspirational head called Mr Greenland for many years. Discipline tended to be harsh and there were stories of boys being suspended out of the upper windows of the school by burly staff in an effort to frighten them into behaving. Incidentally, it was always Alice not William who went up to the school to confront authority if the boys were in a scrape. She was a formidable mother.

Eddie passed the school certificate exam to go to Grammar School in 1935 but refused to go, perhaps influenced by the fact that the family could not afford the uniform or any of the other trappings of a grammar. It is equally possible that Eddie, who was extraordinarily stubborn, decided that he did not want to leave his mates. The cost of the uniform was certainly a factor in prevented Paddie going to grammar school when she in turn passed the exam in 1946. Eddie's life would evidently have been different if he had seized the chance, and I think that he regretted it; as it was, when he finally left school in 1939, he became an apprentice blacksmith and metal worker.

A Long Way from Tipperary

Chapter 13.

The Outbreak of War

Castle Street After Bombing

As the 7th largest urban conurbation in Britain and the main administrative centre for the south west, it was clear that Bristol would become a major target in the event of war. And this was before consideration is given to its status as a westward facing port which would be vital for the connection with the United

A Long Way from Tipperary

States and indeed the westerly sea routes. The aircraft industry based at Filton with the Bristol Aircraft Company and at Yate with Parnalls simply underlined its strategic relevance.

We can only guess at the thoughts running through William's mind as the probability of war grew during the 1930s. After the carnage of Flanders, he would have had no illusions about the likely human cost of conflict again with Germany and although he would have known that his age militated against being "called to the colours" (the kind of terminology with which he would be familiar as opposed to the more prosaic "being called up"), he could not be sure. Moreover, he would have been anxious about the potential exposure of his children to the conflict.

Fortuitously, William's eldest child, Eddie could not serve in the war because he had a foreshortened leg from a childhood accident in which he was hit by a bus in Russell Town Avenue. I believe that this perfectly valid reason for not being able to fight was a source of embarrassment to him. I am sure that he would have been happier in the Army or Air Force where he had friends (one, a rear gunner in Bomber Command was killed over Germany) and that he was sorry to have missed out on what was the most exciting event happening for his generation. As a metal worker, he was in any event in a reserved occupation which would have made enlistment impossible even if he was fit. Terry took a 5 year apprenticeship as a chef on leaving school in 1941 which he started at the Mauretania Hotel at the foot of Park Street. He was called up in 1944 however and not surprisingly, was drafted into the Royal Catering Corps,

A Long Way from Tipperary

serving in the UK, Palestine and Egypt. Graham did his military service on reaching conscription age after the war.

Preparation for war had begun in 1938 when everyone was issued with gas masks and communal bomb shelters were started. Initially, Bristol was thought of as a relatively safe place by the Government, notwithstanding the strategic significance of its port and aircraft factories, because of its distance from German airfields. However, after building trench shelters throughout the city for 40,000 people by the end of the year, basements of buildings, churches, tunnels and even caves were turned to good use. Three types of domestic shelter were eventually introduced. The strongest was a shelter constructed of brick and a reinforced concrete roof; three of these were put up in Cattybrook Street each containing a primitive bucket lavatory. Our neighbours, the Coopers also had an Andersen shelter of which over 41,000 were supplied around the city. This consisted of an assembly of curved corrugated sheets which were designed to be buried in the ground to a depth of 3 feet and then covered with 1.5 feet of soil and turf. This created a space measuring 6 feet high, 5.5 feet wide and 6.5 feet long. It was an uncomfortable billet in which the family huddled with the Coopers during the night raids – and as it could take only 6, the rest of our family joined the other neighbours in the street shelters. The family had little faith in the third option, which was the Morrison shelter consisting of a large metal table like structure with mesh sides into which 4 people were supposed to fit. It was intended for those who had no garden. None of the shelters available were proof against blast but they ensured survival from falling debris and incendiary bombs.

A Long Way from Tipperary

1938 also saw the introduction of the Warden Service which was the backbone of Civil Defence. Its objective was to help the victims of bombing, to issue warnings of danger and to offer general advice. The Wardens liaised closely with the Emergency Services, reported damage and did their best to deal with panic. Over 5,200 had been recruited by the end of the war. Most were unpaid and many of the men had First World War experience. William found unpaid service impossible with a family to keep but he served as a Fire Watcher. He was soon to have an early taste of what this war would bring when he was caught out in the open in Filton during a raid but of course, he had experience already of what it was like to be under shot and shell from his time in France. William's role meant that when everyone else trooped off to the shelter when the warning sirens blew to indicate an imminent raid, he grabbed his Stirrup Pump, bucket, shovel and tin hat and headed for his post, where he could watch for incendiary bombs. It took guts to stand out in the open, pick up incendiary bombs and cover them with sand, put out small fires with the pumps and water buckets and marked the dangerous butterfly bombs that the German planes dropped.

In 1938 recruitment to the Police was stepped up as was the creation of an Auxiliary Fire service to support the Fire brigade. For the first time in our history, every individual was issued with a personal identity card. There was a severe shortage of effective anti-aircraft guns in Bristol at the beginning of the war, most were old and had an operating height of only 14,000 feet – the new Vickers guns which could reach targets at 25,000 feet were not widely available. Searchlights were supposed to be stationed at 3,500 yard intervals but it was June 1940 before

A Long Way from Tipperary

anything approaching a full complement was in place. Balloon barrages eventually covered Avonmouth, Filton and the airplane manufacturing facilities at Filton and Yate. But in the early years, the guns had to be guided by sound location equipment which was not nearly as effective as the radar direction that was too follow. Alarmingly, the strategic BAC factory at Filton was not provided with on-site fighter cover, a mistake that was soon to prove tragic.

In January 1940 rationing of food was introduced beginning with bacon, ham butter and sugar and meat appeared on the list in March. By July tea, cooking fats jam and cheese were added and milk and eggs were soon in short supply as they were supplied to shops based on the number of people registered with them. Initially people were allowed weekly rations amounting to a shilling's worth of meat, 8 ounces of sugar, an ounce of fat, an ounce of cheese and two ounces of tea. Each person had 20 points to use on whatever food they wanted most and everyone had to register at a shop and take their ration card along to have points deducted when they made their purchases. Substitutes were introduced such as margarine for butter, saccharine for sugar and powdered forms of milk, potatoes and eggs. Beer, bread and potatoes were not rationed but were often in short supply. The "Dig for Victory" campaign was a big success in ensuring the production of vegetables from gardens and allotments as Parks and open spaces in the City went under the spade.

In about 1943 Graham got a part time job at Thornes the butchers on the corner of Jane and Church Street when he was still at school and then took full time employment when he

A Long Way from Tipperary

reached 15 in 1946. This connection was a godsend to the family both during the war and in the years after with the continuation of rationing – there were frequent opportunities for him to bring home extra food although this was usually in the form of bones and scraps. The quality of meat supplied through the ration book became increasingly contentious as the war progressed; sometimes it had an alleged "sweet" character which was usually attributed to an equine origin. Later on, I used to love being propelled down the street riding in the basket of his butcher's bike with my chubby legs hanging over the front whilst he put the heavy old thing through its paces. William cultivated his allotment assiduously and we kept chickens in our small yard fed from boiled potato peelings and other kitchen waste.

The outbreak of war created a new dynamic for everyone. Bristol was to become the fifth most heavily bombed British city of World War II. The fall of France brought Bristol within range of German bombers in their new French bases and the Blitz in London starkly indicated the potential consequences. A clue of the future should have been picked up as early as 1939 when a German spy had been arrested in Barrow Road, not far from Cattybrook Street, photographing the railway yards and the gasometer; he was armed and was carrying a map of targets. The identity of this man is not clear from the list of spies shot at the Tower of London or hanged in one of the major prisons, so either the story is apocryphal or he collaborated in the "Double Cross" game played by the Security Service whereby captured agents reported deceptive information back to their German masters. (A copy of the alleged German target map identifying Lysaghts Steel works and ICI at the Netham, the St

A Long Way from Tipperary

Phillips Marsh railway yard and Lawrence Hill Bus Garage was auctioned in 2011 in Bristol.)

When the bombs finally began to fall they were a lot less destructive than people feared – most were incendiaries mixed up with blast bombs their weight varied between 50 kilos, the majority, and 250 kilos. The Lawrence Hill area was lightly hit with bombs early on which hit the railway, the goods yards and the rows of houses in the Moorfields area behind the house in Cattybrook Street. Easton was less fortunate. The most devastating weapon was a small 1 kilo Incendiary which was dropped in profusion and which created veritable firestorms when mixed with blast weapons. They burned with a temperature sufficient to melt steel. The outcome tended to have a pock marking effect – some houses were burned to the ground whilst their neighbours were just scorched. For children, oblivious to the suffering, the bombsites just provided new and exciting areas to play after the cinders had cooled down. Later larger explosive incendiaries were used carrying more weight and delayed fuses to catch out the Fire services.

In the early days, Luftwaffe operations were on a small scale and usually at night. The operation of the "blackout" (all buildings and homes had to mask their lights so as. to prevent light escaping into the street), the shutting off of all street lighting and minimal lighting for vehicles made it difficult for the bombers to locate their targets especially as their navigation aids were fairly primitive. Also efforts to jam the radio beams that helped guide the bombers from France to their targets were frequently successful. William's sole contribution to the war effort at this point was to ensure that houses that caught fire

A Long Way from Tipperary

had been properly evacuated and that any stray incendiaries that fell in the street were covered with dirt or sand. Water was ineffective against magnesium bombs. On 24 June the Germans claimed to have successfully attacked the Filton factory at night with 5 Heinkel 111s but in fact they hit St Phillips and Brislington. German daylight raids were vulnerable to fighter attack but the night fighters of the time were useless. Night raids throughout the summer however were little more than a nuisance. Although Luftlotte 3 had over 480 aircraft for their attacks on the west of Britain between June and September 1940 they inflicted little damage. This was about to change.

On Wednesday 25th September 1940 an attack was made against the Bristol Aeroplane Company works by sixty-eight Heinkel bombers with an escort of 52 Messerschmitt twin engine 110s. Fighter Command wrongly assumed that the raid was intended for the Westland Works at Yeovil so the raiders had an uninterrupted run in from Weston Super Mare in near perfect conditions. Only one bomber was shot down by ground fire (only two aircraft were destroyed by Bristol's defences during the whole war, but arguably, at least the enemy was forced to fly high). The raiders aimed for the distinct rectangle made by the railway lines just to the east of the Filton airfield to making sure of an accurate bomb run; this was exactly where William was laying track at the time.

Just as twelve Hurricanes of No 238 Squadron bore down on the formation from above and behind, the He 111s opened their bomb doors. 350 high explosive bombs rained down from 15,000 feet into an area some one-mile by three quarters of a

A Long Way from Tipperary

mile amounting to 80 tons of high explosive in 45 seconds. As the bombers sped away, below at the factory, chaos reigned. It was over in one devastating moment. The death toll was horrendous. In the factory 72 were killed and 166 injured. Nineteen died later from their injuries. Immediately outside the factory another 58 people were killed with 154 seriously injured. A further 118 people were reported as slightly injured. The bombs had fallen at an estimated four per second and the whole raid had lasted just 45 seconds. William had thrown himself into a ditch and watched the devastation unfold.

The factory death rate was high due to a series of direct hits by high explosive bombs on six crowded air raid shelters. The scenes confronting the rescue parties were horrific; shelters had caved in burying the occupants. Others had been blasted wide open, mutilating the occupants almost beyond recognition. The Germans lost 4 bombers and 3 fighters to the Hurricanes after the raid but knew their operation had been a success. The conclusion drawn by the RAF was obvious- Filton had to have its own squadron and so by the second raid on Friday 17 September when 52 Messerschmitt tried to attack Parnalls at Yate, the result was different. Uniquely the ensuing dogfight was seen over the City itself and remained long in the memory of its people; the raiders were routed and lost ten aircraft and a number of distinguished pilots before jettisoning their bombs in the vicinity of Filton and heading home. Two of their number, Tiepelt and Brosig were buried with full honours in Greenbank Cemetery just along from the grave of William Turner.

The German High Command changed attack in November 1940 so as to focus not only on London but also to target night

A Long Way from Tipperary

raids against Britain's manufacturing base and ports. On 24 November 1940, 148 bombers left France to bomb Bristol and to eliminate it as an "importing port supplying much of the Midlands and the south Of England". The attack started at 6.30pm with waves of aircraft passing over Bristol dropping some 12,000 incendiary bombs and 160 tons of high-explosives; within an hour 70 fires had started and the flames were visible to enemy aircraft approaching through a clear sky from 150 miles away. They lost two aircraft. But neither night fighters, balloons nor anti-aircraft fire made much difference. The City was badly hit. Castle Street, Wine street, and High Street were gutted - the ancient heart of the City. Park Street was smashed; the Bristol Museum was hit; 207 people were killed and thousands of houses destroyed or damaged. The area that is now Castle Park was extensively damaged. The Jacobean St Peter's Hospital was destroyed, and the 17th century timber-framed Dutch House was damaged and subsequently demolished. Four of Bristol's ancient churches, St Peter's, the interior of St Nicholas, St Mary-le-Port and Temple Church were also badly damaged. The St James' Presbyterian Church of England was gutted.

In December further large scale raids took place of involving more than 130 aircraft - by the 6th the City was into its third raid in two weeks at little loss to the Luftwaffe. The MORI Observation teams responsible for assessing civilian opinion began to report an effect on morale. Bristolians were less phlegmatic than other cities and there was a lot of rumour spreading and defeatist talk. Some of this stemmed from well founded dismay over the poor quality of the air raid shelters. The BBC was regarded as giving less credit to the suffering of

A Long Way from Tipperary

the City compared to other towns. A lot of people were said to be listening to the German propagandistic transmissions of " Lord Haw Haw" (William Joyce, executed for treason after the war) I find this rather surprising as although the family listened in to "Haw Haw" , it was as a form of light entertainment and he was regarded as a joke. There was competition amongst the adults, which extended after the war, to give the best impression of his rather oily pronunciation.

January and February 1941 brought no respite. The temperature fell and attacks were pressed by combined aircraft from two Bomber groups of over 200 aircraft on 3 January which amounted to the largest raid launched against the city. Again the harbour and the centre of the City were targets and over 150 tons of bombs and more than 50,000 incendiaries were dropped. The flames could again been seen from over 100 miles making target marking unnecessary. Total casualties were close to 500, many amongst the Emergency services. Night fighter cover was improving but was still not very effective – fortunately follow up attacks on Avonmouth were impacted by bad weather. Interestingly "pirate" attacks of single aircraft operating in daylight probably had more strategic impact than saturation bombing as two such sorties caused severe damage to Parnalls at Yate and another narrowly failed at Filton – the latter crew earned infamy by machine gunning streets in the surrounding area .It seemed clear to Bristolians that the air defence systems were completely unable to protect the City against this kind of attack.

Better off Bristolians dubbed "Trekkers" sloped off to the

A Long Way from Tipperary

countryside now that threat of air attack had became real following the end of the "phoney war". It is estimated that in some areas, 10 per cent of the population moved out into rural areas country at night. But the people of Lawrence Hill were poor and without private transport so they were going nowhere.

On 3 – 4 January 1941 Bristol had its longest raid lasting 12 hours; during this raid the Luftwaffe dropped their biggest bomb

A Long Way from Tipperary

on the city. It was nicknamed "Satan", and weighed 2,000 kilograms (4,400 lb), measuring 8 feet (2.4 m) long (without the tail), and 26 inches (66 cm) in diameter; it did not explode and was recovered in April 1943. The bomb disposal crew had to dig down 29 feet (8.8 m) to get it. Not all raids involved big bomber fleets. Probably the most successful was on February 27 1941 on the Parnalls factory at Yate where William was to work after the war for many years after it changed to a peacetime occupation of shop fitting and cabinet making. Parnalls had made over 1000 planes during the First World War and light aircraft thereafter. From 1939 it moved from making light aircraft into hydraulically operated gun turrets designed by Frazer Nash for bombers as well as air frames for Spitfires and other types. A lone Heinkel dropped 7 high explosive bombs on the factory on 27 February, of which 5 hit the workshops, killing 54 workers and injuring another 105. The same plane unbelievably, returned on March 7 bombing from 80 feet with similar success.

The most lethal raid of all took place on 16 March involving 184 aircraft. Many parts of the city were hit but the Murphy's neighbourhood of Moorfields and Whitehall, as well as Easton, Fishponds and Eastville were saturated. Due to poor visibility over the target the bombers drifted east and unloaded much of their cargo over the working class districts. It did not help that a false " All Clear " was sounded at 1.40 am causing people to emerge prematurely from their shelters. 257 people were killed that night and a further 391 were injured.35 Fire brigades from the surrounding counties came in to assist their beleaguered colleagues. Between 0830 pm and 3.25 am the Luftwaffe

A Long Way from Tipperary

The Dead under Sheets at Easton.

managed to drop 165 tons of high explosive and 34,000 incendiaries This was the raid that made the war personal for the Murphy family when the damage came closer to home with the bombing of Barton Hill and Easton. The newly married Aunt Ada whose husband was in the Army as a Despatch Rider and Military Policeman had her house completely destroyed in Eve Road Easton, fortunately whilst she was in a shelter. There was a gallows humour side to this experience, which she frequently related afterwards, although she was greatly distressed at the time. After emerging blinking from a

A Long Way from Tipperary

communal shelter in the dawn hours, she started to walk towards her house when she encountered a neighbour who asked her where she was going. "Home", she replied. "No you are not", came the response. "Your house has been bombed flat".

Bomb Damage in Easton Road Close to Eve Road

Bad weather reduced the impact of raids in the later part of March as cloud covered the target. The move of one of the German Air Groups from France to the Balkans also reduced the Luftwaffe's strength. RAF night fighters also began to exact a toll. On 3 April another raid was mitigated by poor visibility and rain and the Fire services showed during this raid that they were now gaining control through improved techniques over incendiary fires. The creation of Street Fire Fighting Parties with

A Long Way from Tipperary

which William was involved contributed to the avoidance of significant damage although the National Smelting Company at Avonmouth was badly hit. By putting out fires quickly, the German pilots were prevented from using previous bombings from serving as navigation aids.

The Good Friday air raids of April 11 1941 involving 177

A Long Way from Tipperary

aircraft from two Air Groups caused further damage to the centre of the city, Knowle, Hotwells, Cotham and Filton, and lead to the permanent closure of the Bristol Tramways following the destruction of St Phillips Bridge.

A Fire watcher like William called Bill Hares kept a diary right through the Blitz and it interesting to get something of the flavour of the experience from his writing.

"The siren goes and we stand to as usual. In come the planes. The barrage opens up immediately, but unlike the first blitzes, there are now plenty of fire watchers. Matters are now more organised, the novelty of being subjected to aerial bombardment has faded and we know our own capabilities. Orange and red flares drift slowly down; the red bursts of ack ack shells followed by drifting white haloes light the sky whilst we wait for the more devastating part of the play to begin. With a terrific shriek, a large bomb falls on Broadmead, a very early present. Then a string of incendiaries swishes across Cotham and beyond... In quick succession 5 are plotted. There are big fires raging in Cheltenham Road, Stokes Croft and Kingsdown. In the distance, the blue incandescent light of exploding fire bombs is seen down across the roofs and streets, starting from Stokes Croft and then taking a south west turn towards us. We watch them come nearer, Brunswick square, Rosemary street, and up Quakers Friars. I shout to my mates to duck under the table, expecting to have one through the roof. Seconds pass and we get a shock because there in the office is an incendiary! I let the bomb have a full bucket of water, Harry comes in with some sandbags and dumps them on the top and Bert bring up

A Long Way from Tipperary

the rear with two more buckets"

The "All Clear" goes but then the sirens go on again. As Hares observed -

"We get ready for the second half of the show. The barrage opens up again with fresh intensity and whilst watching the innumerable bursts in the sky, we get the surprise of our lives. The great black shapes of a couple of German bombers come sailing in well below the balloons. With their guns firing, they pass right overhead and let their load full of hate fall near the City centre. The attack now shifts to the middle of the city and fires spring up in Redcliff street, the Centre and Park Street. They quickly get out of hand and become beacons for more terrific bombing. A few more incendiaries across Stokes Croft, St Michaels Hill and Park Row. A big fire starts near the gasometer at the back of the Eye Hospital. Hell let loose again; terrific bomb attack. Fire in Park Street now assumes huge proportions and flames fly high in the area, reminiscent of the first blitz. Raid goes on until early morning, by which time the early fires have died down and I think that everybody has just about had enough".

Churchill visited the City with the US Ambassador on 12 April 1941.The last air major raid of the Blitz on Bristol was on 25 April 1941, when Brislington, Bedminster and Knowle were bombed. It is speculated that these suburbs were not the targets themselves but that bombs intended for Filton's manufacturing areas were mistakenly dropped on other areas. The Germans switched their priorities to other Cities and the

A Long Way from Tipperary

Luftwaffe was beginning to move East in preparation for its onslaught on the Soviet Union

In early 1941 after much prevarication, a scheme was introduced to evacuate children from the worst effected areas to families in Devon and Cornwall. 6,370 children were despatched, amongst them Graham who was sent by train to a farm in St Agnes in Cornwall, departing Temple Meads station like many other children with labels in their lapels like little parcels in case they got lost. Although he was big for his age, he had never been away from home before and was only 8 and quite shy so he found the experience quite shattering. He was

Bombed Out

A Long Way from Tipperary

properly fed but was otherwise treated like a street urchin which he found humiliating so he began to fret. It was not long before William went down to Cornwall to bring him home. He was better off taking his chances with the family. Although the number of evacuees, including those with private arrangements, reached at least 20,000 by March 1942, around 10,000 drifted back like Graham over the same period. The countryside was an alien world to them, Paddie was lucky to be deemed too young to be evacuated.

Clothing began to become an issue by mid 1941 because of the shortage of raw materials so rationing was extended to most items, including shoes. Lots of well meaning guidance was issued on cloth making and careful washing and mending, but this was completely lost on the working class community whose wardrobe had never been exactly extensive and who were steeped in the art of making things last. Alice was good with a needle so turning collars, cutting tails from shirts to make patches and use of a much perforated wooden "toadstool" to help darn socks, was second nature. The disappearance of stockings heralded the innovative introduction of gravy browning to women's' legs as a cheap substitute with a darker line drawn down the calf to simulate a seam. This practice lasted well into the late forties as I remember as a young boy finding it quite odd.

Following a devastating RAF raid on Lubeck on 28 March 1942, and subsequently on Rostock, the Germans were stung into attempting to destroy the British cities listed in Baedeker's tourist guidebook – hence the name " the Baedeker raids". In the West Country, they started with Bath which was virtually

A Long Way from Tipperary

undefended, but then extended themselves to Exeter, Weston Super Mare and Bristol on an opportunity basis. York, Norwich and Cowes were also attacked. By the summer however the cost of these operations in downed aircraft became high and the momentum fell away. But a lone aircraft plunged on the City on 24 August in the form of the new high altitude Junkers JU 86 bomber; its bomb fell on buses and cars killing 45 people and wounding the same number. This became an isolated German success as the Junkers were not seen again once a further sortie was intercepted in September by a specially modified high altitude Spitfire.

Whilst undoubtedly the experience of bombing must have been pretty terrifying for all concerned, it needs to be remembered that outside of London, few cities received the treatment meted out to German towns. The most recent German estimate for the death toll in Dresden was 18,000 victims (a major reduction from the numbers once banded about in the 1960s). On 13 February 1945 the RAF dropped more bombs and incendiaries in one night on Dresden than had fallen on Bristol for the length of the war (1,400 tons of high explosives and 1,200 tons of incendiaries). 50,000 people died in Hamburg from various raids. The RAF attack on the night of 28 March 1942 on Lubeck was one of the first to take place under the area bombing strategy designed to take the war to the German civilian population. It created a firestorm that caused severe damage to the historic centre, the bombs destroying three of the main churches and large parts of the built-up area. The German police reported 301 people dead, 3 people missing, and 783 injured. More than 15,000 people lost their homes.. Although a port, Lübeck was mainly a cultural centre and only

A Long Way from Tipperary

lightly defended. Arthur Harris Commanding Bomber Command, described Lubeck as "built more like a fire-lighter than a human habitation."

The attack on Lubeck later came unexpectedly close to home for the Murphys when William's son Terry married Olga after the war, as she came from Lubeck and the fate of the two cities had the potential to be an inflammatory issue. Olga once said to me rather forcefully when I was a small boy that in Germany civilians had suffered too and that there was no military justification for the flattening of her home town. I was steeped at the time in the notion that the loss of so many churches in Bristol could not have been accidental, being wholly ignorant of the lack of precision in operations by both sides. No doubt the children's comics of the time had a rather less than nuanced view of Germany perfidy. William however was a singularly fair man and remarkably unprejudiced. He never let the fact that he and Olga's father could well have spent their time at the front shooting at each other in the First World War bother him in the slightest. Alice was more ambivalent.

The last raid on Bristol was on 15 May 1944. 91 aircraft set out from France that night but the night fighter defence was now formidable and 13 failed to return; only 5 bombs fell anywhere near the City boundary. The City was in danger of being hit by V-1 flying bombs, and by the V2 rockets, whose launching platforms already had been built on the Cotentin peninsula in Normandy in 1944; but D-Day on 6 June 1944 put an end to this danger. The platforms were quickly overrun by the Allies, so Bristol was safe from the V1 and V2. In total Bristol received 548 air raid alerts and 77 air raids being hit by 1,237 tons of

A Long Way from Tipperary

high-explosive and oil bombs and 248 tons of incendiaries. 1378 people were killed and 3,240 injured as well as 697 rescued from debris. 89,080 buildings were damaged, including 81,830 houses destroyed and over 3000 later demolished. The casualties in Bristol were almost exactly the same as those in Coventry, whose fate is better known.

A Long Way from Tipperary

Chapter 14.

Looking on the Bright Side

Alice and William did not let the small matter of war dismay them. They remained keen dancers although Alice often went dancing alone with her girlfriends at the church halls of St Agnes, St Saviours and St Mathews where small bands played, with occasional excursions further afield. William often turned up late from work for the last few dances. They went frequently to their favourite pubs as always. William particularly liked the Kings Arms on Lawrence Hill which is the oldest building in the road dating back to the 18th century. But the Forge and Hammer and the Packhorse (founded in 1787) all on Church Road, also had their moments. The Glasshouse was favoured by Terry and Graham when they were older.. At the end of Jane Street and less than 80 yards from our front door was the Globe Cinema which was built in 1915 and owned by Joseph Pugsley

The Globe contained 1,200 seats and had an ever changing double bill of films which provided a ready means of escape. I remember that whatever the weather, the long roofed arcade on the Jane street side of the building provided shelter for queues of patient people as they waited in the rain to get in. After the war, we used to brandish a few pennies and ask to be "taken in" if the film had a PG type rating and needed children to be accompanied. I always found pitching couples a good wheeze as the men rarely wanted to be seen by their girlfriends as mean spirited. A more desperate measure was to wait until people banged out of the exits in the course of the show (as the

A Long Way from Tipperary

The Globe Looking towards No 47

programme was continuous, and the cinema was not cleared between films, customers would often go in part way and then stay until they had seen everything). The trick then was to grab the door before it closed and slip in behind the curtains that closed off each exit. And then - not immediately – slide into the cinema and take a seat. We were rarely caught as the lavatories were near the exits and it was always possible to claim that we had just come from there. This manoeuvre worked best in winter when it fell dark outside early.

Later when Alice died, Paddie who was 17 years old and who was working in the Maypole, concluded that as I was only 9 and William was working, she needed work that gave her more During the 9 months that she worked there, Paddie did everything from selling tickets, to showing people to their seats and selling ice cream in the intervals. The latter role was jealously regarded by the Chief Usherette (there were 6) who

A Long Way from Tipperary

relished her moment in the spotlight at the front of the cinema crowd, holding her ice cream and cigarettes tray in front of her and giving to the audience her best "Betty Grable" impression. (Grable was the wise cracking Hollywood start of the moment) When she was not around, the others took a turn. Cinemas in those days were often pretty full as alternative entertainment was sparse on the ground and for a good film, customers would queue not just up the side of the building under the arcade but also in tight circles inside the foyer. Paddie remembers being on the till early on in the job, merrily selling tickets until the message came that she should stop as all the seats had gone and customers were lining up at the back, standing up!

The Manager of the Globe was a rather porcine individual who was having an affair with the chief usherette. He was cordially loathed by the other staff. The Relief Managers had "wandering hands" but the doorman was an ex Great War veteran who warned Paddie to keep the office door open when she handed in the takings to the Manager and who was kind enough to stand outside of the office to intervene if he misbehaved. On Saturday nights and on special occasions when a new big film was being launched (Gone with the Wind, for example), the Manager would wear a dress suit and bow tie, whilst striding about the foyer as if he was greeting his customers at the Ritz. The Globe and the Granada further up Church road were also owned by the Pugsley family whose principal business was the Boiler Makers in Russell Town Avenue and the scrap yard alongside Cattybrook Street which was my playground. Their engineering business also used offices just up from Max Williams, the toy shop on Lawrence Hill. It was clearly a lucrative activity as Joseph Pugsley had a chauffeur driven car

A Long Way from Tipperary

in which the driver wore a full uniform, cap, boots and gaiters. The car was garaged at the end of our block of houses in Cattybrook Street, turning the corner towards the cinema.

The cinema was often visited by predatory males; two in particular always bought the best two shillings and sixpence tickets which were intended to be used in the Balcony but which gave access to all parts of the cinema. They would move about the auditorium looking for females on their own, would slide themselves alongside, and then try to feel up their victims in the dark. The usherettes in turn would try and track their movements and then shine a light on them from the aisles, telling them loudly to " cut it out", although as they kept coming back to the cinema, this would not appear to have been very effective.

The usherettes had responsibility to ensure that the behaviour of "courting "couples did not get out of hand. The cinema was probably the only place at the time in an impoverished community with high density living where some measure of privacy was obtainable. In summer of course, the parks and the greensward of Troopers Hill or the riverside meadows at Hanham Weir on the Avon offered alternatives. Couples were no doubt grateful for continuous programming whereby the cinema was not emptied after each showing; this enabled them to stay in the warm for a double bill rather than be kicked out into the rain and cold after two hours.

The radio was an important source of entertainment during the war and many of the programmes continued afterwards into the late forties and fifties, such as "Music While You Work" and "Workers Playtime". ITMA ("Its That Man Again") featuring the

A Long Way from Tipperary

comedian Tommy Handley and his team who had an audience of 16 million."War Report" was heard every night after the news and was immensely popular. Military Bands played regularly on the Downs and in the Parks which also provided venues for circuses and carnivals. Dancing was not just an evening activity- there were lunchtime dances on College Green in the heart of the city with music supplied by dance melody vans.

The family were strong supporters of Bristol Rovers which was the team of choice for those living in the East of the city. The rivalry was as strong and bitter between the supporters of the Rovers and Bristol City at Ashton Gate as anything one might encounter today in Manchester. Both Will and Alice went to the stadium to stand on the uncovered terraces in the bitter wind which I remember well from the early fifties as there were holes in the fencing which made it very easy for small boys to get in without paying. People were oblivious to the strong smell of town gas that emerged from the nearby gasworks. But this gave rise to the nickname given to Bristol Rovers supporters of "Gasheads". "The Gas" was originally coined as a derogatory term by the supporters of rivals Bristol City. The Club song was "Irene Good Night" usually sung to a defeated opponent to speed them on their way home.

The highlight of my support was a famous FA match between Rovers and Manchester United. This was perhaps the most impressive win in the history of Bristol Rovers with a 4 – 0 FA Cup victory over Manchester United, managed by Matt Busby, on 7 January 1956. Five of the United players on that day were later to die in the Munich air disaster. In the same competition during the 1957–58 season Rovers reached the quarter-final for

A Long Way from Tipperary

the second time, where they lost 3-1 to Fulham at Craven Cottage. In the next year in front of a crowd of 35,000 at Eastville, Rovers put City out of the 5th Round of the FA Cup with a thrilling 4-3 win.

Football was very much part of the culture of Easton. Cattybrook Street was en route to the stadium for a lot of the crowd and on Saturdays, the street reverberated to the sound

The Rovers Ground at Eastville

of the feet of thousands of people walking to Eastville with a buzz of anticipation in their voices, broken by the exuberant sound of a wooden football rattle. After the match, the return crowd could be either boisterous or subdued, depending on the result. You knew the outcome without going on to the street.

A Long Way from Tipperary

The Rovers played in blue and white quartered shirts which seemed to be as stiff as canvas, white shorts and enormous boots by today's standards and used heavy leather balls made in "T" panels. The key players were a roll call of West Country names, Geoff Bradford, Harry Bamford, Ray Warren and George Petherbridge. The only "Foreigner" in the team was Herbert (Bert) Hoyle who came from Yorkshire. He joined in 1953 for a transfer fee of £350 and he became a favourite at Eastville Stadium thanks to his outgoing personality. He became known for chatting with the fans behind the goal before, during and after matches, and after revealing a fondness for oranges (he always placed one in the back of the net as a lucky charm) he was inundated with gifts of the fruit at every home game, usually thrown by the spectators behind the goal. He wore the kind of heavy green pullover that would have weighed a ton after a shower of rain. Hoyle played in an era when many footballers had to take second jobs during the summer, and he worked on local farms during the close-season throughout his career. He died in Dawlish on 6 July 2003, aged 83.

The summer highlights of the pre war period were day trips to the south coast to places like Paignton, Teignmouth, Seaton and Sidmouth which were curtailed during the war; but the old Bristol to Bournemouth line via Bath which no longer exists, must have offered great excitement, particularly if William's employment with the GWR reduced the cost of the tickets. More affordable holiday destinations were Severn Beach which was a short trip down the line from Lawrence Hill to the Severn and to Weston Super Mare. The former was a rather tawdry place which had a fairground next to the station, a large holiday camp

A Long Way from Tipperary

of wooden chalets and a swimming pool filled by the muddy waters of the Severn which was the scene of drowning every season as the water was so opaque that people in difficulty could not be seen once they had gone under. Weston was favoured by the various churches for their annual day excursions but you were fortunate to see the sea and the Lido was deep and too dangerous for anything but accomplished swimmers. But riding the donkeys was great fun. A more exotic pleasure was to take the paddle steamer that plied its trade between the City Docks and Ilfracombe, but this trip was suspended "for the duration" of the war. The Bristol Channel approaches had been dangerous because of German submarines in both wars, notoriously sinking two marked hospital ships (then against established war time convention) in 1914-18.

The Boys Brigade Band in Cattybrook Street

A Long Way from Tipperary

The most disastrous family holiday I can recall was when we went to Highcliffe on Sea not long after the war. We took rooms with a family whose personal hygiene left a lot to be desired and after suffering innumerable bites from bedbugs, retreated to Bristol after a couple of days. I loved the seaside although the water always seemed very cold; my most mortifying moment was when I was about 7 and could not swim – I was paddling on a pebbly beach in my clothes and fell into a receding tide that was about to take me to France before William realised what was happening. He dashed down the beach, plunged into the sea fully clothed and brought me up from under the waves by the collar. His and my clothes had to be dried off in a hotel kitchen and I felt embarrassed to be partly clad in the charabanc on the way home.

The war had little impact on another feature of working class life in Bristol, which was the brass band. The Salvation Army band was a frequent visitor to Cattybrook Street and used a full array of impressive instruments. The most declamatory were the Tubas and the Big Drum that always had ornate Christian paint work around the rim. They used to march down the street past the house and then form an incongruous circle outside of the Victorian cast iron urinal that was tucked away at the end of the road close to the entry to the scrap yard. It must have been quite disturbing to find your self using the urinal at the moment that a blast of "Jesus Saves" music went up into the atmosphere - the psychological damage would have been immense!

The street was also visited by the Boys Brigade Brass band that was usually less polished than the Salvationists. Later I was

A Long Way from Tipperary

proud to be a "Life boy" aspiring to be in the Brigade, so I took particular interest in its repertoire whilst recognising that it was more limited than the competition. However their shoes were cleaner as the prevailing ethos of the Brigade equated godliness with cleanliness. The annoying aspect of both bands is that they moved around the neighbourhood to various sites in the streets around and behind us, so were in earshot for hours. As if this were not enough to upset a working man trying to have a Sunday nap, we had the Dean Lane City Mission immediately behind us where the Reverend Shrubshall gave (loud) voice with his flock to the Christian message. Never had the fallen sung so well or so loud…… Music was not limited however to the missionary zeal of the brass bands; St Georges Park our local green space , which lost all of its fine ornate rails for scrap as a contribution to the war effort, had a marvellous Band Stand that was in frequent use by the Army to more stirring effect.

Dean Lane Mission

The Dean Lane City Mission. This was halfway along the present day Russell Town Avenue. Bristol City Mission Society was founded in 1826 to communicate religious knowledge to the poorer areas of the city. By 1900, this red brick structure had been built in Moorfields. Soon afterwards Arthur Shrubsall became the preacher/pastor, a well known figure in Moorfields. He dominated the Mission's work for over fifty years. The City Mission building in Russell Town Avenue was acquired for demolition in 1962.

A Long Way from Tipperary

William left the railway in the middle of the war to become a cellar man at the Mauretania Hotel; he was entering his 50's and it could be that track construction was just becoming too much of a physical challenge. It is clear from some of our photographs that he had worked bars when he was much younger, possibly at Territorial Army summer camps so he was no stranger to the trade. The Mauretania on Park Street was built in 1870 by Henry Masters some of the furnishings from the RMS Mauretania were installed there. The lounge bar was the ship's library with mahogany panelling: above was a first-class Grand Saloon with French-style gilding. RMS Mauretania (also known as the "Maury") was an ocean liner launched on 20 September 1906. At the time, she was the largest and fastest ship in the world. She held the Atlantic speed record for twenty-two years. William would of course have been working alongside Terry who was taking his apprenticeship in the hotel's kitchens. There were few good hotels in Bristol so stories came back to Cattybrook Street of the celebrities that stayed at the Mauretania. It also became a haunt of the US Military once the United States entered the war in late 1941 and for scenes of licentiousness in the street on VE day when all sexual inhibition was temporarily lost.

William was witness to one of the more unpleasant incidents involving US forces in Bristol where both black and white forces were stationed. British attitudes to blacks at this point were far more enlightened than was the case in the US where levels of anti-black discrimination were intense. Bristol people had a ready acceptance of US black servicemen but this toleration was not understood by white American GIs. In July 1944 troubles between black and white troops in the Bristol area had

A Long Way from Tipperary

been simmering for a long time. Part of the problem was that the organization of the leave areas was complex, and seen by many blacks as discriminatory. In addition Bristol was one of those areas where racist white Americans were busiest, and blacks were driven to using the least desirable pubs. The big explosion came on Saturday 15 July when a black aviation truck battalion was joined at their base, the Müller Orphanage camp, on 10 July by white paratrooper replacements. The blacks claimed that two of their men were beaten up without provocation. This was followed by several incidents involving blacks and whites in Bristol over the next few days. As usual the cause of the problem was not difficult to find: the white paratroopers resented the easy relations that had developed between the white British girls in the town and the black soldiers.

On Thursday 13 July, the discontent spread. Men from the 545th Port Company, based at Sea Mills Camp, tough city blacks mainly from Detroit and New York, mutinied by staying in their billets and refusing to turn out for reveille even when the Articles of War were read to them. The eruption finally occurred on 15 July around Park and Great George Streets, just next to the Mauretania. A large number of black GIs had gathered there on that Saturday evening and brawling had broken out. Extra MPs were drafted in and some calm was restored. The black troops were then marched off to the Tram Centre where trucks were to take them back to their camps. This procedure in itself must have been an awesome sight for the onlooker. Both streets slope quite steeply and the 'march' down to the Centre about a quarter of a mile away may well have induced some panic in the GIs. Bullying by MPs did not help and the result

A Long Way from Tipperary

was, a 'mob spirit' which broke into a riot and shooting at the City centre. The disturbance involved 400 black and white troops and it took 120 military policemen and many arrests to bring the situation back under control. One black GI was killed and dozens wounded. Bristol remained under military curfew for several days.

US military law always came down harder on black troops. Rape was a hanging matter (it had not been so in Britain since the mid 19th century) and a wholly disproportionate number of black Americans featured amongst the 26 soldiers of all nationalities hanged at the Prison at Shepton Mallet in Somerset for this offence during the war. Under the provisions of the United States of America (Visiting Forces) Act 1942, a total of eighteen American servicemen were executed within the prison walls. Sixteen were hanged in the execution block and two were shot by firing squad in the prison yard. Three of the hangings were double executions i.e. both condemned prisoners stood together on the gallows and were executed simultaneously when the trap-door opened. Of the 18 men executed, nine were convicted of murder, six of rape and three of both crimes. Although the American army was 90% white, 10 of the 18 men hanged there were black and three were Hispanic.

Notwithstanding their non-married status, and Alice's own Protestant faith, the couple decided to bring up their children as Catholics – this was a commitment to which Alice strongly adhered. So it was Mass on Sunday for the kids whether they liked it or not. The house in those days was regularly visited by priests and by Nuns from the local Convent wearing their

A Long Way from Tipperary

massive wimples which floated in the air like the top gallant sails of a windjammer. William respected the Church but he was not overawed by its servants, but the family came to have good relations with an outstanding Parish Priest for Moorfields called Father Dillon who founded St. Patrick's Parish in 1923 when he was based at St. Nicholas' Church, Lawford's Gate. There was no house or church then - and only six parishioners initially! Father Dillon lived with parishioners until a presbytery house was purchased on Blackswarth Road.

It was a proud day when the new church was opened in 1923. It cost £14,000. Father Dillon became a prominent public figure and was honoured by both his adopted city, where he was elected on to the Education Committee and by the Church - he became both a Monsignor and a Canon. He never moved from St. Patrick's and remained parish priest for 32 years until his death in 1955. His funeral was one of the largest ever seen in Bristol. The police lined the streets from the City Centre to Avon view Cemetery and over 100 cars followed the Hearse. In 1933 a School was founded also by the Canon at a cost of £40,000 paid for entirely by donations and the fund raising efforts of the parish - at the time of the great depression. Originally the school was for children aged five to 14 years of age and at its peak over 500 pupils attended it. When the secondary modern and later comprehensive school system was introduced for

A Long Way from Tipperary

pupils over the age of 11, St Patrick's became an infant and primary school for a roll of 240 pupils.

Dillon was an immensely popular man with a gift for dealing with people; Will and Alice liked him a lot. He called frequently and was a man who liked a drop to drink; he did not seem bothered that William was neither a regular churchgoer himself nor communicant. Whether or not he knew their secret, he was regarded as a tolerant person and this went also for his curate, Father Carol, a giant bear of a man who had the broken nose of an ex boxer. I remember having to take catechism classes with Farther Carol in order to get up to speed for going to my secondary school, St Brendan's. He was always extraordinary generous – on one occasion, seeing me eyeing hungrily a banana during lessons, he gave me a whole hand to take home. Bananas were exotic fruits in 1953, especially for us.

It was assumed that the children would marry in the Catholic Church, an assumption that was challenged by Eddie when he announced in 1944 that he was going to get married, without taking the precaution beforehand of introducing his wife - to - be to his parents. He also said that they would not be marrying in the Church. The response was clear; he was underage (21 was the age of majority at this time and Eddie was only 19) and required parental approval to marry. Moreover, William and Alice made it clear that his side of the aisle would be empty unless they married in a Catholic Church, preferably St Patricks. He wisely capitulated but not with good grace; Paddie was not invited to accompany Doreen, Connie's sister as bridesmaid, which seems unkind today.

A Long Way from Tipperary

The position adopted by Will and Alice was somewhat hypocritical now that we know that they married secretly in October 1943 in a registry office, not in the Church and in Catholic terms, had been "living in sin" for 20 years. I am not sure that the outcome did much Eddie's regard for Catholicism! It is certain that the hardliner over the issue was Alice who was not even a Catholic at this point. She only joined the Church on

Eddie - Reluctantly at St Patrick's Church

her deathbed so that she could be buried in Catholic ground with William when his turn arrived. After her death, William fell out with the Church, kicking a rather obnoxious Catholic priest from Northern Ireland out of No 47 because of his anti – British attitudes. The priest wrongly assumed that William would share his view of British oppression in Ireland and alleged Army

A Long Way from Tipperary

atrocities during "The Troubles". A new Concordat was eventually achieved after the priest moved on.

Alice had a particularly difficult relationship with Eddie; they loved each other, but disliked each other at the same time. Eddie was unbelievably aggressive as a young man, always picking fights with people and losing his temper. On one occasion, he got angry with Alice over some trivial matter and happened to have in his hand some extra meat beyond the ration that he had been given by Alice through Graham's job at Thornes, the butchers. He promptly threw this meat in rage straight at the closed kitchen window, cracking the glass. Eddie was feared at school right from a tender age because he was frightened of no one and was always ready for a fight. Terry who was one year ten months younger, benefitted from this protection at school but said many times in later life that he was often bullied by his older brother. The tender photograph that we have of the pair at school speaks better than words. It is interesting however that whatever the travails that divided the two brothers for some of their adult years, they came together in a much warmer relationship later in their lives.

Eddie had a more uncomplicated relationship with Will – he loved his father and spoke often of his sense of loss after William died in 1965. He was never heard to speak of Alice in similar terms. We can only speculate, but Eddie must have resented the fact that Alice's affection for Terry was transparent and that he was the favourite one among the five. This was probably because Terry was very much like William - very openly warm and a bit of a softie at heart. Both boys had some nasty childhood experiences; Eddie had the accident with the

A Long Way from Tipperary

bus and Terry fell from Lawrence Hill Railway Bridge and split open his head. Granma took him all the way on foot to the Bristol Royal Infirmary to have his scalp stitched back again. But in all these tales of scrapes and woes, Eddie gives the impression of being pretty indomitable and hard Terry's distress was more expected and normal.

When I was about 10, I managed to pour a kettle of freshly boiled water on my ankle whilst making tea at no 47. After a trip to the BRI, it looked like I might need a skin graft because the

A Long Way from Tipperary

damage was serious. As the skin repaired itself, it was essential to keep the joint moving , whatever the pain and Eddie was quite relentless in keeping me at it. He was right of course but it did not make him lovable! Underneath however, Eddie was very much like William, given greatly to emotion but perhaps perceiving it as a weakness. He had a big heart but concealed it pretty well until he was much older. Eddie was a bundle of contradictions; on the outside, he was very hardboiled but he studied French with the WEA, attended Ruskin College Oxford on a WEA programme and towards the end of his life was fascinated by ballet, taking Connie to London to see one of the last performances of Rudolf Nureyev in "L'Apres Midi d'un Faune. He could appear prejudiced but admired James Baldwin the black gay writer of the sixties – he was a complex man.

Alice managed the family finances and was very good at it – she was resolute in not falling into debt; but times were often hard. Granma Alice had resorted frequently to the pawn shop when she was bringing up her family, but not Alice. Clearly the railway allotment was helpful and we kept chickens in the back garden which stretched the budget but even with several wages coming in, it was a challenge to manage. On one occasion, in about 1945, she served Sunday lunch without any meat, just vegetables, as clearly there was no money for anything else. When the family reacted with disappointment, Alice broke down and wept. She was a proud woman and must have felt keenly our relative poverty. But the family tended to be mutually emotionally supportive. William and Alice were very tactile; the whole family would kiss Alice on leaving and returning to the house. When they were out, the pair always walked arm in arm.

A Long Way from Tipperary

At Christmas time, the principal meal was chicken and Uncle Arthur came over to despatch the chosen bird as my father was rather squeamish about ringing its neck. The curtains were closed so that the ghastly deed could not be seen in the yard by the family. But on one occasion, Arthur rather scuppered the subterfuge by using a chopper instead of ringing the bird's neck and reported loudly afterwards that the headless chicken had run around the yard for a while before expiring. This was rather an upsetting Christmas for me because I had been given a grey kitten as a present which played under the table during dinner - sadly, my mother moved her chair back suddenly and broke it's back. I was inconsolable – well, until the replacement arrived.

Tobacco was expensive during the war and in the immediate post war period and so I was grateful to Arthur for the small fee that he gave me for collecting cigarette stubs for him in a small tin. He then mixed up the middle part of the discarded stub with fresh tobacco and rolled out new cigarettes with a Rizla machine. With the benefit of hindsight, the carcinogenic let alone bacterial downside of this practice must have been lethal (although he lived into his 80s) and no sooner had I begun to become accustomed to my new source of income than Alice put a stop to it.

We had a gas supply to the kitchen but all of the heating was through open coal fires. As there was no space in the back yard, this meant frequent visits from the coalman who loaded up his cart at the yard at Lawrence Hill station. His horse was often given a carrot and rather expected it, such that when the coalman was carrying the sack of coal through the house into

A Long Way from Tipperary

Arthur- Middle of the Middle Row

the backyard, the horse would inevitably follow, shoving his great big head and bushy, iron clad feet into the passageway to great excitement. This inevitably dragged the cart onto the pavement and lead to high irritation by the coalman, particularly if this caused a bag to fall off and burst..... The horse was always watched rather closely as it came down the street, in the hope that it would decide to defecate; horse dung was highly prized for the garden and housewives would be out with a shovel and bucket, loading up almost before the stuff hit the ground. But there was etiquette to this – it was considered bad form to pinch dung that had fallen outside of someone else's house although I am sure that this lead to demarcation disputes.

Straightened circumstances caused Alice and William to fall prey to temptation during the war through a scheme brought about by Uncle Charlie. He was working at St Anne's Board

A Long Way from Tipperary

Mills on the River which pulped paper. I loved Uncle Charlie but he was a rather dodgy character. He was married and eventually had three children, Michael, Margaret and Carol. He was an inveterate gambler and would lay money on anything as well as being willing to back himself at darts and snooker or billiards; he achieved near professional standards on the tables and gave his opponents odds to make it more interesting. "Hustler" would be an appropriate word to describe him today. I believe that his track record on the race track and with the greyhounds was less impressive. In between gambling, he worked at the Board Mills – he had terrible lungs so he was unfit for military service (he eventually died young of pleurisy which was not surprising because he refused to wear a top coat, whatever the weather).

He noticed one day at work whilst cleaning a perforated drum that was used to mulch ration stamps that a large number of these had fallen behind the machinery and had not therefore been destroyed. As everything, food, clothing, petrol was rationed by this time, these coupons had real value on the black market. So Uncle Charlie brought them back to no 47 where they were ironed dry by his sister Alice so that he could dispose of them through

A Long Way from Tipperary

his contacts. There is no indication how long this little earner went on, but at some point the existence of the loophole was discovered and it was closed. Charlie's exploitation of the situation was never disclosed – if it had been, he would probably have gone to goal for black marketeering and Alice and Will would have been in the soup also.

William and Alice in Park Street

A Long Way from Tipperary

This is an interesting photograph which could have been taken by a street photographer on the day in October 1943 when they married in the Bristol Registry Office but it may be later.

Alice was a very attractive woman as can be seen from all of the photographs of her. Even though the family were poor, she had flair for clothes from a young age and was always able to add an item to her dress that gave it a touch of distinction. I have a pair of earrings belonging to Alice that are really stylish, even though the "diamonds" are simple glass. She was quite a slim young woman in her earlier years but obviously lost that svelte line as a consequence of having children. Her weight appears to have swung wildly; it looks from the picture of her on the beach with the three boys as young children that she had become almost stout by the mid '30s but by the time I was born in 1943, she was significantly underweight, gaunt even as can be seen by the poor photograph with me sitting on her knee in the back garden. She gained weight again of course and the photograph of her and William at the bottom of Park Street towards the end of her life shows that she was in good shape again. William obviously liked to give her good things; in one photograph she is wearing a simple mother of pearl broach at her throat; he also gave her a watch with an elasticised bracelet that was given an outing on special occasions.

A Long Way from Tipperary

Chapter 15.

Death and Bereavement.

It is doubtful whether after having lost two infants, Alice really wanted another when I arrived in 1943. I was very underweight and my Grandmother (who died herself 6 months later) assured Alice that I would not survive "You'll never save him Alice!" It could not have been easy having another mouth to feed at the end of the war and she was probably permanently tired. My early infant memories of being cherished owe more to the warmth I felt from Paddie and my brothers (especially Graham) than Alice.

My recollections are that Alice was permanently stressed which was a lethal condition in an age when the only "treatment" for high blood pressure was "rest" – there was no medication for her illness. It was of course impossible for a woman in Alice's position to rest and having a lively toddler and then little tearaway did not help. I was full of little tricks like hiding behind the coats hanging in the hallway, waiting until she passed into the scullery and then jumping out at her. On one notorious Christmas occasion, when I was about 7, I offered her a chair at the table and then pulled it out of the way so that she sat on the floor (too much matinee cinema!) When I was arrested by the Police hiding in the scrap yard after firing stones with my catapult at the boilers of the steam trains in Lawrence Hill Station and then attempting to escape, a life of juvenile crime might well have been predicted for me. It was more embarrassing to be frog marched down the street to no 47 by the Police in front of all of the neighbours standing on their

A Long Way from Tipperary

doorsteps than to be whacked by Mum. But she was quite a whacker. Paddie who had good connections with the law, sweet - talked the police into making sure that my "crime" was not reported to the station.

On another occasion (I must have been around 9) I went to Weston Super Mare with a bunch of kids for a Sunday school outing on the train, taking with me a length of clothes line that I intended to use to climb some rocks. I was accompanied by my cousin Clive with whom I had a close but taciturn relationship – Clive was a quiet boy.

Alice , Ada, Clive and Ralph

There must have been next to no supervision as I managed to take my small gang off to some low cliffs which we scrambled up with Clive hanging on to the end of the rope. Regrettably, just short of safety, the rope broke and Clive rolled to the bottom of the cliff, promptly concussing himself and ending up in hospital for observation. I reported back events to my mother when we got

A Long Way from Tipperary

home with some trepidation and was told to hurry around to Eve Street tell the bad news to Aunt Ada. Poor Ada became hysterical with fear over the fate of her only child and rushed down to Weston to the hospital. Fortunately Clive had come to no permanent harm.

<u>Cattybrook Street – The Excitement of a Bus Diversion</u>.

As far as William was concerned, I had no doubt that I was the apple of his eye. When he started to work as a labourer in the tobacco factory at WD and HO Wills in Bedminster, I used to wait impatiently at the front door for his return at night, watching for him to emerge at the head of the street, flat cap on his head and gas mask bag (in which he took his lunch) over his shoulder before running up the street to meet him. When he sat down for his dinner at the table, I would invariably sit alongside of him. Although I had already had my tea, he would feed me from his plate (which may explain the somewhat chubby boy

A Long Way from Tipperary

who appears in images of the time) to the background warning from Alice, "Will, you are going to spoil that boy!". When I was not eating my meals on my own with the plate on my knees in the stairs, I was in the street, on the wall, in the scrap yard or in a hideaway under the ticket office at Lawrence Hill station that dropped straight down onto the track. I liked to put pennies on the rails to have them flattened by trains. My other favourite haunts were the lily ponds beyond the "Beat 'em and Whack 'em" Pub at Speedwell which was a marshy area of wet ground near the Peckitts engine works that was full of frogs. The "Brillos", an area of derelict ground alongside the river that was a spoil heap from the ICI chemical works, was also an adventure ground for the bike. So, I was not the easiest of children. I attribute this to the need to correct the image conveyed by the embarrassing studio photographs of me as a child with girly hair looking like a Pears soap advert.

Graham in the RASC

A Long Way from Tipperary

Graham was a tremendous presence in my childhood before he was called up to do his National Service. He was always full of life and seemed too large to fit into the small house that was no 47; he loved to sing and joke and throw me up in the air as well as ride me about in his butchers basket on his bike, whether or not the basket contained sausages or joints of meat that he was delivering somewhere! He was also one of the helpful hands at the ready when I learned to ride on two wheels. He seemed to have had a personality transplant in his early teens as he had been a bit of a misery when he was little. There was no angst however around Graham. He was finally called up to do his National Service in 1951 when he joined the Royal Army Service Corps and was taught to drive heavy vehicles. Most of his time was spent in East Anglia where he had a bad accident

Gray, Paddie and Terry

Eddie and Christopher

A Long Way from Tipperary

with another army vehicle for which he was punished by spending several weeks in the "Glasshouse" at Colchester – it was a pretty dreadful experience as Army prisons were notoriously punitive in their approach. He then met Olga from Lubeck who was working for an Army family in Thetford and eventually brought her back to meet the family in late 1951 shortly after which they became engaged. I believe that she was greeted by polite acceptance but by this time, Alice's health had become a major preoccupation. Alice suffered from high blood pressure all of her life. The first stroke was just after the war in about 1947 during a visit to "Cousin Edna" (the granddaughter of Great Aunt Eva, who was not of course related to us at all). Eva was married at that time to a Chef on the Great Western Railway and the two couples were great friends. Paddie and Alice had gone to see Variety Bandbox in Hammersmith and got lost. Paddie (who was 12) was not

Bournemouth ;Eddie, Mrs Towson, Alice and Graham

A Long Way from Tipperary

worried as they only had to get to Earls Court. The next day Alice had a blinding headache which the family GP, Dr Evans later diagnosed as a minor stroke. She became a bit more fragile. In 1951 Alice went into the General Hospital for major surgery for a prolapsed womb. She could only be given a small amount of anaesthetic because of her high blood pressure and she became conscious halfway through the operation (which continued). Afterwards, the surgeon told Paddie that Alice was on of the bravest women he had ever met – she certainly had a very high threshold for pain. William was worried and distraught.

After her surgery in 1951, Alice went to Branksome, near Bournemouth, for convalescence. Coach seats were booked on a coach for me and Paddie to go down and see her but when the coach failed to arrive at Lawrence Hill, the coach company gave us a chauffeur driven car, taking us down in high style. We spent a lot of time waving at people as if we were royalty. The photograph that we have for that visit are amongst the last we have of Alice. She looks much older than

A Long Way from Tipperary

her years and the fatigue can be clearly seen. Alice made a friend of a lady called Mrs Towson, who is in the photograph and also of another lady whose subsequent death from cancer at the General Hospital in 1952 upset Alice a great deal. After her convalescence, she continued to visit the General Hospital at intervals for examination. On her way back one day from a visit to the General Hospital, Alice called on Paddie who was working at the Maypole in Clarence Road, to say she was not feeling well. Paddie took her back to number 47 by taxi where she had a seizure. This was the beginning of her final decline.

Alice was visited by her GP Dr John Evans who in the absence of paralysis, called in a specialist, who confirmed the diagnosis of a major stroke. She was sent to the BRI where she stayed for 10 days; I recall that she was in a bed in a ward on the third or fourth floor facing the door. It was jam packed with people who were seriously ill or dying. Alice witnessed the slow death of a woman in an adjoining bed. This probably contributed to stress and to a brain haemorrhage which lead first to paralysis of her hands and feet and then her death. Paddie was in the ward when this occurred; Alice started to throw off her bed clothes and this signalled a major intervention to save her which failed.

Paddie sent her friend Jean Walsh to get William by taxi but Alice was dead by the time that he got there. I remember going to the hospital earlier and saying goodbye to Alice at some point; she had high colour and was conscious but woozy. I had the definite sense that this was going to be for the last time as the family knew that her chances were not good. She looked unwell but had a bloom on her face which gave her an

A Long Way from Tipperary

unnatural appearance of vitality. I took her loss hard but seeing William's distress was even harder.

Alice was laid out as was traditional with the coffin open at No 47 before she was taken to be buried in the Catholic plot at Avonview, there to wait for William who would have another 13 years to live. I was kept away at Auntie Ivy's house (the wife of Uncle Charlie) and did not attend the funeral. The partnership of Alice and William was over with Alice's death at the shockingly young age of 49.

Boring Bournemouth

William was devastated by Alice's death, almost unmanned. I went with him on holiday to a boarding house in Bournemouth

A Long Way from Tipperary

that summer accompanied by Paddie and her friend Betty. The boarding house was quite smart, its rear backing out on to a ribbon of garden that went right through the town and which contained a deep cut stream which was great for playing. But Bournemouth was quite sedate and frankly boring. The owners of the boarding house were very pretentious and got upset when they caught me sliding down their banister. The house speciality was thin vegetable soup and silence was expected in the dining room. There is immense pathos in a contemporary photograph of William, embracing his grief, dressed in a tidy suit and trying to sleep in a deckchair. We were all relieved to get back to Bristol.

William was now working at Parnall's as a uniformed security guard. He worked three shifts and apart from manning the gate during business hours, had to walk around the factory after close down, clocking in at various points. At night he was accompanied by a very docile Alsatian dog called Linda. He often walked to work (carrying a small attaché case for his sandwiches) which

A Long Way from Tipperary

was quite a way as the factory was in Fishponds and we were still living at 47 Cattybrook Street. I liked visiting him in his gatehouse where we would make toast over an electric fire, toasting one side only and buttering the other side. I sometimes walked with him to work. . Conversation was pretty limited as William's natural taciturnity seemed to have deepened with the death of Alice. He did not seem to have any mates with whom to share his grief, I doubt that he knew how to do so.

Terry on finishing his National service in 1946/47 had decided to take his career off shore by joining the Merchant Navy where over the next 6 or 7 years, he worked as a chef on the P and O passenger line on such ships as the Orion and the Orcades (the company operated a fleet of ships to the Far

Terry in the Merchant Navy

A Long Way from Tipperary

East each one beginning with "O"). But he also worked on tankers, general cargo vessels and tramp ships that plied their trade from port to port and cargo to cargo. There is a great photograph of him with a villainous crew in Palermo, Sicily. For a spell during the Korean war he served on a hospital ship. Terry was a romantic figure to me, full of tales of the Orient and adventures in foreign ports and this suggestion of the exotic was appealing both to the family and to the " girls in the 'hood."

When he first returned from sea, he always bought presents for everybody, gave lots of housekeeping money to Alice and stood rounds of drinks in the pubs. When the money ran out, and a loan taken out against the housekeeping for the next trip home, he left for sea again. It is impossible to overestimate the appeal of the seafarer – or the excitement of being given your first pair of roller skates with real ball bearings. Terry remained Alice's favourite until the day that she died.

A major rift threatened however when Olga was introduced to Terry by Graham and the two promptly fell in love with each other. Ironically, Graham had asked Terry to look after Olga when he went back to barracks, so the relationship acquired an almost Shakespearean quality. Olga first told Graham of the change in her affections and then the brothers talked it through.

A Long Way from Tipperary

William was much more understanding of the situation but it had been important not to engage the volatile and ill Alice in the affaire . She was to die shortly and after her death, Terry and Olga's decision to marry became less contentious. This time, Paddie became a bridesmaid at the marriage ceremony which again took place at St Patrick's Church.

Again at St Patricks.

Graham behaved with magnificent restraint. He left Bristol and went to work in South Wales labouring for Haydens the pipefitters who were running a major project in Pembrokeshire. There he met Jim who was a Policewoman and his life was transformed; he joined the Police himself, rapidly progressed up the ladder and the rest is history. He eventually became the youngest man in the force to achieve the rank of Chief Superintendant when the South Wales Forces were

A Long Way from Tipperary

amalgamated into Dyfed Powys. Eventually, as far as family relations were concerned, time healed all wounds – both brothers were lucky to have found life fulfilling partners and there was reconciliation in due course.

Terry and Olga decided to immigrate to Toronto in Canada in 1953 where they could rely on the temporary support of Olga's eldest brother who had settled there after the war. Terry had a deceptively good first summer working as Chef/Manager at a golf club, but could find no work in winter. He even applied to join the Fire Service but did not have sufficient time in the country to qualify. Then Olga fell pregnant. As soon as the cry for help went out, William liquidated his savings and paid for the couples return, thoughtfully depositing cash with the shipping line so that they had money to spend during the crossing. It must have been mortifying for them to return to No 47 with Olga pregnant with daughter Leigh and having to start again. Terry did a stint on the railway laying track before going back to sea on the Bristol City Line with whom he made trips to New York and then later to Ireland. The ships were small ex Liberty vessels and after one particularly perilous Atlantic crossing, Terry opted for closer European destinations.

The slum clearance of Cattybrook

A Long Way from Tipperary

Street in 1956 was helpful to Terry because he was quickly re-housed in a prefab in Frenchay having been moved up the housing ladder. I loved their presence in No 47 but the lack of privacy must have been tough for them, and also difficult for Olga in view of Terry's prolonged absences at sea. But then he moved into the hotel trade and eventually into the Health service. Jim and Graham married at the Chapel in Trevine in Pembrokeshire, the village where Jim had been brought up. This lead to one final skirmish with the Catholic Church however when the local Catholic Priest, a certain Father Green

The Wedding at Trevine

in Haverfordwest, where Graham was stationed at the time, spoke to him discourteously in the High Street, saying that he had heard about his marriage plans, but that he should know that his marriage would not be recognised in the eyes of God and that any children would therefore be illegitimate! Graham's response can only be imagined.

A Long Way from Tipperary

Chapter 15.

Brave New World

Cattybrook Street was one of the last streets to be cleared, so we had the wonderful excitement of having free access to streets of derelict houses before the bulldozer did its work. There was a very old row of early Victorian cottages next to the Infants School in Russell Town Avenue which were a particular pleasure. After they were emptied, we made "dens" in their gardens and swung from mature trees on makeshift ropes. The big "dare" in one house was to pile abandoned mattresses in the garden and then jump onto them from the first floor. But these pleasures were short lived and soon we could not wait to move out from the eerie ghost town around us.

Enjoying The Dereliction

A Long Way from Tipperary

One casualty of this move was my love affair with Margaret Perram, a little girl with a pigtail who lived in Cattybrook Street close to the lamp post. We had known each other since we were 5 or 6 and my mother encouraged us by giving us jam sandwiches and tea in the back garden on a makeshift table made from an orange box; this little idyll was sometimes destroyed by clods of earth thrown by a concealed hand from the next door garden which I knew belonged to little Johnny Cooper who was too small to regard as a rival. I nonetheless whacked him whenever possible. I kept for many years a letter written on a scrap of paper by another young girl with whom I used to consort in the exit passages of the cinema, out of the rain. It only amounted to one sentence.

The Gang

A Long Way from Tipperary

I still attended the local primary school at Whitehall but then I passed the "Eleven Plus" and decisions had to be made about grammar school. I decided for entirely quixotic reasons (I liked the badge and the title of the school) to go to St Brendan's College, a Catholic school in Berkeley Square. This meant passing an interview with the Head and taking a quick course from our local priest in the Catechism. It is a testimony to William's humanity that when the Head produced a leather black strap at the interview to indicate what happened to those who failed to toe the line (Brother Crease called the strap, humorously " Dr Black") leading me to burst into tears, William asked me on the bus going home if I really wanted to go to that school?. I did.

William's friends tried to keep him busy and possibly as a consequence of that we were invited to watch the Coronation of Queen Elizabeth on television. I remember sitting dressed up in my best jacket and short trousers on a hard chair lost amongst rows of other chairs in someone's living room. The set was tall and definitely a furniture statement but unfortunately the screen was tiny and it was very difficult to see anything at all. I felt that we had nonetheless paid our respects to the Monarch, dressed up as we were in our Sunday clothes.

In mid 1956 we moved to 18 Avening Road which was a semi detached council house on a small estate in Kingswood. We were relieved to get the house because the risk was that when Moorfields was knocked down, we would be sent to Hartcliffe or Knowle or one of the vast housing estates that were constructed around the City following the wave of slum clearances. These were known to be without soul and suffering

A Long Way from Tipperary

from poor bus services, had few shops and little community life. Ex neighbours would sometimes return disconsolately to Moorfields to advise against following them to these places. William threw himself into gardening at No 18, inheriting grassy neglect and turning it into a vegetable and fruit garden of distinction – everything was grown along military lines. ("Carrots and beans, 'shun!").

No 18 was positively luxurious compared to Cattybrook Street. It had an indoor lavatory, a small bathroom, a large scullery, a through - sitting room and three bedrooms. We could scarcely believe our good fortune. William chose the middle size bedroom in which the marital bed just fitted, I had the smallest bedroom and Paddie took the third and  biggest which oddly had its own fireplace. By now Paddie had joined the Territorial Army and started to learn to drive 3 tonners. In 1958 she left us to work in the Prison Service which was definitely the right thing to do and from there built a very successful career in social work. It would have been better if William had been encouraging about this opportunity but he always found it difficult to say the right words.

A Long Way from Tipperary

It was not easy living with William as the loss of Alice seemed to have penetrated to the marrow of his bones. There were times when he was so miserable that I joined him in bed just to cuddle him and to try to make him feel less lonely. He was a man however of his time, born in the 19th century and unable to express his feelings. In later years as I became more independent and started to make the transition to adulthood, he began to fear that he would have no role and started to talk foolishly of ending his life notwithstanding the fact that he had a large extended family around who cared for him.

I had all the excitement of going to Grammar School and enjoying the fun of becoming a teenager, first as a bicycling fanatic and then at 16 buying my first motorbike – a Royal Enfield 500cc single cylinder ex Army bike which I acquired for £5. This was paid for from my first week's wages at Chapple Allen, the bra factory in Avonvale Road where I had a brief and innocent liaison with a young woman in the sewing department, encouraged by her older workmates. Dad was worried about me having a powerful motorbike, but bikes ran in the family - Eddie and Terry both had bikes and sidecars; Graham had a police bike. Dad allowed himself to be "conned" by the suggestion that I would get a sidecar in due course.

William's moodiness and general state of depression would have been hard for any adult to endure but we managed quite well between us – neither was a brilliant cook but we coped and when the depression lifted, William was good company. He had lost his old companions from the pubs of Lawrence Hill but developed a close friendship with Eric "Jock" Finlayson, a refrigeration engineer who had been in the Machine Gun Corps

A Long Way from Tipperary

with the Cheshire Yeomanry in 1914-18 and then became a fighter pilot at the end of the First World War. Eric was a hardened bachelor, constantly being pursued by his elderly landladies, or at least that was the standing joke. He told great

stories about operations in his Bristol Fighter against Von Richthofen's squadron; I was able to establish later that his operational experience was genuine. William lunched occasionally with Terry and with Eddie's family and visited Pembrokeshire from year to year to be with Graham. He would gruffly press small amounts of money into the hands of his grandchildren "to buy something". His quiet time was with books (he loved westerns, especially Zane Grey) and television or radio.

The house was always kept pretty immaculately and we had rose bushes in the front garden and gladioli around the back.

A Long Way from Tipperary

William gave me a pleasant surprise on one occasion when he decided to paint my bedroom/study when I was away on holiday. He had obviously seen in the papers that the new style of decor was for bright hues so he painted every one of the walls and the ceiling a different and clashing colour – it made the place quite psychedelic.

We had some lunatic neighbours in Avening Road, Mr and Mrs Scrase and their son Bert were right next door in number 16. Mr Scrase was a tiny ex sailor and he rolled down the garden path to inspect his cabbages as if pacing the deck of a destroyer in a heavy sea. There was gentle competition over the garden especially when we made an effort to move ahead by constructing a smart shed on the foundation of an old Anderson shelter. Unfortunately, I constructed it at my then height so within a year or two, it was useless unless I was prepared to cut a hole in the roof for my head. Mr Scrase worked for the Bristol Corporation and accumulated a grandiose quantity of useless blunt garden tools that had been sent to the dump which were going to be invaluable one day. Mrs Scrase looked like Methuselah and took impressive quantities of snuff, much of which hung from beneath her nose making accepting food from her (which was always genuinely pressed) a difficult proposition. She also had a voice like a foghorn which carried her unique Bristolian accent and sayings well beyond the neighbourhood. Bert had a labouring job and was a soul of geniality; unfortunately, he liked a pint or two after dinner and his noisy snoring rattled the wall between our respective bedrooms.

A Long Way from Tipperary

I worked during every school vacation once I reached 15 and even before then had a newspaper round and cleaned cars for cash. The Post Office and the Railway were reliable part time employers, but I also made concrete staircases and worked in garages and bars and drove ice cream vans. I was never without pocket money but the cost of staying on at school after 15 obviously fell on William. He was proud however that I was at St Brendan's and although I made two attempts to leave early (once at 15 to join the Police Cadets and later at 17 to become a Fighter Pilot), neither was caused by William's desire to lift the financial burden. The gap in age between us was too great for him to bridge with useful advice; it was Graham who intervened cleverly on both occasions to keep me on at school. The school itself was keen not to see me leave and sensing (wrongly) that money was the issue, proposed that we apply for Council funding. William was difficult to persuade because he did not believe in hand outs, but Eddie got around him....He was then told that he was not poor enough to get a grant which made him feel even more humiliated.

When William reached 65 in 1956, he retired from his security job and became a factory postman; he delivered mail around Parnalls for the next five years until finally retiring in 1961 at 70. The postal job was probably more demanding physically but he clearly preferred to work rather than face an empty house. I went to University in 1961 and returned home to live during the vacations increasingly less as time went by. I do not believe that William ever got his mind around the idea of a son at University and he decided not to attend my graduation. Graham did the honours instead. William died in 1965 on 8 August, his birthday, just after I joined the Foreign Office. He had a stroke,

A Long Way from Tipperary

went into a coma and was nursed at home with the family around him for a week before taking his last breath. I had nursed stroke victims at Barrow Gurney Hospital one vacation so I knew what to expect if he made less than a full recovery; I am glad that he did not have to face that indignity.

William left everything in his one - page will to Eddie – but the sad fact was that he had nothing to leave. He had subsisted on his state pension since retirement and had no savings. There was nothing of any value to pass on. The house was cleared of furniture and handed back to the council; a few things like pictures were distributed around the children as well as some few items of Alice's jewellery. The piano which had been mute since Alice's death was given away. The one mystery was the whereabouts of William's medals from the First World War which everyone claimed to have seen and which had therefore "disappeared". The air was thick with suspicion. It was not until April 1988 that I was able to establish that the medals had never been issued and therefore were available to be claimed by his next of kin. They are now with us.

The strong narrative that I hope runs through the story of William and Alice is of a couple whose families emerged intact from the worst that the 19th century had to offer to working class people, that they endured wars and poverty in the course of the 20th century and that they left a host of descendants of whom they have every reason to be proud. Every time that I look in the mirror, particularly as I get older and closer now to his final age, I see reflections of my parents and I am reminded of the past and of the sacrifices that they made. I can recall now every vein in William's broad and strong hands; he had fingers

A Long Way from Tipperary

like spatulas and nails like tombstones. He loved Alice and his family only too well and gave himself throughout his life to their wellbeing. He was above all a kindly man who passed on to his children a strong sense of morality which I believe endures through the generations. Some of this is undoubtedly due to his catholic upbringing and stern mother but the rest is owed to the character of a man who knew instinctively the importance of doing right and respecting himself.

William's Eldest Sons in Flanders 1995

A Long Way from Tipperary

As the details of William's origins and his wartime experiences emerged over time, they have served as a means of drawing the family together in recognition of a shared history. William's children have visited Flanders together to walk the bloody fields on which he fought, followed by his grandchildren on their own expeditions. The extended family has explored its Irish and Welsh heritage and have recently connected with the descendants of William's brothers in Wales. There are still stories to be told about German connections going back to the beginning of the 20th century. These adventures have enriched the family's sense of knowing who we are.

William's Son and Grandsons in Flanders 2005

A Long Way from Tipperary

William's three eldest sons lived on for a further 30 years and more and then passed away with startling rapidity. Graham died on 1 April 1998 in his mid sixties which was very young for this age after having retired from a very successful career in the Police. Eddie died on 18 December 1999 and his brother Terry died on Christmas Eve 1999 during the night following Eddies funeral whilst being cared for by Paddie who will be 80 in 2015. Eddie had spent many years as a stevedore until falling victim to a horrendous accident whilst unloading timber from a vessel at Bristol Port. The lorry was unsecured, the baulks of timber shifted and fell, pinning him to the quay. Only the fortunate presence of a small area of mud which cushioned his skull against the concrete saved his life. After he recovered from his injuries, he became a Swimming Bath Superintendant which arose tangentially from his role as life saving team coach of the Port of Bristol.

Following his colourful early career, Terry became the Catering Superintendant of the Stoke Park Psychiatric Hospital which ironically belongs to the same group as Fishponds, where his grandfather William Albert Turner had died. Olga pre-deceased him, Eddies wife Connie has now died but Jim, Grahams widow lives on.

William would have been proud not only of the professions chosen by his grandchildren but by the contributions that they have made in their various ways to their communities. There are in fact two words which best cover a common attribute of William and his descendants. They derive from the motto of his Regiment which some historians believe dates back to the Battle of Crecy when the Black Prince took the Three Feathers

A Long Way from Tipperary

emblem of the mortally wounded blind King of Bohemia and also his motto. They became attached to the Prince of Wales in the 14th century and later to the Welch Regiment. They are "Ich Dien" – "I serve" which is a near homophone for the Welsh phrase "Eich Dyn" meaning " Your Man".

William served.

Made in the USA
Charleston, SC
15 January 2015